RAVE CULTURE;

an insider's overview

By Jimi Fritz

A primer for the global rave phenomenon

Published by SMALLFRY PRESS, Canada.
Printed and bound in Canada

Published by SmallFry Press, Canada
email: smallfryenterprises@home.com

ISBN 0-9685721-0-3

Canadian Cataloguing in Publication Data

Fritz, Jimi, 1955-
Rave Culture; an insider's overview

ISBN 0-9685721-0-3

1. Rave culture. 2. Techno music-Social aspects.
3. Youth-Drug use. I. Title

HQ799.2.R38F75 1999 305.235 C99-901043-3

LAYOUT AND DESIGN

Davin Greenwell / arizOna
Contact: wk805@victoria.tc.ca
http://arizona.cjb.net
1-250-477-3549

ARTWORK

Virginia SmallFry
Contact: thesmallfrys@home.com

PHOTOGRAPHY

Tristan O'Neill
Contact: tristan@dircon.co.uk
Trent Warlow
Contact: 250-704-0098

Dedication:

For Virginia, without whom none of these things would be possible.

PEACE, LOVE, UNITY AND RESPECT TO EVERYONE WHO PARTICIPATED:

Chris Cowie, Dave Jurman, Terrence Parker, Rick Doblin, MAPS, James Lumb, John Digweed, Dave Ralph, Paul Oakenfold, Davin a.k.a. arizOna, Wayne Grimwood, DJ Billy, Topher and Tracy, DJ Daniel, DJ 608, Michael Elewonibi, Tim Laughlin, Lieneke Marshall, Trent Warlow, Generic, Ohmit, Chika, Solstice Productions, Noble House Nigel, The Alien Mental Association, Damien a.k.a. DJ K-Rad, Gina Womack, Kim Stanford, T.R.I.P., Brent Carmichael, Dan Serpa, Anne Marie, Surfer Bob, Logan, DJ Davie, DJ Mis-Chief, Pappa Smurf, George Storm, Jane of Art, Gil Oliveira Santos a.k.a. Ravehunter, SkyLab2000, Lubna, J.C., The Shulgins, Sylvia Thyssen, Dan Merkur, XLR8R Magazine, Andrew Rawnsley, Laura La Gassa, Brian Behlendorf, Jonathan, Leandre, DJ Robinod, Muzzy, Raevn Lunah Teak, Rennie"Dubnut"Foster, Nicole Makin, Tristan O'Neill, V.I.B.E. Productions, Philosophers of Phunk, Kamal, Digniti Productions, Fi-ance Productions, Joe Bazooka, Holger, John Beaumier, B-Side, Janne Leino, Will from Greece, Alan Smith, Jussi Mononen, Juuso Koponen a.k.a. DJ Mekaanikko, Veny Veronika Vere, Veikko Watia, Erkki Rautio, Esa Ojansivu, Dj Jules Nerve, Dj Drenalin, Alex Martyshev, Stardiver a.k.a. Alex, Tomá1 Rádl, Foka, Scotto Ba Gotto, Tomasz Wileñski, Maya, Jonas, Berelowitz, Sandro Markovic, Lloyd Morgan, Pyc, Marko Vajagic a.k.a. DJ Mark Wee, Stargate Group, Veteroski Goran, Stevan "STeW" Fryd, DJ SCIENCE, Jo Fruitybits, Petr Nejedly, Ivan Arar, NoRuleZ, Mladen Alajbeg, Damon, DJ Marcore, Sonic Intervention, Nicole A. Tobias, Federico Sommariva, Marek, Fredrik Larsson, Alison Maria Clemens, Nico Claes, Jari Savander, Damir Ludvig, DJ Sylk, Petar Mimica, Katherine Wheatley, Peter from Lodz, Jari Nousiainen a.k.a. Super attaK, Olivia Ball, Hannele, Leyolah Antara and Nathan Kaye, Karl Munns, Lotars Lodzinsh, Oleg Ilyushin a.k.a. DJ Vint, Frank Zelaya a.k.a. DJ SoR, Dominique, Brewster B., Daniel a.k.a. Earthguy, Kevin Dempsey, Sebastian Zillinger, Amit K., Tony Horner, Ferid Abbasher a.k.a. DJ Lord Ferdi the Despiser, Nexus, Hernando, Vix, Norman NG, a.k.a. Nomskii, Mikael Jergefelt, Rich, Chrissie, Dj Lory Traxx,
and all the people who make the scene happen.

CONTENTS

CHAPTER 1: THE BEGINNING OF A BEAUTIFUL FRIENDSHIP

photo: jason dyck

"Life is either a daring adventure or nothing. To keep our faces toward change and behave like free spirits in the presence of fate is strength undefeatable."

- Helen Keller, deaf and blind author and lecturer, USA. 1880-1968.

1
The Beginning of a Beautiful Friendship

In one of the last interviews before his tragic suicide, Abbie Hoffman was quoted as saying that the nineties would make the sixties look like the fifties. Coming from one of the most colourful, committed and effective revolutionaries in recent history, this was an intriguing and provocative statement. As a person who experienced the sixties, I found it an exciting prospect to think we could come full circle and re-kindle the spirit of revolution which had transformed the world more than three decades ago. However, at the time, I could see very little evidence of a cultural, musical or political revolution of that scale anywhere in sight. Our culture still seemed obsessed with superficial material pursuits and, as far as I could see, nothing new had happened in music since the explosion of creativity which marked the peace and love generation so long ago.

I stopped listening to the radio around 1974. For the next fifteen years or so, new musical ideas in popular music appeared to be virtually non-existent. The spark of originality and unbridled creativity so apparent in the sixties had become drowned in a sea of derivative pop music as we were mercilessly subjected to one fashion conscious, egocentric musical fad after another. Even rock music, once the alternative voice of an anti-establishment fringe, had become painfully predictable. The spontaneous and instinctive qualities that originally made rock music exciting had become overly sophisticated to the point of boredom. For the most part, the music industry was being run by fifteen-year-olds, who bought records and therefore dictated what was being promoted and played on the radio. The so-called new music seemed to consist of half a dozen musical formulas, derived from 60's music, being endlessly reworked and recycled. As far as I could tell, we had been listening to the same catchy radio pop songs, the same head-banging metal machinations, the same sugary sentimental ballads and the same old rock and roll anthems for more than twenty years. Musical innovation had been treading water for two decades with absolutely no evidence that things were about to change. I began to think that perhaps Abby had taken one too many hits of LSD and had finally lost his once legendary razor-sharp perception. Until one fateful night several years ago when a friend's son piqued my interest by inviting me to a rave.

I had just turned forty and was already well into the throes of a classic mid-life crisis. As an independent filmmaker with "several projects" in development, rejection had become a way of life. The cumulative effects of being treated like a leper on the streets of Calcutta had begun to take its toll. My once budding career as a filmmaker was grinding to a painful halt, and Macdonalds began to look more and more like a viable career alternative. No one was interested in buying any of my screenplays, no one would give me a dime to make another film and I had collected enough rejection slips to wallpaper Michael Jackson's romper room. On top of this, my children had just entered their teen years and were exercising their newfound independence by becoming rude and surly. Everything worth living for was in the past and the future looked bleak and meaningless. My nose, once wet and cold and shiny, had become warm and dry with a dull, matte finish.

Wayne, whom I had known since he was in diapers, was now twenty-one years old and already a seven-year veteran of the rave scene in England and Canada. He convinced me that a rave would do wonders for my nasal condition. He told me everyone was extremely friendly at raves, and he told me that the music was truly new and exciting. And he told me that a nice big hit of MDMA would open up my heart chakra and enable me to dance all night long.

I was somewhat skeptical to say the least. I had never particularly liked electronic music and as a musician myself, was faithfully devoted to the acoustic, organic qualities of the guitar, piano and bamboo flute. My experiences with electronic keyboards had always been very disappointing. No matter what instrument they attempted to reproduce, they invariably sounded like the disturbing whine of low-tech kitchen appliances. An annoying electronic buzz is not improved by varying its pitch or frequency. This merely turns a high-pitched annoying buzz into a low-pitched annoying buzz - a wing into a wang. The sounds being produced by synthesizers in the seventies seemed to lack an important human quality that I believed was essential to good music. When mixed with other "real" instruments synthesizers could produce some interesting effects, but on their own, were somehow cold and sterile.

artwork: virginia smallfry

Another thing - I had not found any music worth dancing to in twenty years. The last time I danced with total unbridled enthusiasm was at a rock concert in 1973 when The Who were in their heyday, and I and twenty thousand hippies and leftover mods went berserk in a soccer stadium in London, England. That night I also learned a valuable lesson about thermodynamics; you can not use the plastic packaging from a refrigerator box as a sleeping bag, especially if you are sharing it with a close friend. That was the last time I would sleep in a plastic bag and the last time I could remember dancing with complete abandon. Since then, I had rarely come across any music that inspired me enough to express myself on a dance floor and had consequently become labeled as a chronic, non-dancing person. I had certainly never danced all night.

I patiently explained my position on electronic music and my limited dancing experience to Wayne who remained undaunted. I detected a mischievous twinkle in his knowing eye and he remained steadfastly convinced that I would benefit from the experience. I countered with a host of good reasons as to why my worldly wisdom would render me impervious to this fleeting teenage fad. Wayne listened patiently as if he had heard this story before. A wry smile crept playfully across his boyish face. Or was it an impish grin? "Check it out!" he challenged. And so I did.

Armed with a capsule of ecstasy, I marched downtown to a building that until recently had been home to The Salvation Army. Around 11:30 PM a crowd of twenty-somethings began filing into the building that had been slated for demolition in a few weeks. From outside, the music sounded like a muffled and messy explosion of bass drums. What the hell, I had nothing to lose. If it failed to turn my crank, I could always go home and watch a movie instead. I popped my pill and went in.

My nose, once wet and cold and shiny, had become warm and dry with a dull, matte finish.

Once inside, the music was very loud and crystal clear. At first I thought it sounded a little stuck in a groove, but I had never heard anything quite like it before. These were not the depersonalized electronic sounds of the seventies. I heard nary a wing nor wang. They were rich, textured sounds - fat and juicy and warm and friendly. Later, I would learn that many of these sounds had never been heard by human beings before.

The main room that had once served as a chapel for the soldiers of salvation was now packed with several hundred dancers. Swirling coloured lights and lasers buzzed the room and psychedelic animations flickered on every wall. At the far end of the large rectangular hall was a raised balcony where the DJs were set up. I wandered up the stairs to have a closer look. For a while I sat behind a DJ and watched him spinning records on two turntables while fiddling with a mixer between the two decks. Although I had some experience with sound systems and recording studios, I could not quite figure out how all the sounds were being created but was fascinated by this mysterious process. I finally gave up trying to figure out the mechanics and began to listen to the music more closely. It was now about twelve-thirty and the place was packed. Wayne was right, everyone seemed very happy and friendly. And this music was definitely growing on me.

As the ecstasy began to produce a warm glow throughout my body, I began to hear complexities in the music that I had not previously noticed. These new sounds began to pervade my body, seeping into every pore. I felt myself beginning to move to the music so I headed back to the dance floor and waded into the throng. The mood on the dance floor was electric. I had never before seen so many people dancing so enthusiastically and with such fervor. The energy level in the room could have easily powered a small town. People were dancing hard and smiling from ear to ear, as if amazed at the ability of the music to affect them so completely. The heavy tribal beats continued to grow, building in intensity. Just when any increase in power seemed impossible, a plateau of swirling sounds suggested an ultimate zenith. Then, suddenly, the music exploded into another rhythm even more penetrating and profound than before. This upward spiraling cycle of pulsating sound continued to build relentlessly hour after hour throughout the night. Like a musical river, it swept everyone along with an irresistible momentum. An incredible sense of optimism and enthusiasm pervaded the room as we surrendered to this new musical form.

I was completely astonished at the intensity of this new experience and by the look on everyone's faces, I was not alone. The atmosphere in the room was one of turbo-charged celebration. Complete strangers came up periodically and introduced themselves to me with a warm hug. They told me they were glad to see me and wished me a great night. From time to time, experienced ravers approached me with a reminder to drink plenty of water or to offer me a piece of candy. I felt protected and safe, as if surrounded by close friends and family.

photo: tristan o'neill

I was almost twice the age of most of the ravers that night but it made not the slightest bit of difference to any one, least of all myself. I felt like I had walked into a different world. A world where the social rules had changed. A world where people had transcended their petty, superficial differences and evolved to the state where they could accept everyone else for who and what they were, without judgment or fear. We are all familiar with theoretical notions of brotherhood, ranging from the ancient Christian ethic of "love your brother," to current new age philosophies that advocate opening our heart chakras and seeing God's light in others. Though we all know how it's supposed to go, apart from a handful of saints and sages, it is extremely rare to see these practices manifest in daily life. But here I was in a sea of six hundred radiant souls putting into practice five thousand years of religious and philosophical hypotheses. Beyond the conceptual world of ideas and dogma this was a direct experience of tribal spirituality practiced by our ancestors. I could feel the pulse of the shaman's drum and almost smell the pungent wood smoke from an ancient fire.

That night, I danced for seven hours straight with barely a break. By seven a.m., as the dawn light flooded into the room, the party was still in full swing and the music was still climbing to impossible heights. When the plug was finally pulled and the music faded away, I stood in a room of exhausted and exhilarated people, said fond farewells to a few new-found friends and walked out into a crisp new morning.

The next day I found it difficult to relate my experience accurately to family and friends. I had never experienced a party quite like this one. I felt changed. My growing cynicism and frustration with the world had been replaced by a new optimism. A friend, who like myself, had experienced some wild parties and psychedelic experimentation of the sixties, nodded knowingly and said, "Oh, yeah. Been there. Done that." But she was wrong. Although there were obvious similarities, we had never quite been *there* and done *that*. This really was something new.

I had experimented with various psychedelic drugs in the past and had some powerful and inspiring experiences but this experience had an immediacy and intensity that set it apart. It felt more real than the fantastic, illusionary worlds of LSD or magic mushrooms, as if the effects were activated by the ecstasy but ultimately came from somewhere deep inside. Coupled with the influence of the music, it seemed that, rather than feeling a

photo: trent warlow

direct effect from the drug, it seemed that the feelings were generated from my own being, merely triggered by the drug, making the experience seem more organic and less drug induced. But the effects of the ecstasy were only one part of the equation. The music also had a powerful influence and was key to the overall effect. It was a combination of the people, the environment, the music and the drug all conspiring to bring about a unique set of circumstances with the power to create a powerful and meaningful group experience.

I can honestly say my experience that night changed my life for the better. During the writing of this book, I have spoken to hundreds of ravers about their first time experiences and found my story was far from unique. The majority of ravers had a very similar story to tell.

It seemed amazing to me that this life-changing ritualistic, cultural phenomenon was going on in almost every large urban center in the western world and beyond, making it a truly global phenomenon. It has been estimated there are now many more ravers in the world than there were hippies in the sixties. Even more amazing was that the rave scene was still almost entirely underground even after a decade of phenomenal growth. The mainstream press and media have only sporadically reported on rave culture and have consistently missed the real story, choosing instead to focus on raves as out-of-control drug fests.

The underground nature of the movement is deemed by ravers as essential to protecting the scene from over-commercialization and contamination from mundane, mainstream mind-sets. While I understand and applaud the motives of such a stance, I felt that the movement might be a little too underground for its own good. There is a lot of opposition to rave culture, from biased, sensationalist reporting, to parties being raided and shut down, to dramatic stories of drug overdoses and corrupted youth. Over the past few years, my experiences with the rave movement have proven to me that most of the fears that mainstream society has concerning rave culture are largely based on ignorance and fear. It became obvious that people outside the scene simply had no idea what was really going on.

If we are to grow and develop as human beings, it is essential that we strive to replace ignorance with knowledge. We must base our opinions on what we know to be true while remaining open to new truths. Resistance to new ideas is nothing new but we must first understand an idea to be able to accept or reject it. I believe something wonderful and worthwhile is happening within the culture of rave and its voice deserves to be heard above the clatter of misinformation and hysteria.

An incredible sense of *optimism* and *enthusiasm* pervaded the room as we surrendered to this *new musical form.*

In response to the largely negative and uninformed reports about rave culture, this book is intended to be a positive, realistic, general overview of the global rave scene of interest to ravers and non-ravers alike. For people who know nothing about the scene but what they may have heard in the press or on the news, it will give them information with which to shape their own informed opinions. For ravers, it will give a voice and context to powerful experiences they may have had but been unable to verbalize or fully understand. Because the movement is growing and evolving so fast, it is impossible to be completely comprehensive, but it is my intention to present as complete an overview as possible while placing the movement in an historical and cultural perspective. For anyone interested in a more detailed, critical history of the rave movement, I can highly recommend "Energy Flash" by Simon Reynolds.

We have arrived at a point in history where people are losing touch with themselves and others with disastrous effects. The young people of today are busy creating new tribal rituals as the old religions continue to lose their appeal and meaning. The rave experience is as valid and powerful as any tribal ritual or spiritual practice from the past or present, and can serve to fulfill our basic human need to feel connected to our families our communities and ourselves. Does that sound so bad?

The material for this book has been gathered over the last three years from many varied sources in keeping with the spontaneous and eclectic nature of rave culture itself. What is presented here is a compilation of subjective notes and opinions that collectively, will give you a taste of what rave culture is all about. If you want the real thing however, you will have to try it for yourself…

DJ Linus, Germany

photo: trent warlow

CHAPTER 2:

THE WINDS OF CHANGE

- the roaring twenties
- the swinging sixties
- the revolution of rave

photo: tristan o'neill

"You say you want a revolution, well you know, we all want to change the world."

- From "Revolution" by The Beatles.

2
THE WINDS OF CHANGE

As we near the end of the twentieth century and look back at the last hundred years, it is hard to believe that we have come so far in such a relatively short time. Never before in history has our world gone through a period of such rapid growth. So many areas of our daily lives have been completely transformed by new advances in science and technology it is now hard to imagine a world without televisions or computers or telephones. At the beginning of this century, our brains could not have even conceived of such changes that today seem commonplace. In retrospect, these changes seem to occur with lightning speed but while we are in the throes of cultural and social transformations, they appear more gradual, giving us the time we need to adjust and adapt. But this is not always the case. Every now and then a set of circumstances conspires to make sweeping changes that reverberate to every aspect of our lives and ultimately change the way we think. To understand the current rave phenomenon and place it in an historical context, we have only to look back at the last hundred years to see that history does indeed repeat itself.

Every now and then a set of circumstances conspires to make sweeping changes that reverberate to every aspect of our lives and ultimately change the way we think.

There have been many micro-revolutions which have influenced or changed specific areas of society, e.g. the agricultural revolution, the industrial revolution, the technological revolution, the information revolution, etc. Although these new developments have had a major impact on certain areas of society, their effects are not total, in that they do not necessarily permeate or influence all areas of human endeavor. Sometimes however, we see a set of circumstances start a chain reaction which touches every level of society and actually affects our collective consciousness. These revolutions have an effect on, and eventually transform our politics, social order, sexuality, psychology, spirituality and the arts. If we look back over the last three centuries, these major changes can be seen to take place approximately every thirty years. For our purposes it will suffice to examine the twentieth century, beginning with the first of three such revolutions which began in the twenties.

The Roaring Twenties

The first cultural and social revolution of the twentieth century began shortly after World War One and effectively brought us from the Victorian age into the modern age. Previous to this, we were living in a restricted, limited and restrained climate where conformity was valued above all else. It was a society that embraced repressed sexuality, an oppressive and controlling church and a stifling class system. Life was relatively sweet for the small minority of privileged, rich landowners and aristocracy who maintained almost total control. However, for the vast majority, life was a struggle from birth to death, living conditions were horrendous and the life of a peasant amounted to little more than slavery.

artwork: virginia smallfry

After the devastation of the First World War, a shift in consciousness took place. The end of world war gave way to a new climate of liberty, tolerance and optimism. The world was once again free from tyranny. And the twenties began to roar.

Easy credit, technological ingenuity, and war-related industrial decline in Europe caused a long economic boom in which ownership of new products such as automobiles, phones, radios, etc. became democratized. Prosperity, an increase in the number of women workers, women's suffrage and drastic change in fashions created a wide perception of social change.

These cultural changes were considered decadent and socially disruptive by right wing conservatives struggling to maintain control, but to the people who were busy creating a new society it was a time of celebration and experimentation, with people stretching the limits of new found social freedoms. New musical explorations resulted in a move away from formalism towards the expression of individuality. The formal approach of classical music that had been dominant for a century gave way to new popular forms, as the traditions of folk music were transformed into the improvisation and experimentation of jazz. This new climate of artistic freedom also marked the birth of modern dance, as couples moved away from dancing in pairs and learned to express themselves through movement. New dances like the Charleston and the Black Bottom were causing scandals and disapproval from old school traditionalists and had as much to do with sexuality and politics as partying.

Theatre, fine arts and literature also entered a new era of self exploration in the twenties as the stifling veil of Victorian morals were finally lifted. Bauhaus, a famous German school of design, that had an inestimable influence on modern architecture, theater design and the industrial and graphic arts, was at the height of its influence. Paul Klee, the Swiss painter, watercolorist, and etcher, one of the most original masters of modern art, taught at Bauhaus between 1920 and 1931. Pastoral landscapes, iconic Christian imagery and photo realism were being rejected by a new generation of avant-garde artists who were not just pushing the envelope, but tearing it up altogether and reassembling it into something completely different.

New dances like the Charleston and the Black Bottom were causing scandals and disapproval from old school traditionalists and had as much to do with sexuality and politics as partying.

The Dada movement, which began in Germany spread to America by the early twenties. Dada was an artistic and literary movement reflecting a widespread nihilistic protest against all aspects of Western culture and became the inspiration for the Surrealist movement, founded by the French poet and critic Andre Breton. Breton, who published his Surrealist Manifesto in Paris in 1924, had a huge influence on the creative world, asserting the superiority of the subconscious mind and the importance of dreams in the creation of art. Like Dadaism, Surrealism emphasized the role of the unconscious in creative activity and inspired many artists of the day including Salvador Dali, Rene Magritte, Man Ray, André Masson and Joan Miro.

The world of literature was also witnessing a revolutionary boom in the 1920s as prose writers explored radical narrative modes related to dreams and the internal monologue. Poets and novelists were writing about modern alienation, as in T.S. Eliot's Wasteland and Lost Generation. Gertrude Stein was busy both exasperating and thrilling critics with her challenging word play. The great German writer Herman Hesse, wrote Siddhartha in 1922, Steppenwolf in 1927 and Death and the Lover in 1930. And one of the twentieth century's most influential writers, James Joyce attained international fame with the publication of Ulysses in 1922.

The transformation of literature at this time did much to change the way people thought about themselves and the world around them, while at the same time gave a voice to some of the anxieties being experienced due to the rapid societal changes taking place. Franz Kafka, the Austrian/Czech master of alienation, wrote The Trial in 1925 and followed it up with The Castle in 1926. Jean Paul Sartre, the French philosopher, dramatist, novelist and leading exponent of existentialism, was also teaching and studying philosophy during the twenties. Outer worlds were also being explored as writers of the day gave birth to a whole new genre called science fiction. In 1921, George Bernard Shaw wrote five plays under the collective title, Back to Methuselah, exploring human progress from Eden to a science-fiction future, while H. G. Wells was inspired by the times to write a vision of the future called The Shape of Things to Come.

photo: tristan o'neill

Cultural revolutions are invariably fueled by artist's attempts to expand their consciousness into new realms. Indeed, this process is essential to push the boundaries of both art and science. In the twenties, free thinkers everywhere were exploring the themes of dream worlds, the subconscious and altered psychological states. In 1923, Jean Cocteau, poet, novelist, dramatist, designer, and filmmaker, known for his versatility and unconventionality, became addicted to opium, an experience he described in his book, Opium, published the same year. During this time he produced some of his most influential works - the plays Orpheus (1926) and The Infernal Machine (1934), the novel Children of the Game (1929) and his first film, Le Sang d'un Poète (Blood of a Poet, 1930). Exploration of the inner realms led to the increased use of psychedelic drugs as the artists of the day explored new realms of human consciousness. Aldous Huxley, the English novelist and one of the earliest experimenters and proponents of psychedelic drug use, wrote Chrome Yellow in 1921, Antic Hay in 1923 and Point Counter Point in 1928, all of which illustrate the revolutionary temper of the 1920s. Huxley was most famous for his prophetic vision of a futuristic utopia in Brave New World. It is no coincidence that the name of this book has been borrowed repeatedly for articles about rave culture. During the last few years I have read countless pieces with the phrase "rave new world" in their titles.

Cultural revolutions are invariably fueled by artist's attempts to expand their consciousness into new realms.

The arts were also being used as political arenas as people struggled with the growing pains of a new age. In the theatre, Bertolt Brecht's early plays showed the influence of expressionism, the leading dramatic movement at the time. In 1928 Brecht wrote a musical drama, The Threepenny Opera, with the German composer Kurt Weill. This musical was a caustic satire on capitalism and became Brecht's greatest theatrical success. Eugene

O'Neill, American dramatist, Nobel laureate, and winner of four Pulitzer prizes is often considered the most important writer in the American theatre, a playwright whose works attempted to define fundamental human problems. O'Neill wrote many of his most famous plays in the twenties including, The Hairy Ape, Beyond the Horizon, The Emperor Jones and the nine-act play, Strange Interlude which won a Pulitzer prize in 1927.

By the late 1920s, a new climate of social freedom was making waves as sexuality came out of the closet and challenged our old notions of relationships and marriage. In the popular theatre, burlesque was evolving from musical comedy to a more ribald and risqué form of entertainment, and it was during this time that striptease was introduced into the theatre for the first time. The politics of sexuality were also on the move as the second-class status of women was finally being addressed by a burgeoning women's movement that took to the streets to demand equal rights. In the dance halls of America, the flappers styled their hair in mannish bobs, wore short dresses revealing their thighs and showed the world that women could party as hard as men. It is somehow fitting that some of the fashions of the twenties - feather boas and tight fitting, short dresses with spaghetti straps - are re-surfacing in the rave scene today.

It is somehow fitting that some of the fashions of the twenties - feather boas and tight fitting, short dresses with spaghetti straps - are re-surfacing in the rave scene today.

In the realm of psychology, Carl Jung, the Swiss psychiatrist and father of psychoanalysis, superseded Sigmund Freud as the new authority on the human psyche. His work emphasized the importance of dreams and formed the basis of his theories on the collective unconscious. In 1921 he published a major work entitled Psychological Types in which he dealt with the relationship between the conscious and unconscious, a work that still dominates psychoanalytic thought today.

In the world of science, advances in knowledge and technological aptitude increased exponentially with the increase in the number of practitioners. Einstein's general theory of relativity was published in 1915 and revolutionized scientific thought and challenged our very notion of reality.

Collectively, all these changes represented a quantum leap forward in human social evolution, as if the hundredth monkey had just received prescription glasses, instantly enabling everyone to see the world with renewed clarity. But there was another factor that had a powerful effect on people's perception of both the world around them and the world within. The revolution of the twenties also marked a quantum leap forward in recreational drug use.

By 1900, alcohol was regarded as the most dangerous threat to society. The Anti-Saloon League of America endorsed candidates for public office and demanded that their state governments allow the people to vote on the question of continuing to license the saloons. By 1916, 23 of the 48 states had adopted anti-saloon laws that closed the bars and prohibited the manufacture of any alcoholic beverages. But this “war on booze” did little to stop the use of alcohol, and its use became fashionable in underground speakeasies across North America. It is now clear that the ban actually caused people to drink more rather than less. It also promoted widespread disrespect for the law and generated a wave of organized criminal activity, with bootleggers selling liquor illegally, making huge profits available to gangsters who, in turn, corrupted almost every level of government. The proponents of today’s “war on drugs” would do well to learn from these past mistakes.

Meanwhile, the freedom loving sectors of society were partying harder than ever. It was during this time that hashish and marijuana became popular with free thinkers and artists throughout society. After the power play of the opium wars at the end of the century, opium too had resurfaced as an underground drug and was enjoyed by the privileged class, as was morphine. Sir Arthur Conan Doyle wrote his last Sherlock Holmes book in 1917 (The Last Bow) and often portrayed his sophisticated hero using morphine or cocaine to ward off boredom between cases. Amphetamines also became widely available in the twenties and gained popularity both as a prescription drug and for recreational use. Whether increased drug use is a result of rapid social change or part of the cause is hard to say, but it seems apparent that wherever and whenever there is a shift in consciousness, experiments with mind altering drugs are never very far away.

The revolution of the twenties not only changed the social, political and cultural landscape forever but also changed the way people thought about themselves and the world around them. The massive changes that reverberated throughout society not only had a profound influence on the society of the day, but would continue to have a powerful influence and fuel changes in society for the next thirty years.

artwork: virginia smallfry

The Swinging Sixties

artwork: virginia smallfry

After the Second World War, a period of reflection and inertia gave way to a return to family values and right wing politics. The booming post-war economy led to a feeding frenzy of consumerism that promised a chicken in every pot, a car in every driveway and a television in every room of the house. With the world once again cleansed of evil, people strove for an ideal of goodness, and strict moral standards became the order of the day. Men shaved off their beards, wore their hair short and sported dark and serious suits. Women hid every trace of cleavage and wore their dresses well below the knee. Once again, sex went underground as families desperately tried to keep up with the Cleavers. But beneath this squeaky-clean facade, subtle evolutionary forces were bubbling up through the collective consciousness, stoking the boilers for the next major revolution of the century.

By the late fifties, the American dream had begun to fade and a growing number of people became disillusioned with what they saw as a paternalistic, rigid system that was insensitive to the changing will of the people. The fifties saw a return to the puritanical values of the Victorian age, and once again, people reacted with a pendulum swing to the left in a move toward more personal freedoms and demands for social justice. As before, there would also be an explosion of creativity in all areas of the arts and a huge increase in recreational drug use. The Cleavers were history as the stage was set for the revolution of the sixties.

photo: tristan o'neill

As with all social revolutions, personal freedom was at the heart of the changes sweeping through North America and Europe but this time it came with a social conscience. People not only wanted freedom for themselves but also demanded equality for others, including minorities, women and homosexuals.

Once more, a war provided the catalyst for change. The conflict in Vietnam began in 1959 and by the early sixties it became apparent that the war could drag on indefinitely. Watching the body count on the six o'clock news became a national pastime and eventually led to a strong anti-war sentiment. The Vietnam War became less and less popular with many Americans but it was the youth that took to the streets that gave birth to a vibrant and active peace movement. Numerous social movements came into being as a significant portion of the population voiced their concerns and demanded change.

The peace movement, the civil rights movement, the women's movement, gay rights and racial equality were the issues of the day, and an army of young people marched in the streets to demand these rights and freedoms. The shocking realities of war gave way to the philosophy of peace and love as flower power bloomed and hippies organized and showed their strength in numbers. Outdoor music festivals attracted record numbers, culminating at Woodstock, where four hundred thousand people came together on a farm in New York state for "three days of peace, love and music."

Again, an explosion of creativity from the arts community celebrated, challenged, reflected and commented on a society hungry for change, as new found freedoms gave way to new ideas. The rebellious rock-and-roll of the fifties had paved the way for a complete transformation of popular music. The rulebook went out the window and originality became the prime objective, as musicians explored new musical technology and pushed the boundaries of creativity to outrageous extremes. The Beatles, Jimi Hendrix, Bob Dylan, The Doors, Joni Mitchel, The Rolling Stones, The Who, Janis Joplin, Led Zeppelin, Pink Floyd and a host of others too numerous to list, gave birth to new musical ideas that formed the basis of our musical culture for the next twenty-five years. Ninety percent of all the so-called original songs played on FM radio today are direct copies of musical ideas originated in the sixties.

Ninety percent of all the so-called original songs played on FM radio today are direct copies of musical ideas originated in the sixties.

Rock music had also become a powerful political force and was used effectively to communicate the ideas of a world in transition to a mass audience of receptive young people. Never before had youth been so vocal or organized about social change, and it became common place for thousands of hippies to congregate in "be-ins" or "love-ins", using their sheer numbers as a form of passive resistance. More active forms of political revolt were taken up by the Youth International Party, also known as the Yippies, who staged many defiant and even militant demonstrations, culminating in a mass protest at the 1968 democratic convention in Chicago. It was at this convention that the Yippies, led by Abbie Hoffman, Jerry Rubin and five others, who collectively became known as the Chicago Seven, were arrested on charges of sedition and intent to overthrow the government. The subsequent court proceedings became a media circus, bringing global attention to the issues, and ended with The Chicago Seven behind bars. But it would take more than jailing a few ringleaders to stop a revolution now supported by a generation on the march.

Attitudes towards sexuality were once again transformed as the philosophy of free love permeated society. Sex was no longer the exclusive domain of committed relationships and could also be used to express casual friendship or enjoyed as just plain fun. The women's movement took another quantum leap forward in the sixties as women moved away from traditional roles as wives and mothers and opted to take their place in the workplace alongside men. The liberation of women continued in other areas too, with the fights for equal pay for equal work and abortion rights. The bra became a symbol of male oppression and women took to the streets to stage media bra burning events to express their new found sexual and social freedom.

The sixties revolution probably did more to change the way people think and act today than any other time in the twentieth century and the paradigms that were created at that time have continued to fuel our social and cultural changes for the past quarter of a century.

Once again, as people's minds were opening to new ideas, the process was enhanced with drug experimentation, this time in the form of marijuana and LSD. Psychedelic gurus such as Harvard professor Timothy Leary experimented widely with these drugs and hailed them as new teaching aids to higher consciousness. Leary urged a generation to "Turn on, Tune in and Drop out," and many young people did exactly that, leaving behind traditional lifestyles to create new models of communal living. The hippies became the spokespeople for a new generation of freethinkers, embracing a philosophy of peace, love and freedom which for many people, young and old, became a welcome antidote to the conservatism of the fifties and the antithesis of the war in Vietnam.

The political influences of the hippies, as well as other revolutionary political groups of the time such as The Youth International Party, and even the more extreme and violent organizations such as The Weathermen and The Black Panthers, collectively helped change the political climate away from right wing policies towards a more liberal left wing sensibility. And the thousands and thousands of people who voiced their concerns and demands in the streets of America and Europe forged the way to a new kind of democracy and political activism, creating new models that are still relevant today.

The sixties revolution probably did more to change the way people think and act today than any other time in the twentieth century and the paradigms that were created at that time have continued to fuel our social and cultural changes for the past quarter of a century. From the environmental movement to current world politics, we owe much to the peace and love generation of the sixties. But like all social revolutions, we can only bask in the glow of past glories for so long. Sooner or later, another shift in consciousness will create waves in our popular culture and begin to manifest at all levels of society.

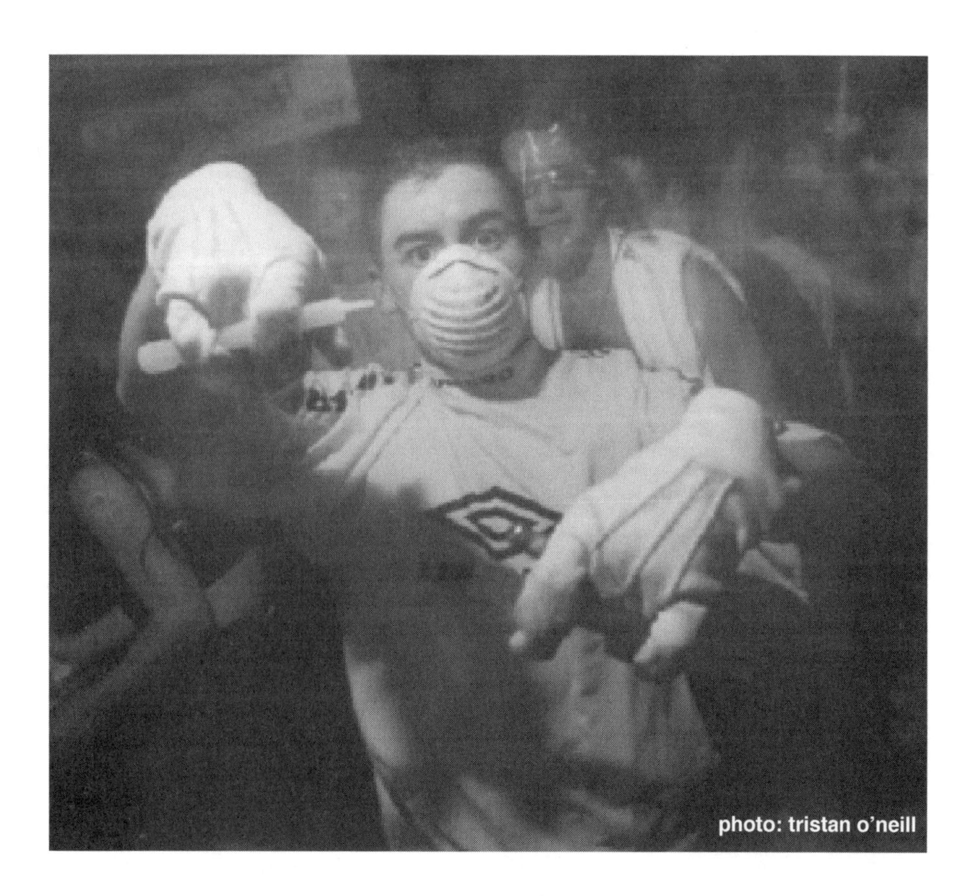
photo: tristan o'neill

THE REVOLUTION OF RAVE

Looking back at the social and cultural changes of the twenties and sixties, and comparing them with the current trends in rave culture, we can see all the same elements resurfacing. Once again we are experiencing a fascination with the subconscious and dream worlds, the rejection and transformation of political ideas, experimentation with mind expanding drugs, the creation of new technologies, new directions in music and art, a change in attitude towards sexuality, issues around personal freedom and the creation of new tribalistic rituals.

Although rave culture has been almost exclusively underground for the past ten years, it is now far too big to stay that way for too much longer. There are now millions of ravers worldwide and their influence is just beginning to infiltrate and effect societies throughout the world in the same way that the two previous revolutions of this century have done. First through music and the arts, and more recently, impacting politics, sexuality and fashion. It can also be shown that rave culture is bringing about changes in technology, particularly in the digital domain where it is pushing the boundaries of computer technology in areas of music production and distribution, advertising, computer art and communications.

Rave has been incubating in the underground caldron of popular culture for almost a decade and a half and we are now beginning to see evidence of its influence impacting on many levels of society. In every corner of the world, the global rave movement is fast becoming a significant force in the evolution of world culture and is now poised to become the revolution that propels us into the next millennium.

A universal symbol of rave culture: the glowstick.

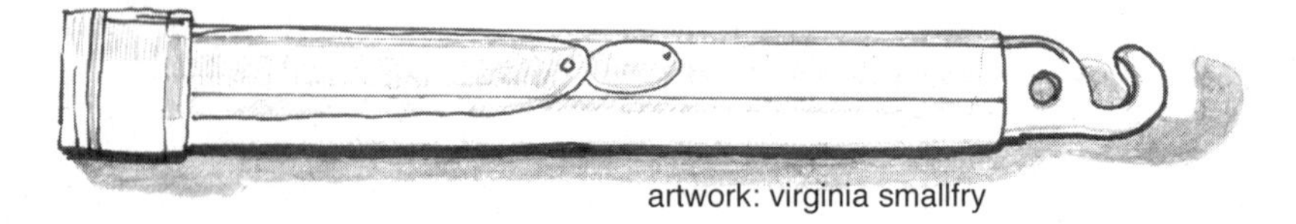

artwork: virginia smallfry

CHAPTER 3:

WHAT IS A RAVE?

photo: tristan o'neill

"Dance is the hidden language of the soul."

- Martha Graham, dancer, choreographer, 1894-1991.

3
WHAT IS A RAVE?

If you look up the word rave in the dictionary you will find very little that relates to rave culture except perhaps "unbridled enthusiasm." The word usually conjures images of mad people frothing at the mouth and was probably originally coined to be controversial - to shock and scare away the straight people. If this was the idea, then it has been very successful. Some would say too successful. But whatever the historical or semantic origins of the word, its definitions have since expanded to connote a unique cultural phenomenon, one which involves a new electronic musical form, and the ritualistic, neo-tribalistic gathering of people who dance all night to achieve a collective trance state.

photo: tristan o'neill

Even within rave culture the term brings with it a certain amount of controversy. Some ravers believe the word has been a hindrance to the movement for too long and have abandoned it in favor of more ambiguous alternatives. Raves are now often referred to as "parties" or "events." The music is designated as "electronic dance music", or more recently "electronica." The movement itself is sometimes described as "dance culture." But all of these terms can be ambiguous, taking on different meanings and interpretations depending on who is using them, and therefore are not always specific to the rave scene. Club DJs for example, tend to shy away from the term "rave" and even when they play at a rave prefer the term "warehouse party." This is largely because the word has been sullied by bad press, and when dealing with people outside of the scene, ravers would rather avoid the issue than deal with the inevitable banal questions. To confuse the issue further, rave is also used to describe a specific type of electronic music that became popular in England at the beginning of the rave movement in 1987 and has since become extinct.

Despite the confusion, "rave" still seems to be the most specific term to describe this cultural phenomenon. And from talking to hundreds of ravers, promoters, musicians and DJs worldwide, it is clear that its meaning is clearly understood by a massive global community of people whose lives have been forever changed by their involvement in the movement.

For those who have never been to a rave and only know what they have read in the local newspaper, the imagination can run wild with mysterious goings on in the dead of night in secret locations. But the truth is far less mysterious and scary than the sensational and myopic reporting of our disaster obsessed media. So leave your preconceptions at the door and let's take a tour through a typical rave...

Earlier in the evening we called the info line on a flyer we picked up at a local electronic music store and listened to a recorded message that gave us directions to the location. This information is only given out on the day of the event or, in some cases, only an hour before the doors open. Although this is a tradition dating back to the early illegal raves of the eighties, the practice continues today, even when parties are held in totally legal venues. The idea is to create a little anticipation of discovering a new location, a sort of magical mystery tour that harkens back to the excitement of bygone days of break-in, warehouse parties. Apart from the traditional aspects, the extra effort required also serves to screen out unwanted guests such as gang members, drunks and other non-ravers who may not take the time to find a flyer and call the info line but might show up after the bars close if they knew the location of the event in advance.

When parking is limited at a venue, shuttle buses are often provided to ferry people to and from pre-arranged pick-up points. Tonight the location is a warehouse in an industrial area on the outskirts of town. A larger rave for five or ten thousand or more might be held in a sports arena or community center. In the summer it could be outside in the woods, in a farmer's field, on top of a mountain, or in the middle of the Mojave Desert.

A larger rave for five or ten thousand or more might be held in a sports arena or community center. In the summer it could be outside in the woods, in a farmer's field, on top of a mountain, or in the middle of the Mojave Desert.

The flyer gives the start time as ten o'clock but we are some of the first to arrive as we drive up and park at the back of the building just past eleven to the accompaniment of a muffled, booming bass. Small groups of people are hanging around the unlit entrance to the warehouse and as we get closer, we see that two of them have walkie-talkies and jackets with security company logos. A school bus now pulls into the darkened parking lot, and a stream of ravers pile out and head to the door. Most of them are wearing backpacks or carrying sports bags full of essentials for the evening's entertainment. Supplies can include a change of clothes, a towel, incense, candies and gum, glow sticks, a water bottle, sparkles and stickers, etc. Once through the door, there are more security people in a makeshift foyer. After giving our tickets to the door person, we stand in line to get frisked. One by one, a security person pats us down, looking for glass bottles, alcohol and drugs. Raves are non-alcoholic events and are not required to be licensed, but if alcohol is found on the premises, the police have a legitimate reason to instantly close the party. Consequently, promoters are very careful to make sure that not even one can of beer makes it inside the venue. At a smaller party, the security might be handled by volunteers or ravers working for a free ticket. At a purely underground event there is usually no security at all. After the body search, we file past a long utility table and present our bags for inspection. Arrests and charges are rarely made at the door, and if any alcohol, drugs or glass bottles are found, they are duly confiscated. A large waste paper basket on the table already contains a couple of bottles of booze, several cans of beer, a dozen joints and various containers of pills and powders.

Ravers have a penchant for candy and it is common to have someone pop up on the dance floor to offer you a hard candy or a gummy worm or a lollipop to suck on.

photo: tristan o'neill

Once inside, the music is loud and clear and the first DJ of the night is spinning records on a raised stage at one end of the cavernous building. A mountain of speakers flank the stage and a live video image of the DJ is projected on a giant screen behind the stage area. The DJ's name is also dancing across the screen in expanding and exploding letters. It is now twenty past eleven and there are about a hundred people milling about in a space that can easily hold two thousand. This is typical of the late night rave crowd who usually arrive en masse around midnight. For now the place looks almost empty as we set out to explore the environment.

The main room is huge and reminiscent of an aircraft hanger. Large screens are hung from the ceiling and a tower of scaffolding in the middle of the floor houses half a dozen film projectors that throw a constantly changing collage of images on to the screens and walls of the warehouse. Footage of outer space is intercut with tribal imagery while on another screen, a newborn baby spinning in space is superimposed on a computer-generated futuristic landscape. Japanese animation, pirated from the local video store, transforms the back wall into a moving panorama of colour. At a larger party there may be two or more dance rooms featuring different kinds of music. Above the stage is a gantry loaded with intelligent lights, strobes and spots, operated from a computer terminal. Only a few of them are activated now, but later they will transform this room into a psychedelic, three-dimensional light environment.

It is now a quarter to midnight and people are beginning to arrive in droves. There are squeals of delight and much kissing and hugging as people meet friends they may not have seen since the last party. Others are wandering around looking for a place to dump their coats and bags. A group of about three hundred are now dancing in front of the stage. Some of the girls are dressed as fairies with gossamer wings and magic wands while others wear feather boas or outrageous make-up and hair-dos. Another has a transparent plastic backpack filled with flashing coloured lights. Over by the entrance there is a coat-check area where for one dollar you can leave your possessions in safekeeping. Some people will use this service but many will not, preferring instead to find a convenient spot to pile up their stuff in a dark corner or behind a speaker. Theft is rare at raves and in any case, most ravers are smart enough not to leave their life savings lying around unattended.

DJ Hype, UK

photo: tristan o'neill

Across the back wall of the warehouse there is a line of vendors. One is a candy store. Ravers have a penchant for candy and it is common to have someone pop up on the dance floor to offer you a hard candy or a gummy worm or a lollipop to suck on. The sugar provides a welcome energy boost and the chewing or sucking action can help to alleviate jaw clenching, an occasional side effect of ecstasy. At another stall, an enterprising young woman is selling glow sticks, sparklers, glow in the dark stickers and an array of other rave toys and accessories. Her partner is painting psychedelic patterns on people's bodies with fluorescent paints.

The biggest area in the market is reserved for a smart bar where fresh vegetable and fruit juices can be purchased. These drinks will often come with herbal additives such as spirulina, ginseng or other energizing herbs. This is also a place where you can buy bottles of mineral water. Before long, almost everyone at this party will be carrying around, and periodically swigging on, a bottle of mineral water. At another table, a harm reduction group is handing out flyers and offering information on safe sex and drug use. These organizations are a common presence in the rave scene and throughout the evening they will be talking to whoever will listen about how to be safe and avoid problems with irresponsible drug use. They will also give out free condoms and offer emergency first aid when needed. Most legal raves might also have ambulance personnel on hand and even a few special duty police officers in addition to the professional security team.

These measures are one of the reasons that raves have one of the best safety records of any public event.

It is now twelve-thirty and people are flooding onto the dance floor. More people are finding each other amidst enthusiastic screams as if finally reunited after years of separation. The next DJ of the night is picking up the pace as the music intensifies in speed and volume. The DJs will change every two hours throughout the night, each more intense than the last. The crowd is now a thousand strong and you would have to be flat lining not to pick up on the excitement in the air. After dancing for a while we decide to take a break and wander through the far door into the chill-out lounge, an area where people can relax, cool down, or mingle and chat with friends. The DJ in this room is playing ambient music designed to create a soothing atmosphere. The room is lined with old couches and chairs scrounged from the local Salvation Army and the many black lights that hang from the walls give the space an ethereal glow. People are lounging everywhere, laughing, talking, hugging and grooving to the music. Just off the chill-out is a smaller, dimly lit room equipped with several massage tables. For a couple of dollars you can get a professional massage therapist to loosen up your aching muscles at any time during the night. At bigger events you might find an inflatable room to bounce around in, or a cyber station, or even midway rides.

Hour after hour, the intense pace continues as the dancers meld into one living, breathing, dancing organism.

It is now one thirty as we head back in to the main room. The scene is now truly amazing. Almost two thousand people are dancing ecstatically to the wild, pounding electronic beats. The lights are now going full blast, filling the room with shafts of coloured light thick enough to cut with a knife. Several smoke machines mounted underneath the stage are pumping out a white fog that engulfs the dancers nearest the stage and creates a soft focus effect in the rest of the room. The swirling smoke acts as a medium for the pulsing and piercing lights, transforming them from a transparent medium to an almost solid form. A giant disco ball suspended from the ceiling is illuminated by a powerful green spotlight, filling the space with laser like points of light. As the music rises to a crescendo, hundreds of people begin screaming at the top of their lungs. The place is alive with writhing forms, some deep in their own personal experience, others openly sharing their feelings in spontaneous outpourings of warmth and affection. Complete strangers hug each other with the same intensity and sincerity as they would embrace long lost love ones.

The music doesn't miss a beat as the featured DJ steps up to the decks at two a.m. The crowd nearest the stage acknowledges his arrival with whoops and hollering. Another musical build begins, and once again the crowd begins to scream and yell in anticipation of the climax. This time the sounds of whistles are added to the chorus and help punctuate the thumping bass drum. With two thousand people dancing flat out, the party is now in full swing and will stay that way until the sun comes up. Hour after hour, the intense pace continues as the dancers meld into one living, breathing, dancing organism.

In the morning, when the sun finally begins to filter into the room, the pace actually picks up, and for the last hour, even people who have spent most of the night in the chill-out lounge will join the throng to dance in the dawn. When the music finally ends, the floor is a sea of empty plastic water bottles, and the cool morning air is a welcome antidote to the sauna-like conditions of the night before. Outside in the parking lot hundreds of ravers are milling around, saying their good-byes, re-grouping with friends and preparing to leave. Many will go on to an after hours party that will continue all through the next day. Outside, other promoters are handing out flyers for the next party that might be twice, or ten times as big. The next event might be held in an arena, on a private yacht, under the stars in a forest or on a remote beach. But wherever it is, you can guarantee that hundreds or thousands, or even hundreds of thousands of ravers will be there, bursting with enthusiasm and anticipation of another chance to touch something larger than themselves, to be a part of a neo-paganistic tradition that is putting people back in touch with themselves and their tribal ancestry.

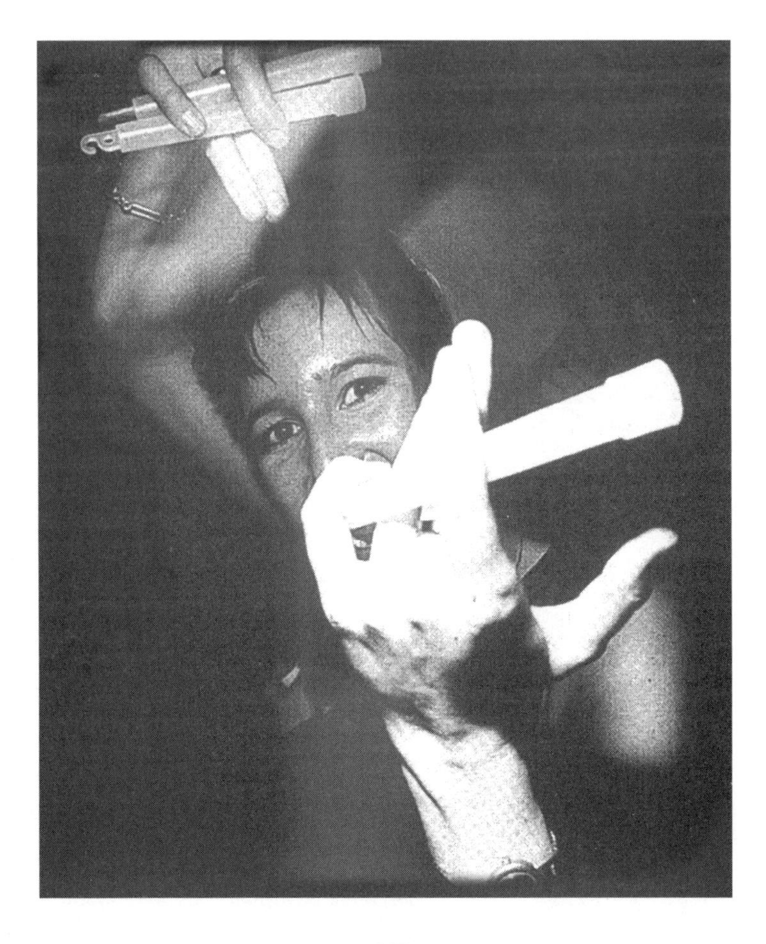

"A rave is any place where a group of people come together to dance to a variety of musical styles with the idea of Peace, Love Unity and Respect. If the people who come to party do not have Peace, Love, Unity and Respect towards their fellow ravers and do not come together with a feeling of acceptance and an open mind, then it is not a rave."

- Maya Berelowitz, student, raver, Cape Town, South Africa.

"Raving is a perfect anti-stress experience. When all is perfect, I mean the music, place, people and 'vibes', it makes you dance for hours in a "ecstatic" mood that multiplies your energies during the event and leaves you feeling relaxed for days after."

- Federico Sommariva, rave promoter, DJ, Milan, Italy.

"A general definition of a rave would be a modern high-tech form of an ancient tribal ritual where shamans gather to dance themselves into deep trance or self-hypnosis. Raving is a very deep spiritual experience, almost like the enlightenment states in many religions. For this one single reason, raving is not actually dancing at all and techno is not really music at all, but something much, much more."

- Janne Leino, raver, Helsinki, Finland.

"A 'rave' is a spiritual event which is capable of uniting everyone. It's a place where you can drop all illusions and dance without any judgment."

- Jo Fruitybits, magazine editor, raver, Melbourne, Australia.

"At a rave you feel free to express everything. You can dress as you like, you can behave as you like, you can do you hair as you like and you can dance as you like. Everything is free, there is no limits and when the music is great, a rave party is a beautiful trip."

- Ivan Arar, raver, Zagreb, Croatia.

"A rave is what you make it. It is somewhat built up around what the person throwing it means to do. The parties we are involved in are about family, about community, about self expression and about freedom."

- DJ Drenalin, Salinas, California, USA

"A rave is a physical manifestation of a gathering of a number of people, regardless of origin, race, background, social class, age, etc. using peaceful techniques to reach a higher state of consciousness and humanity through the revival of ancient ritual."

- Ferid Abbasher a.k.a. DJ Lord Ferdi the Despiser,
Nexus, Indjija, Yugoslavia.

"A rave is... motion filled, energetic movement. A way of having fun without any alcohol or drugs. Nice, friendly people, smiling and dancing all night. Something wonderful..."

- Esa Ojansivu, student, raver, Ilomantsi, Finland.

"A rave is a gathering which is a totally autonomous zone. Basically there is no authority telling you what you can and can not do. If the energies of the participants are strong enough and the music pushes them far enough, it is possible to take the party into another dimension."

- Will, computer technician, raver, Athens, Greece.

"A really good rave party is something that you can't define. Just be there and feel it..."

- Federico Sommariva, promoter, DJ, Milan, Italy.

"A rave is a dance party with beautiful people and lots of expression, creativity and love."

- Katherine Wheatley, computer sales rep, raver,
Melbourne, Australia.

CHAPTER 4:

THE HISTORY OF RAVE

photo: tristan o'neill

"History is a relentless master. It has no present, only the past rushing into the future. To try to hold fast is to be swept aside."

- John Fitzgerald Kennedy, 35th president of the United States, 1917-1963.

4
THE HISTORY OF RAVE

The history of rave should properly begin around forty thousand years ago when early man still lived in caves and breathed wood smoke. At some point in primitive man's social evolution, people began to express themselves musically, probably vocally at first, then later experimenting with making sounds by banging sticks together and so on.

The first musicians would have responded to their mostly rhythmic musical attempts by swaying back and forth, stamping their feet and bobbing their heads, etc. Through this process of self-discovery, music and dance were born. Humans quickly discovered that this new activity created a common shared experience which was not only pleasurable but also served as a method of communication and a powerful bonding ritual, one that could readily express emotion and a range of other non-verbal messages. Almost every primitive culture embraced group dancing as a form of community building and most still do in some fashion.

In more recent times there has been a growing tendency to move away from ritualistic group bonding practices with disastrous results. Although modern alternatives like sports events, nightclubs, rock concerts and other mass public events have a group experience in common, they are apt to be dominated and motivated by egotistic tendencies and therefore ultimately create more division than unity between the participants. Even the churches are falling short in their attempts to create a common spirituality. It comes as no surprise then, that the same basic human drive that urged and inspired primitive people to stomp around the cave and bond on a Saturday night are once again resurfacing in rave culture to fulfill the same fundamental needs.

It is commonly believed that the birthplace of rave was Ibiza, one of the Balearic Islands comprising an autonomous region and province of eastern Spain in the Mediterranean Sea. The story goes that itinerant British and European lotus-eaters populated the island and put it on the map as a place for international travelers to hang out and party on their way to and from Morocco, bringing with them slabs of hashish, the drug of choice at parties on Ibiza at the time. By 1985, ecstasy was making its first appearance in the dance clubs of Dallas and other North American cities where at the same time, house music was evolving from underground disco in the gay clubs of Chicago.

Meanwhile, disciples of the Indian guru Bhagwan Rajneesh had discovered ecstasy in America and adopted the drug as an aide for spiritual advancement. They are credited with bringing ecstasy to Amsterdam in 1985. By 1986 the drug and house music had found their way to Ibiza and were immediately embraced by the party community, transforming late night laid back parties into all night dance parties. Shortly afterwards the parties migrated back to England with the itinerant Brits and rave culture was born.

While there is a lot of truth to this sequence of events, the history of rave is also inextricably linked to the birth of house music that evolved in the dance clubs of America. The truth is, it is hard to say where a musical idea truly begins because every so-called new idea has a long and illustrious genealogy and is closely linked to the history of music itself. This is especially true today, where communications technology makes it possible to instantly transmit ideas on a global level. A new musical idea may come to light in the bedroom of a beat mixer in Baltimore, be posted on the Internet as a sound file ten minutes later and a few minutes after that, can be influencing a producer in Poland or inspiring a Japanese techno artist in Tokyo. Even so, it is possible to chart the growth of house music from the accounts of people who were there at the time. (See: The History of Electronic Dance Music.)

The clubbers in Dallas may well have been among the first ravers because they were dancing to early house music while under the influence of ecstasy as early as late as 1984, just after the drug had leaked out of Alexander Shulgin's laboratory in Berkley, California and before it made its legendary voyage to Ibiza. This was a natural progression from disco DJs and MDA use popular in disco clubs all over America in the seventies and early eighties. The first house tracks were also being produced in Chicago at about the same time. But the dancing was still confined to the clubs and there were no full-scale raves in Texas or anywhere else in the United States at that time.

In more recent times there has been a growing tendency to move away from ritualistic group bonding practices with disastrous results.

The first underground raves were probably held in Ibiza in 1986, but spread quickly northward to England. The first English raves are said to have been impromptu, clandestine parties in warehouses around the English countryside in the outskirts of London and the Manchester area in early 1987. The music being played was acid house and the parties were known as acid house parties. These events moved outside in the summer of '87, marking the birth of the free party movement, a natural progression from the free festival movement that was prevalent in England at the time. Free parties are still an important part of rave culture today and are a reminder of the movement's political roots and its commitment to operate on a non-exploitive basis.

Thousands of young people from all over the country began showing up in remote and secret locations to be swept away by the new music and dance the night away. It didn't take too long before the authorities caught on to what was happening and made moves to stop the parties. Because of the illegal drug use and the lack of permission or permits from city councils, the official "war on raves" began and continues to this day.

By 1987 rave parties were springing up all over England and were catching on at an incredible rate. This spate of early parties kick-started the rave scene in England and became known as the Summer of Love, a name recycled from the Summer of Love in 1967 that marked the peak of the hippie culture twenty years before. Parties were set up in a makeshift fashion and held in garages, deserted warehouses, disused buildings and farmers fields. DJ Robynöd from England remembers one of the early parties in the Midlands of England, *"One of the first parties I went to was a BWPT event just outside of Loughborough in England. BWPT were one of the original groups of traveling underground rave promoters doing events in the Midlands. Four of us drove around for miles to find a farmer's field. After being lost for an hour or more we had nearly given up when we saw some cars parked by the side of the road and then we could hear the music. They had the decks set up in an orchard, some strobes, and a backdrop hung up in the trees. About two hundred people were there and a group of about seventy people were really going off in front of the decks. It was a great party and went 'til the sun came up."*

photo: tristan o'neill

It was during this time that groups like Schroom and Genesis P. Orridge's Psychic TV began throwing all-night dance parties in England along with a host of other underground party promoters. At the same time, the rave phenomenon was taking hold in Germany and in particular, Berlin. Holland, Belgium, France and Italy were not far behind and in less than a year, raves had sprung up in every corner of Europe and made the journey across the ocean to North America.

In the early days, the parties were almost always illegal. A group of loosely organized promoters would descend on the location a few hours before the event was scheduled to begin to set up the sound and lights. Lookouts, armed with cell phones or walkie-talkies were posted at strategic locations around the area to give early warnings of approaching police. It was also common practice to monitor police activity by eavesdropping on the police band radio frequencies with a CB rig. If the promoters were organized enough, they could turn off the music and have everyone be quiet while the police did a drive by of the area. Often, the party would go undetected and when the all clear was heard by lookouts scattered around the neighboring rooftops, the sound system would be turned back on and the party would instantly kick back into high gear. Sometimes parties could survive two or three visits a night from the police and still continue until morning.

The early raves were advertised strictly by word of mouth with networks of ravers communicating on cell phones, giving secret location information hours or even minutes before the party began. Sometimes the location was given out directly but as the police began to learn the rules of the game and began monitoring cell transmissions, the ravers responded by inventing new tactics. One of these evasive techniques involved giving out meeting locations on cell phones, places where ravers would gather and mingle to share location information face to face. Intermediate locations could be parking lots, farmer's fields or city parks, and these wild goose chases could sometimes involve more than one intermediate location, often resulting in convoys of cars racing around the countryside or city streets for hours in search of the party. But rather than being a deterrent, these hardships were all part of the thrill of illegal parties. Ravers embraced the chase and were excited and empowered at the prospect of discovering a secret new location while at the same time outwitting the police.

photo: trent warlow

DJ Billy was attending parties in the burgeoning scene in Vancouver, Canada in the early nineties. *"In '91 in Vancouver the parties were still underground. There were no flyers. Everybody would get on their cell phones, go to a meeting place, get the location and drive off in convoys to the gig. It was a hilarious adventure back then."*

Kim Stanford of The Toronto Raver Information Project (TRIP), a harm reduction organization, also remembers the excitement of illegal venues. *"I think that with the illegal warehouse parties, to take over an empty space normally used for something else was symbolic of a new way of being. To take something that is old and run down and a part of what used to be and creating something completely new and phenomenal in the same space. You lose that excitement with clubs and legal venues. It was exciting to always be going to a new space and not knowing where it was 'til the last minute. Of course with legal venues you gain things like running water and adequate fire exits so I have to support that."*

As the parties became bigger, it became less practical to have everyone chasing around searching for the location information. Some promoters started to print flyers as a more efficient method of communication. The flyer contained information on the DJ line up, some information on the production and an info line; a phone number that accessed a recorded message giving the location on the day of the event, a method that is still exclusively used today. The flyer method, like the cell phone/tag team method before it, ensures that only dedicated ravers make it to the party. The flyers are passed out from hand to hand and are left at select locations such as electronic music stores where ravers are likely to hang out. Flyers act as a screening process to filter out the bar crowd and other non-raver groups that do not embrace rave philosophy but may be looking for something to do after the clubs shut down. This is one of the reasons why there is very rarely any violence or other problems at raves. The flyer system also keeps the location a secret until the day of the event to keep the authorities in the dark until the last moment. Even with a legal permit in a licensed building, local authorities still have a nasty habit of closing parties.

The early raves were advertised strictly by word of mouth with networks of ravers communicating on cell phones, giving secret location information hours or even minutes before the party began.

By 1989 raves had spread across Europe and were beginning to make waves in North America. Although early house music was being created in Chicago and Detroit as early as 1984, electronic dance music was still almost exclusively confined to the club scene. It was not until the music migrated across the Atlantic to England that it became associated with raves. By the late eighties, the rave phenomenon had traveled back across the Atlantic to the US where people were already familiar with the music but had not yet been exposed to all night rave parties.

The first raves in America surfaced in California as early as 1988. Gena Womack was involved in the early rave scene in San Francisco and Los Angeles and was also one of the founding members of The Moontribe Collective. *"I went to an early warehouse party in Los Angeles in 1988. We went in through a secret entrance and up four floors in an elevator to a big room with black lights and a smoke machine. The crowd were still mostly clubbers in those days."*

English ravers had migrated to California by 1989 and brought with them the latest music and a new sensibility and style. Gena Womack remembers their influence on the scene in California. *"When the English ravers arrived, they knew what they were up to and turned a lot of us on to the music and the psychedelics. Fraser Clarke's Evolution Magazine and other literature was coming over from England and people would be going over to England, checking it out and coming back with clothes and new sounds. The British were definitely a big influence on the scene in Los Angeles and San Francisco but there was also a lot of groundbreaking Americans involved too. It was a real melting pot.*

The scene in San Francisco probably started in 1991 with a club called Love at Big Heart City, but it was more of a club scene. Next came Tune Town that was run by a guy called Preston and had incredible events with biofeedback machines and guest speakers like Terrence McKenna and Mark Anton Wilson. Shortly after that, Alan Mcqueen started Wicked Productions and produced a lot of big parties. They also produced the first Full-Moon parties on Beaker Beach and Bonnie Dunes in Santa Cruz. Everything was renegade at that time. Tune Town started out as a warehouse thing and later turned into a more commercial venue but it brought in a lot of acts. They worked with Eddie Richards of Dynamix from England to bring in a lot if international DJs. They had loads of visuals and were the first people to do smart bars.

DJ Tyger Dhula
photo: trent warlow

1991 was a real ground breaking year in LA. A promoter called Mr. Coolaid did a huge party called Gilligan's Island on the Island of Catalina which got a lot of national press. Then Doc Martin moved down from Los Angeles and started these after hour events called Flammable Liquid and he would play for hours and hours. Doc was a huge influence and transformed the dance music scene in LA. Another event called Community had just started on Tuesday nights on Folsom Street with two San Francisco DJs, Jeno and Ernie Munson. Everyone came and the place would get packed out. Then there was The Top on Haight Street on Sundays, Housing Project on Wednesdays. Then at DVA on Thursdays was Osmosis with Peter Veela. Pretty much every night of the week something was happening.

After that, things really got cooking and the phenomenon started, other people started doing things like Funky Tekno Tribe, and "A Rave Called Sharon" which was ground breaking for a lot of people and brought a lot of kids in. It was a large party with lots and lots of visual candy and dancers with feathers and paints and computer imagery and slogans like "I am God" and lots of really positive stuff."

On the West Coast the ethos of the rave scene blended nicely with the hippy mentality and values that had been well established in California since the sixties. In no time at all, the spiritual aspects of rave culture were enhanced and amplified by a new generation of techno-hippies. From California rave spread eastward back across America and in a remarkably short time every state in the union had been exposed to this new cultural sensation.

By the end of 1992 rave culture had truly become a global affair and was well established in many countries around the world.

DJ Djanda

photo: trent warlow

One of the most significant developments on the East Coast was a series of parties called the Storm Raves. These parties were produced by Frankie Bones, a DJ from Brooklyn, New York who was one of the first DJs to be invited to play at raves in England. Frankie was so impressed by his experiences in England that on his return, he started the Storm Raves in Brooklyn and turned a huge amount of East Coast clubbers on to rave culture. The parties began in early 1992 with a modest attendance of anywhere between fifty and a hundred people. Frankie would project images on giant screens of the English raves to show people how it was done. Many DJs who are now world famous got their start at Frankie's Storm Raves including Sven Vath, Doc Martin, Keoki, Josh Wink and many others. In December of 1992, Frankie held a party at an abandoned loading dock in Queens that drew over five thousand people. According to rave mythology, this was when Frankie Bones made his famous speech about peace, love, and unity that would later become the acronym PLUR to form the philosophical foundation of the global rave movement. (See: The Philosophy of Rave.)

By the end of 1992 rave culture had truly become a global affair and was well established in many countries around the world. The tradition of the illegal parties continued but as the movement became more and more popular, some promoters were starting to see the economic potential of raves and began to look for legal venues. The break-in warehouse parties of the past had now become a liability for some promoters. It was frustrating to regularly have the parties shut down; the threat of a closure severely limited the kind of production that could be staged. With the greatly increased expenses of international DJs, huge sound systems and a demand for bigger and better light shows, producers wanted a safer investment for their time and money. Large arena raves or "massives" began to emerge, regularly attracting record crowds of anywhere between 500 to 1,500 for an average size party, to hundreds of thousands for a big party. (The Love Parade in Berlin, Germany, the world's biggest rave event has attracted more than a million people in recent years.)

Although the big legal parties are popular, and continue to grow and attract new people to the scene, rave culture has since diversified and now has many levels of involvement. Among seasoned ravers there is a common feeling that the large parties take away an element of intimacy so they purposefully organize smaller more "vibey" events of 50 to 200 people. Some ravers have intimate house parties of only ten or twenty people to create an environment where people can really connect on a deeper, more personal level. In the summer when the weather is mild, more and more outside events take place in beautiful natural surroundings, although I have also seen parties take place outside in mid-winter with crowds of enthusiastic ravers dancing through the night in the howling winds and pounding rain!

Today, thirteen years after the first parties on the island of Ibiza, rave culture is an international movement with a unified vision and global sense of community. There are well developed scenes in almost every country with people of diverse backgrounds raving in every major center in the USA, Canada, Europe, South America, Scandinavia, Japan, Thailand, India, Australia, New Zealand, Russia, South Africa and many other parts of the world. (See: Raving Around the World.)

Rave may well be the biggest pop culture movement in history and it is only recently beginning to move from its underground status to a full blown social revolution with the potential to positively influence a generation and ultimately change the course of human consciousness.

"I think that there was a definite element of excitement when we were running around in farmer's fields to a marquis tent with the decks on the back of a lorry, not knowing if it was going to be shut down, and watching the sun come up in the morning. There was a lot of fun about those days. I've been privileged to have witnessed both side of it. I enjoy playing in clubs like Twilo but I like the fact that I played at those early parties as well. That's where I cut my teeth."

- John Digweed, DJ, producer, England.

"There was this feeling, the smell of the fog out of the fog machine, strobes, the pumping music. It's not like that anymore - it's no longer new, illegal and sneaky, thus exciting. There was Spirit to it. It was rebellion, it was freedom and individuality."

- Jari Nousiainen a.k.a. Super attaK, Helsinki, Finland.

CHAPTER 5:

THE RAVE EXPERIENCE

photo: tristan o'neill

"Occasionally in life there are those moments of unutterable fulfillment which cannot be completely explained by those symbols called words. Their meanings can only be articulated by the inaudible language of the heart."

- Martin Luther King, Jr., American civil rights activist, Nobel Laureate, 1929-1968.

5
The Rave Experience

At the very heart of rave culture is a phenomenon that I will call "the rave experience", and what many ravers refer to as "going off".

The rave experience is what happens when all the conditions and elements are just right and everything comes together to create a transcendental group-mind experience. This is the reason that most people go to raves and why they have become so popular. This kind of experience was once common to the tribal communities of our ancestors and considered essential to the mental health of the community. (See: Neo-Tribalism.)

You do not need to be familiar with any ritualistic practices or esoteric teachings to experience and benefit from the rave experience. In fact, many ravers, particularly the younger set, have little or no knowledge of the cultural and historical significance of rave culture or its tribalistic roots. Even the love-ins and be-ins of the sixties are ancient history to the majority of ravers today. But this is the beauty of the rave experience and why it has been such an effective cultural tool for so long. It is not something that you need to be educated about. It is not something that can be taught or explained or read from a book. It is something that you experience directly, beyond language or even thought. Like meditation, it is the direct essential experience of life itself, beyond the artificial constructs of the ego-based discriminating mind. Thousands of years of practice have proven that when we engage in this type of group ritual, the effects and aftermath can be truly liberating.

artwork: virginia smallfry

Many people unfamiliar with rave have the impression that as long as you take enough ecstasy you will automatically achieve the rave experience. This is far from the truth. Many people who have only taken ecstasy outside of the rave environment - and this includes therapeutic sessions conducted by qualified counselors - have a very different view of the effects. Compared to LSD or other psychedelic substances, the effects of ecstasy are relatively mild, merely producing warm feelings of empathy and well being. In therapy, ecstasy puts the client in a receptive, trusting state of mind that can reduce anxiety and aid in attaining an objective viewpoint from which to discuss psychological problems. At a rave, the user is put under the influence of a very different set of stimulus. So although ecstasy and other psychedelic drugs can serve to enhance and encourage the rave experience, they are only one element of a much bigger picture. Indeed, in Sweden, Finland and many other countries which have a vibrant rave scene, the use of ecstasy is nowhere near as widely used as in other countries, with many ravers rejecting ecstasy use altogether. I have heard from scores of people over the last three years who have been raving for years and describe complete psychedelic trance experiences they have had at raves on nothing more than mineral water. But to create the necessary elements for the rave experience a number of conditions must be met. The most important and significant element by far, is the music.

The music must have the power to generate the momentum necessary to carry the listeners away on a magic carpet of sound. Not all DJs have the skills and sensitivity necessary to create a musical journey that is essential for a transcendental experience. Incompatible or mixed-up rhythms, too many stops and starts or sloppy mixing techniques can all dilute the overall effect. DJs earn their reputation based on their ability to read and respond to the energy of the crowd and provide the required intensity at the right times to be effective as a musical catalyst. It is the job of the DJ to bring everyone to a place where the group-mind takes over. Once this is achieved, a DJ has the responsibility to maintain and/or increase the intensity to continue the journey indefinitely. A drop in the musical energy can drastically effect the atmosphere and send people wandering off the dance floor. Like the tribal drumming that fueled our ancestors community-building rituals, the beats must be continuous and integrated and the transitions seamless.

The music must have the power to generate the momentum necessary to carry the listeners away on a magic carpet of sound.

Just as our tribal ancestors reserved special or sacred places to gather, a successful rave needs the right location. This can be one of the most difficult requirements for today's tribal events given the resistance from most local authorities. Needless to say, it is not very favorable to the rave experience to have a squad of police officers barging across the dance floor, searching people's bags and threatening to make arrests. But regardless of the obstacles, promoters do manage to find suitable locations that are conducive to a meaningful group experience.

The location must be big enough for the number of people attending so there is enough room for everyone to dance and move around freely. A high ceiling is advantageous to create a sense of expansiveness. Adequate ventilation is essential. An overcrowded room with poor airflow can become unbearable very quickly and many of the casualties reported at raves are often found later to be due to overheating caused by overcrowding and/or poor ventilation. Even when there are enough windows and skylights to supply fresh air, promoters are sometimes reluctant to open them for fear of sound complaints, the most common cause of raves being closed down. It is also important to have an area where people can rest and take a break if necessary.

photo: trent warlow

Decorations, projected images and lighting must all conspire to create an alternative environment, one that can transport us away from our daily concerns and help foster a sense of awe and wonder. The environment in general must inspire a climate of freedom, where people can feel unfettered enough to completely let go and yet still feel safe. It is hard to really let go and enjoy yourself with a security guard looking over your shoulder, watching every move. This is one of the reasons why the illegal warehouse parties were so popular and continue to have appeal. In a deserted warehouse, there is only the in-house security hired by the promoters or, more often than not, no security or control at all. This can create some safety problems but at the same time ensures a climate of freedom essential to the rave experience.

Next, if you decide that ecstasy will be part of the formula, it must be as pure as possible and taken in the correct dosage. Much of the ecstasy on the market today is not pure MDMA and the illegal status of the drug makes quality control almost impossible. Although there have been relatively few casualties from toxic additives, it pays to be careful and only buy from people you know and trust.

When all these elements fuse together, the party goes off. At that point - and it is quite obvious when it happens, even to passive spectators - there is a definite shift of energies in the room. It usually begins with a musical build that starts to create an atmosphere of excitement. You can feel the mood change as everyone gets swept up in the upward spiral of sound. As people become lifted to greater heights of awareness, they will often spontaneously begin to shout, whistle or scream in anticipation of the impending musical climax. In some places, sports whistles or party horns are used to make noise. At the height of the climax the music explodes into an intense storm of sound and the dancers go ballistic. At some point the personal experience of the individual dancer then becomes a collective one. It is no longer a group of separate individuals dancing in a room but a holistic group mind, connected by a mystical, universal energy. Like a shoal of fish or a flock of birds, the dancers move as a synchronized whole, far greater than the sum of its parts.

Kim Stanford of the Toronto Raver Information Project has this to say, *"The rave experience is about coming together with a unified vision and a one-mind. It's about raising a huge amount of collective energy for an intensely spiritual experience. And that is far more powerful than any drug."*

The rave experience is about coming together with a unified vision and a one-mind. It's about raising a huge amount of collective energy for an intensely spiritual experience. And that is far more powerful than any drug.

When a party goes off, it is common to see people laugh and smile in amazement as they are swept up in the experience. The amount of energy generated in the room is truly marvelous and continues to build and intensify hour after hour. At the height of the experience language becomes clumsy and is either reduced to simplified terms or dropped altogether in favor of the non-verbal communication of body language. When eye contact is made with other dancers, a knowing look or sympathetic smile is sometimes all that is needed to convey a deep understanding of the shared experience as the awareness of self gives way to a universal feeling of oneness. The dancers experience deep feelings of unlimited compassion and love for everyone around them. Strangers become trusted friends and all superficial judgments are suspended. Social differences that would normally create division become superficial and meaningless. A state of group awareness allows us to identify with others as a part of ourselves and so we share a human experience rather than imposing our own ego based perspective. It is not unusual to see spontaneous displays of affection and caring on the dance floor as complete strangers hug or massage each other. No words or explanations are necessary. Everything is understood.

Along with the deep sense of connection come feelings of elation and freedom. The stress and worries of daily live fall away as the dancers transcend their mindful preoccupations and enter a trance state identical to alpha wave states that meditating monks and other spiritual practitioners strive to attain in their various meditation practices. If approached in this way, the rave experience can be as valid as any other practice designed to achieve a state of transcendence or enlightenment. (See: Rave as Religion.)

While it is true that transcendental group experiences can also happen at a variety of events, what makes rave unique is that an experience of transcendence is their common goal. It is understood through a well-developed philosophy that the objective is to get swept up in the experience and it is important to remember that this is not solely dependent on a drug-induced state. Although ecstasy can be an extremely useful tool to help achieve this transcendental state initially, once we have learned to let go and

photo: trent warlow

trust in the group mind, the music becomes a hypnotic trigger that can induce the same experience without the drug. It is a common for ravers to report that when listening to electronic dance music in a sober state they will often begin to feel the empathetic effects of ecstasy. This is because ecstasy works by stimulating and increasing the secretion of the naturally occurring neurotransmitters, seratonin and dopamine. Seratonin produces the euphoric and empathetic effects while dopamine causes increased energy levels. The music can act as a hypnotic trigger "tricking" the body to boost the normal levels of these brain chemicals. Of course, this triggering effect presupposes that the listener has had an ecstasy experience raising the question of the relevance of using drug-induced states to attain transcendental experiences in general. We know that certain substances can achieve transcendental states that might otherwise take many years of formal and sober practice. I have heard it compared to taking a helicopter ride to the summit of a mountain. We achieve the ultimate goal without the benefits of the long, hard but ultimately rewarding journey. While there is some merit to this argument, I would also add that a peek - or even a good look - at the summit can often provide the necessary motivation to make the rewarding journey in the first place.

The benefits of the rave experience do not begin and end with the dance floor. A variety of positive effects can and do carry over into the everyday lives of ravers. Most commonly, people report that that their relationship with themselves and others improves dramatically. They often notice an increased awareness and empathy with friends and family and become more tolerant of others in general. Many people describe the rave experience as opening their heart chakra, putting them in touch with their emotional side. Many report a renewed enthusiasm and optimism for life in general.

The rave experience can be as valid as any other practice designed to achieve a state of transcendence or enlightenment.

For most people involved in the rave scene, the experience of a group trance state is about personal growth and freedom, about looking beyond the self to identify and empathize with others. It is about the liberation of spiritual energy and a feeling of collective forward motion, a united community moving inevitably towards a positive future. In a world that sometimes appears to be completely insane, the rave experience can give people the advantage of a new and benevolent perspective, one that can offer some sanity and hope to our own lives and ultimately to our troubled planet.

But it is by no means guaranteed that you will have a transcendental experience by simply attending a rave. Not all raves work. In fact, in my experience, less than half of the parties produced, provide the necessary conditions to foster the rave experience. This is why you will find people who may have attended several raves and still don't see what all the fuss is about. They have yet to see one "go off." On the other hand, you will find that practically all dedicated ravers have had the rave experience and this becomes their primary reason for producing or attending parties.

While the goal may be a transcendental experience, this does not mean that the parties that do not "go off" are complete failures. It is an accepted reality among ravers that some parties will not take you all the way and so become relegated to more conventional type, social gatherings. These events can still be great parties and often serve as an opportunity to meet and socialize with people whose names you never learned, with whom you may have shared powerful experiences with in the past without exchanging a word. I have had novice ravers describe their experiences of a non-transcendental rave and claimed that it was the best party they had ever been to. And while it is true that any event is what you make it, when people have their first true rave experience, it can be one of the most powerful and influential experiences of their lives.

One of the important lessons of rave is to be able to assimilate and incorporate this type of heightened experience into our every day lives. This is one of the areas where some ravers fall short of the total benefits of the experience. The powerful or transforming activity of the night before is lost the next day, becoming a separate reality to be put aside until it is recreated at the next party. If this division between the ritual and daily life continues for too long it can create a situation where we can become dissatisfied with our normal lives and become dependent on the ritual in the same way we can become dependent on a drug. What looks and feels like salvation can begin to turn into a dangerous trap.

The tribal rituals of our ancestors also produced powerful group trance states, out of body experiences or other transcendental states of being. (Both with and without mind-expanding drugs). But the next morning, when gathered around the communal yam-mashing bowl, these experiences would be openly discussed and assimilated into daily life. In this way the "real world" and the "trance world" would become one and the same. Both areas of experience would compliment each other to broaden and enrich the experience of the individual, which in turn reflected positively throughout the community. In our society we are discouraged from talking about these kinds of heightened experiences for fear of being labeled as unstable, flaky, or worse yet, a crazed drug fiend. I remember hearing an interview with a sports psychiatrist who had written a book about the supranormal experiences of professional athletes. From hundreds of interviews with athletes competing at world class levels, he had discovered that it was common for athletes to have a full range of psychedelic experiences while engaging in intensive training or while reaching peak performance in competition. Most of the athletes confessed they had never talked to anyone about these experiences for fear of a negative reaction. Many had come to the psychiatrist in the first place worried that they were going insane. Their experiences included hallucinations and visions, overwhelming feelings of euphoria, out of body experiences, and many other symptoms normally associate with heightened states of consciousness or psychedelic drug use. This demonstrates that any kind of peak performance, including dancing all night, can produce these "normal" effects. In so-called primitive societies these experiences were accepted as an ordinary part of life. It is relatively recently that society has relegated this part of human experience to the status of criminal behavior and routinely banned any activities or substances that produce these effects.

Raving is part of our ancestral legacy, indelibly etched into our genetic code.

This innate quality that human beings have to break through perceptual barriers and explore other states of consciousness will not go away. It is part of our ancestral legacy, indelibly etched into our genetic code. The rave experience is merely a modern expression of that ancient and intrinsic human drive. By exploring these non-ordinary states we enhance and expand the realm of human experience and therefore increase our capacity to understand the world we live in.

"The first time was a feeling of total elation and euphoria. I felt such closeness to the friends I was with. We were opened up to each other's feelings but the communication wasn't verbal. I had a great feeling of celebration. Something really happened that night. Fifteen hundred people became very close friends. I met so many new people and by the end of the night we were all friends. It was totally amazing."

- Topher, underground rave promoter, Canada.

"I walked into the main hall and was blinded by the lasers and deafened by the music. I didn't actually start to dance; the music just grabbed me and forced me to dance. I felt the beat gushing in my bloodstream, forcing my whole body to move, to follow every single sound in unison. I closed my eyes, automatically. I fell into myself, getting better in touch with my mind and soul than ever before. I felt no pain, no exhaustion at all. The music was feeding me all the energy I needed and more. I felt the energy pulsate through me with incredible strength, lifting me up above the ground. I danced for eleven hours that night, almost non-stop, without getting tired and I have never taken any drug."

- Janne Leino, raver, Helsinki, Finland.

"Another name for "the rave experience" is "the primal point of contact" when you break through the perceptual barrier into another reality. You are most likely to find this kind of experience at an outdoor, tribal, or full moon event. The conditions are more conducive at that time of the month and the people who organize this type of event are aware of that side of things and program their parties so that it will actually happen."

- Andrew Rawnsley, musician, DJ, editor of XLR8R magazine, San Francisco, USA.

"At a rave every sense is completely and overwhelmingly fulfilled to the point where you can't possibly want more. A lot of people will never experience that kind of joy and total fulfillment. It is complete and utter satisfaction."

- Raevn Lunah Teak, raver, designer, Brisbane, Australia.

"It was my birthday and a girlfriend took me to Players, a rave club in Bath. It was bloody incredible, I couldn't believe it. We danced for hours, stripped down, dripping with sweat and ended up entwined in each other's arms on top of a speaker. We left the club at 5 a.m. and drove off across the Wiltshire downs. We still wanted to dance so we stopped, put a ghetto blaster on top of the car and started dancing on the side of the road in a thick fog. We made our own light show with the hazard warning lights on the car. We were dancing like crazy when a police car drove up behind us. He asked me what we were doing and I said, "Dancing!" "Not here, you're not! Not at 5'o clock in the morning." So we moved along. That was the first time and it completely changed my life."

- Tim Laughlin, rave promoter, Vibe Crew, England.

"My first time at a rave, Laurent Garnier & Sven Vath were playing. I just started moving, dancing, ... I closed my eyes and I saw many stars. It was beautiful. Next to me were some beautiful girls, I thought, this must be heaven! Thanks again, Laurent & Sven!"

- Nico Claes, rave promoter, Antwerp, Belgium.

"I went to a rave bar in Utrecht, Belgium and had one of the most intense experiences of my life. I remember being on the dance floor feeling like I was traveling forwards in an undulating tunnel pulsing to the beat of the bass drum with lights streaking towards me. Each instrument took on a different colour and quality of light. The lead guitar was yellow, the bass was an unbelievable vibrant purple that shook the ground beneath me. I realized that each instrument had a unique story and combined to make the big picture. At that moment I felt like I had a major revelation. After that experience I began to listen to rave music in a whole new way."

- Michael Elewonibi, rave promoter, musician, Canada.

"Rave culture has changed my whole life. I was brought up in Tokyo in a middle-class family and had no appreciation for nature or connections to other people. Rave culture and trance music has given me direction and spiritual fulfillment. My life is more valuable to me now. I have seen other people change too. They become happier."

- Chika, Solstice DJ, rave promoter, Tokyo, Japan.

"The whole rave experience lets you meet and mix with so many different types of people that you ordinarily wouldn't come into contact with. It is this that opens your mind to opportunities in the world that otherwise you would never have considered."

- Karl Munns, DJ, Hertfordshire, England.

"One of the most memorable parties I went to was called Jokers High in Toronto in 1993 with two thousand people. I had never seen anything like it before. I was instantly in love and found the thing that I wanted to do for the rest of my life. I was completely amazed by the energy level. It was so intense, I could feel the love of the people and the love they had for the music. I could never even describe the feelings of joy I had rushing through me. I had been a shy person before and came right out of my shell. I felt so comfortable dancing together with everyone. It was the best time I've ever had in my life. Ever since then, I've been working with my friends promoting parties and DJing so that we can share that experience with other people."

- DJ Davie, The Vibe Tribe, Canada.

"The trance dance provides some form of release and re-charging, while solitary meditation provides similar experiences, the music, social and meditative aspects of the rave combine to produce a uniquely satisfying experience."

- DJ Sylk, Hobart, Tasmania.

artwork: virginia smallfry

"At a rave you get to drop all the bullshit from your life. You can just go and be yourself and have fun with other people and get an incredible sense of being a part of something. In your day-to-day life you may feel like you're all alone in the world trying to figure out what to do. Then, all of a sudden, we're all together and we know what to do. We're going to dance and have fun."

- Surfer Bob, The Vibe Tribe, Canada.

"At a rave you can let go of yourself and feel free of all the baggage you carry around with you most of the time. It helps you to get in touch with yourself and it's healing because it clears your mind. The music makes the experience more intense and you feel a strong tribal connection with everyone."

- Holger, raver, Hamburg, Germany.

"The bonus point is when you look around you on the dance floor and there are other people experiencing the same vibe and you are all united in one big rush and you can hear whistling or air horns. Woah! What a rush, I'm telling you, man!"

- Lloyd Morgan, musician, DJ, Cardiff, Wales, United Kingdom.

"My first rave was an amazing entry into the rave scene. There were lasers, a huge sound system, and friendly people. I was given candy, popsicles and cool little trinkets. It was an entry into a totally foreign and intriguing world and was also one of the turning points in my life."

- DJ Drenalin, Salinas, California, USA.

"My first rave experience was back in '92 at a party in Helsinki. People seemed to be relaxed from their typically rigid Finnish behavior patterns and were able to dance and have fun spontaneously even with strangers. In other countries this would seem normal, but for Finland it was very unusual. What made it special is that many people were able to be into it even without drugs or alcohol."

- Erkki Rautio a.k.a. pHinn, DJ, web master of pHinnWeb, Tampere, Finland.

"My first rave experience was like being a child again. All my blocks were gone. I was goofy, I was loving. I was sharing my energy with everyone through dance. Then I went off on my own and danced on a rock for two hours just as the sun was coming up and I realized for the first time what love really meant to me. I said the word (love) to myself and felt it through every single vein in my body. The first thing I did when I got home was call my mom and told her that I loved her. After that, I was a completely changed woman."

- Gena Womack, founding member of Moontribe, Los Angeles, USA.

photo: tristan o'neill

"I kind of knew that there must be something going on in the rave scene, although acid and smoke sure didn't get me there in the first 4 or 5 parties I went to. I couldn't understand what all the fuss was about with this music and its repetitive, constant bass drum beat. But there was this wickedly good vibe that I felt. My first E experience taught me exactly what was going on."

- Pappa Smurf, rave promoter, Kind Gatherings, Toronto, Canada.

"Music in general has always been able to sweep people off their feet, but what distinguishes raves is the concept of the shared experience; a feeling of unity often arises and people are open and friendly to one another. There is a loss of that "attitude" that is omnipresent in normal clubs and even in life in general. People are celebrated for who they are, not what they are not."

-Brian Behlendorf, founder of SFRaves and Hyperreal.com, San Francisco, USA.

"With the rave experience, intellectual processes are overridden as you surrender to the music and experience a sense of brotherhood and camaraderie and a feeling of unification. You become connected on a molecular level to everyone and everything. All is well with the world."

- Jane of Art, artist, raver, Quebec, Canada.

"The music takes you to incredibly deep subconscious states, particularly when your senses are heightened. Your rational brain and all of the societal, logical programming tells you that this is not happening. But the rhythm latches on to it and it can't think because it's got this pounding rhythm going on. The left brain says, okay, this is something linear I can grasp. And when that happens, it allows the intuition and memory and the entire subconscious realm to have completely free reign. The experience happens in a non-linear, time-space. The displacement of time has to do with the constant rhythm. When it happens on a mass scale, everyone is riding that pulse together and it sucks every body in to create a total group experience."

- Andrew Rawnsley, musician, DJ, Editor of XLR8R magazine, San Francisco, USA.

"The best moment is when the whole mass begins to trance... that's the rare moment, I think."

- Pyc, electronic musician, student, raver, Belgrade, Yugoslavia.

"Whenever you are sincerely pleased, you are nourished."

-Ralph Waldo Emerson, critic, poet and philosopher, 1803-1882.

CHAPTER 6:

NEW MUSIC, NEW TOOLS, NEW SOUNDS.

- early electronic experiments
- an interview with james lumb of electric skychurch
- the history of electronic dance music
- new sounds, new ears
- musical quotes
- an interview with brent carmichael

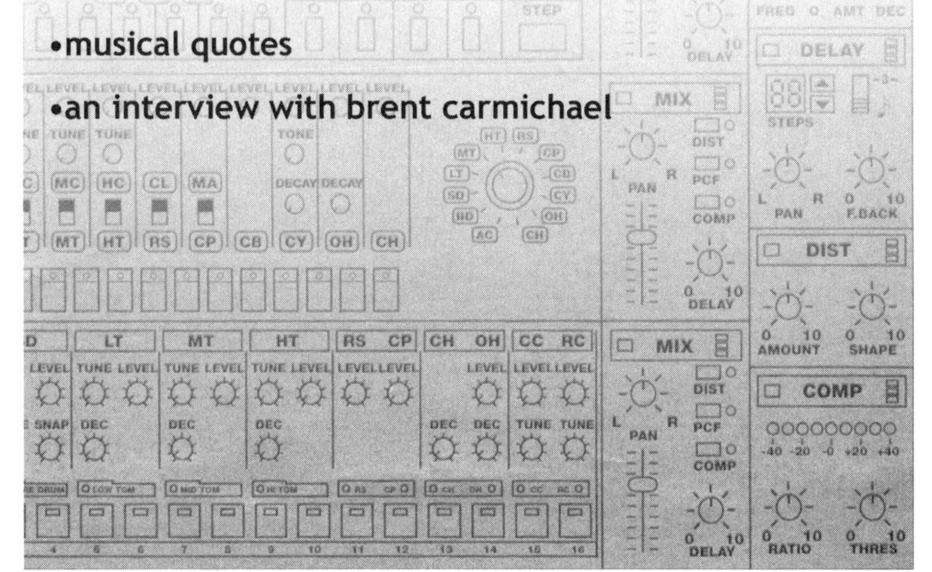

"Music is well said to be the speech of angels; in fact, nothing among the utterances allowed to man is felt to be so divine. It brings us near to the infinite."

- Thomas Carlyle, Scottish essayist, historian, 1795-1881.

6
New Music, New Tools, New Sounds.

Music is without doubt the most exciting aspect of rave culture. Not only are we experiencing new musical forms for the first time in twenty-five years, but we are hearing sounds that have never before been heard by human beings. These sounds are being created by a new generation of technology that has revolutionized the way we create, record, perform and distribute music.

Many people associate rave music with purely electronic sounds but, the sampled sounds being used in today's generation of dance music can originate from any source. Musicians are sampling as many acoustic or "real" sounds as electronically created sounds. The music, like rave culture itself, has become an all-encompassing synthesis of past, present and future. On the same track we can hear ancient hand drumming, beeping pagers, the roar of a lion, snippets of a fifties TV show, or the ancient chanting of Buddhist monks.

On the same track we can hear ancient hand drumming, beeping pagers, the roar of a lion, snippets of a fifties TV show, or the ancient chanting of Buddhist monks.

Electronic music in general has had a checkered past and some of us, myself included, have bad memories of those early experiments with synthesizers. The sounds were cold, sterile and aloof with all the appeal of dehydrated, vacuum-packed space food and spoke of a technological future we were not sure we even wanted. But eventually, electronic instruments evolved and found their place as an adjunct to traditional instrumental line-ups. Apart from a few mavericks operating on the fringes of music, early electronic pioneers tried as hard as they could to fit in with the trends being set by the rock music of the day, trying to imitate real instruments and all too often, falling short. The buttons on the

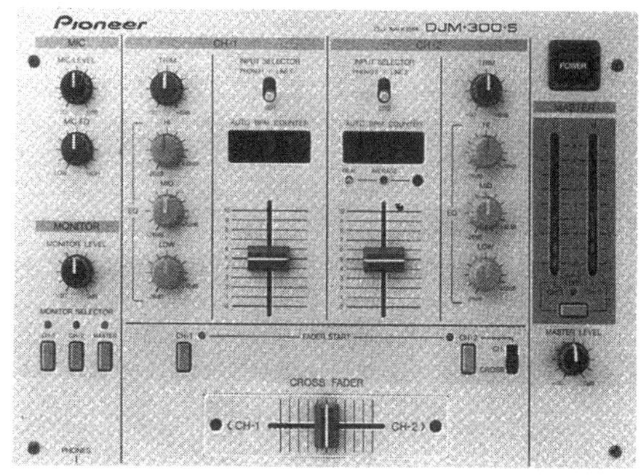

keyboard listed everything from oboes to bagpipes but when activated could only produce a variation or modulation of the electronic tone from the previous choice. With evolving technology and new computer software, the focus has now radically changed. Sounds can now be sampled, created and manipulated in endless ways. Any sound can be digitized into a computer environment and from there, the only limitation is the software and our imagination. We can take a recording of a footstep, sequence the sound, fatten it up, stretch it out to make it longer, selectively manipulate every frequency separately, add and blend any other sound, play it backwards, upside down or inside out. In the end, our solitary footstep can become a richly textured percussion track on which to build a composition. Theoretically, one sound sample can be endlessly manipulated to create an entire symphony. Once the sound has been converted to digital information it can be endlessly reorganized in the computer environment and then output to CD, tape or vinyl. But electronic music is not only about manipulating and transforming existing sounds. It is also about creating completely new and original sounds that have never before vibrated in a human ear.

Over the past decade electronic music has produced an avalanche of new musical ideas, but up until quite recently these exciting developments have remained almost exclusively underground. In the last few years however, we are beginning to see these new musical forms permeating into mainstream musical society, albeit in slightly watered down, sanitized versions. Today we can hear techno or drum and bass used in advertising, on the six o'clock news or in educational videos. The influence of electronic music is also sweeping through the upper echelons of popular music. David Bowie's last album, Earthling, has a heavy jungle music influence and Robbie Robertson new CD entitled, Contact from the Underworld of Red Boy, features early historical recordings of North American Indian chants set to electronic dance rhythms. Madonna is routinely handing over her latest songs to be remixed by electronic musicians, and last year U2 released an

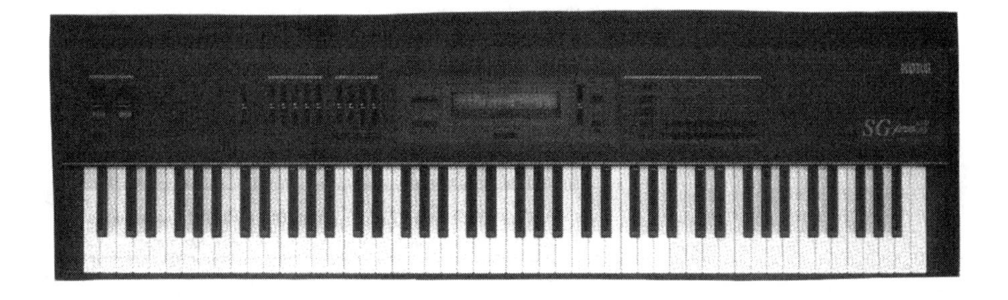

electronic dance music album. Even RuPaul, the transvestite celebrity and self proclaimed "Queen of all Media", is now hosting a national radio show of electronic dance music.

Popular acts like, Prodigy, Underworld, Daft Punk, The Chemical Brothers, Lionrock, The Propellerheads, Represent and the Bentleys are now performing electronic dance music to millions of fans, getting tons of airplay on MTV, churning out hit albums, and playing highly successful world tours. It is now standard practice for record companies to hire electronic musicians or DJs to create dance remixes of existing records that can be pressed in vinyl and played at raves or in clubs. Paul Okenfold, John Digweed, Sasha, James Lumb, Goldie and a host of other high demand remixers around the world spend much of their time creating dance versions of existing recordings. Everyone from Madonna and The Rolling Stones to Led Zeppelin, Cat Stevens and Bob Marley are getting remixed to expand their audience and appeal. 1998 also marked the first year that remixers have been included in the Grammy Awards.

artwork: virginia smallfry

Movies too, have been assimilating new electronic talents in an effort to keep up with the times and appeal to the next generation of moviegoers. A Life Less Ordinary, Spawn, Batman Forever and a host of other Hollywood fare, all contain electronic tracks. Orbital and Daft Punk were featured in The Saint. The Hartnoll Brothers were featured on the sound track to Event Horizon. And who can forget Nicholas Cage going ballistic to Tricky's 'Christiansands' in Face Off.

But while the influences of this new music are making their way into popular culture, the cutting edge artists are still working largely underground, and if you want to hear the latest and greatest you still have to go to a rave or an underground club.

As music expands and develops into new forms it suffers a kind of identity crisis. Each new turn and twist seems to simultaneously defy and demand a new classification. With the speed at which electronic dance music is evolving, yesterday's category quickly becomes tomorrow's outdated cast-off. To date, each new sound has spawned a new moniker.

We now have House, Acid House, Progressive House, Deep House, Happy House, Hard House, Diva House, Techno, Gabba Techno, Ragga Techno, Industrial, Hardcore, Happy Hardcore, Old School, Jungle, Drum and Bass, Hip-Hop, Hard Hop, Trip Hop, Trance, Hard Trance, Happy Trance, Goa Psy Trance, Mojave, Ambient, Somulent, Intelligent, Down Beat, Break Beat, Garage, Raggage, Dub, Acid Jazz, Bhangra, Chutney

Soca, etc., etc., etc. The list goes on, and new categories are being invented on an almost daily basis. (See: Categories of Music and Definitions.)

Most of these categories are used as if they are different genres of music and, while it is true that some have very different musical roots, others are best described as variations on a theme rather than distinct categories in themselves. To understand the inter-relationships we must begin at the beginning, with early electronic experiments and the history of house music.

EARLY ELECTRONIC EXPERIMENTS

As early as 1913, Italian composer Luigi Russolo featured the industrial noises and rhythms of factories and machinery in a piece called Art of Noises. This may well have been the first industrial music but it was in the twenties - which gave us so many new ideas - that the first electronic instruments were invented. The Theremin and the Ondes Martenot were both early electronic instruments invented in the twenties and marked the first forays into electronic experimentation. Composers such as Honegger, Messiaen, Milhaud, Dutilleux and Varese all composed for the Ondes Martenot. The Theremin was also widely used and probably best known for the ethereal and eerie high pitched wailing sounds used in numerous horror and science fiction movies in the fifties. Oskar Sala was another early electronic pioneer who in 1928, together with Dr. Friedrich Trautwein, built an electronic musical instrument called the Trautonium, a monophonic device based on an oscillator with a glimmer lamp. The Trautonium was capable of producing a continuous alteration of the tone colour, controlled by a horizontally stretched wire, which was pressed against a metal rod beneath it. In 1950, Sala went on to invent a more sophisticated electronic instrument called the Mixturtrautonium which he used to compose the music for Alfred Hitchcock's thriller, The Birds. In 1926 Jorg Mager built an electronic instrument called the Spharophon and later created the Partiturophon and the Kaleidophon. In the forties came the Solovox and the Clavioline, the Melochord, the Multimonica, the Polychord organ, the Tuttivox, the Marshall organ and the Electronic Sakbutt.

With the proliferation of new musical tools, the musicians of the day were inspired to think about music in a different way. The sounds being produced by the new technology were unlike anything that had gone before and gave musicians a new musical palette to work with. A good example of an early electronic experiment is John Cage's Imaginary Landscape #1. This 1939 composition was also the first piece of music to be reproduced electronically.

The sounds being produced by the new technology were unlike anything that had gone before and gave musicians a new musical palette to work with.

With the invention of the Moog synthesizer in 1964, the golden age of electronic music was born. The rock musicians of the sixties were already experimenting wildly with both instrumentation and form and had no hesitation in embracing these new tools. Shortly afterwards, the Mellotron was invented which was the first keyboard that actually played samples. The first real digital sampler however, was The Fairlight CMI or Computer Musical Instrument, invented in 1979 by two Australians, Kim Ryrie and Peter Vogul. This crude and bulky instrument was first used by the likes of Mike Oldfield, Stevie Wonder, The Pet Shop Boys and the legendary Jean Michel Jarre. Shortly after, The Ensoniq Mirage and the Akai S900 were among the first affordable samplers to hit the popular market, enabling musicians to capture and manipulate existing sounds. And from 1980 to 1982, Roland introduced the TB-303 bassline machine and the TR-808 drum machine. These machines are still widely used today and have been responsible for many of the innovations in modern electronic dance music.

Since the sixties, the evolution of electronic musical instruments has moved forward with the same break-neck speed as the music itself. But throughout the eighties and nineties, Roland has been the world leader in the development of tools for the electronic musician, offering a dizzying array of technological wizardry. Machines like the Roland TB 303 Bassline with its distinctive "acid" sounds and signature deep bass lines played a key role in the development of electronic music in the eighties and is still being rediscovered by a new generation of electronic musicians today. Many of the classic house percussion sounds that we are so familiar with today came from the Roland TR series of drum machines. The Roland TR 808 is the drum machine responsible for the low-end hum kick and tinny claps and snares found in so many house tracks. Tune the delay of the 808's

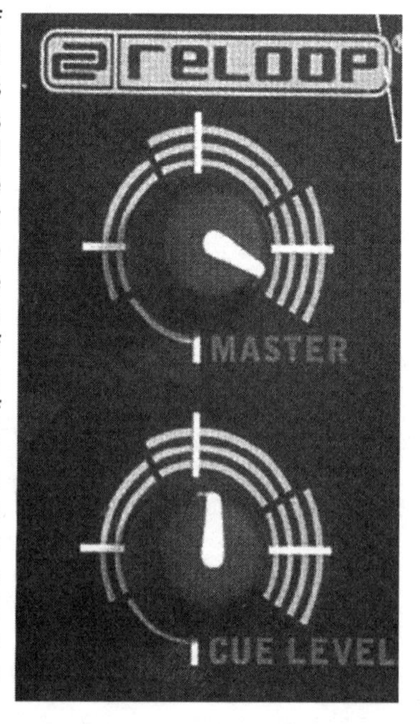

kick drum down and you have the deep, mushy thud that is found in most acid house. The mainstay of many house producers over the years has been the Roland TR 909, a versatile drum machine also responsible for many of the percussion sounds that have become characteristic of a decade of house and techno music. Roland also makes a variety of synthesizers, sequencers and workstations that are specifically designed with the needs of the electronic musician in mind. But although Roland have enjoyed being the industry leader for so long, today the climate is rapidly changing and many other companies - new and old - are now tapping into the growing market for electronic instruments.

photo: trent warlow

DJ Doran using a pair of Technics 1200s

The range of tools now available for electronic musicians is truly amazing, but the basic requirements are largely the same. First, the sounds need to be created or collected. Percussive sounds are usually generated by a drum machine or can be recorded and looped from a real drummer. Looping is taking a sound or sequence and repeating it for as long as needed. Synthesizers generate their own unique sounds and are also used to alter other sounds that can originate from electronic or acoustic sources. Samplers are used to record and store a repertoire of sounds that can then be sent to a sequencer that plays the samples back in the chosen order to produce a finished composition. Up until quite recently, all of these pieces of equipment would have been pieces of hardware linked together with a MIDI system or Musical Instrument Digital Interface. This system was released in 1983 and has since become a standard protocol for connecting musical instruments which can then be controlled by software or hardware driven sequencers. Nowadays, all these elements are available in hardware *or* software. Programs such as Q-Base, Visions or VST (Virtual Studio Technology) give the musician all the capabilities of samplers, sequencers, drum machines, synthesizers and mixers in one software package. Music can be created, mixed and output to a finished product on CD or DAT, with every step of the process controlled from the computer screen. More often than not, today's electronic musician is using a combination of software and hardware and it seems likely that before long many musicians will be working exclusively in the computer environment.

Another piece of equipment which has been enormously influential in the development of electronic music is the turntable. The undisputed industry standard and an integral part of dance culture are the Technics 1200 series. Whether you are a DJ in Paris or Poland, at an underground rave in Finland or a house club in Tokyo, chances are that you will find a pair of Technics 1200s waiting for you. The incredible success and market dominance of Technics over the years has been partly due to a patent the company has held on its unique drive system. When the patent ends this year, other companies such as Vestax who are already making inroads into the DJ market, will be poised to become serious contenders for the most commonly used turntables for playing vinyl records.

"The Roland TB 303 and the TR 606 were originally intended to simulate a bass guitar and a drummer so that you could have backing tracks for your demos. Nobody ever intended for the 303 to become this iconic acid house instrument. That was never part of the plan. It was marketed to straight-up rock and roll musicians. The interesting thing about electronic instruments is that they are usually released as toys and it's the people who use them that find a niche for them and turn them into instruments over time."

- James Lumb, Electric Skychurch, Los Angeles, USA.

"A lot of the reason why the music is so different is in the way it is made. It was never physically possible to do it before. It's all mathematics and computers. Each piece of software or hardware lends itself to a certain kind of sound assembly. So the music came from the technology as much as peoples inspiration. Once you start to use the tools it leads you in new directions. It's MIDI technology, computers and sampling that have made this music possible. Back in the early days, I was using a keyboard-triggered synthesizer that limited your control to what your fingers could do. I used to think if I could only have three of these stacked together, I could do so much more. All these things were in my head and now it's like a dream come true because anything I can think of, I can do. Now I feel like I'll never even have enough time to scratch the surface of what's possible."

- David Ewing, Skylab2000, Los Angeles, USA.

"I think that the whole DIY ethic is a good thing. Music has always been a function of technology and the technology today is getting better everyday. A young person twenty years ago wanted a guitar or a piano, but a child of the millennium wants two turntables or studio equipment to make music and that's a big change. I think that the changes in technology have changed the definition of what a musician is. A musician is no longer defined by a person who strictly plays a conventional musical instrument. The person who is operating samplers and other studio equipment is now a legitimate musician."

- Dave Jurman, senior director of dance music, Columbia Records/SONY.

AN INTERVIEW WITH JAMES LUMB OF ELECTRIC SKY CHURCH...

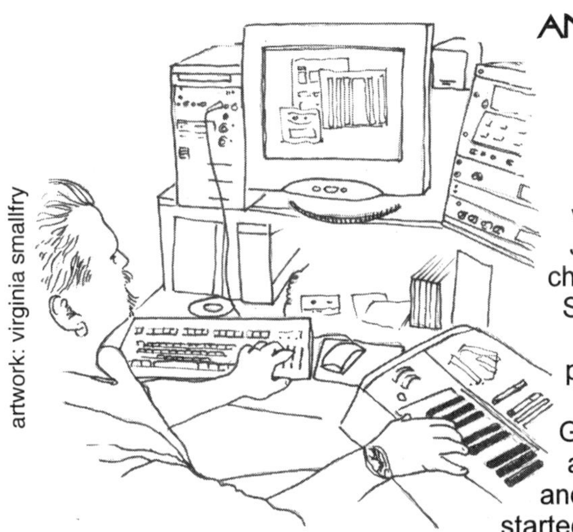

artwork: virginia smallfry

Los Angeles veteran electronica producer James Lumb has been churning out tracks as Electric Skychurch since 1989. James began as a bass player for the underground psychedelic funk band The Groove Trolls, and in 1989, armed with a drum machine and a four-track tape recorder, started writing acid house tracks. In 1993, James was joined by David Delaski and began throwing full moon parties in the desert that evolved into the Moontribe Collective. (See: The Moontribe Collective.)

Electric Skychurch are still one of Americas few big live electronic acts and James Lumb is currently one of North Americas most talented and sought after remixers. For more info on Electric Skychurch, check out their web site at: www.electricskychurch.com.

FRITZ: So does every pop star want a dance remix that can be played in clubs?

LUMB: *No, every pop star's record label wants a dance remix to help keep selling that pop star. It's a straight up business deal.*

FRITZ: How do the pop stars feel about that?

LUMB: *Well, I live in Hollywood and a lot of these people are my neighbours. When I go down the street to get Mexican food, these are the people I see. A lot of the rock guys I run into say that they hear a dance remix and think that it's cool but it's missing the point of the song. What I do is try to figure out what the little tiny nugget of meaning that can not be lost and take that one little thing, maybe a riff or one piece of a vocal, toss the rest out and then build a new song up from that point and try to hold on to what the song is about throughout the remix. If you can pull that off a couple of times then you start to get calls.*

artwork: virginia smallfry

FRITZ: What equipment are you using for remixing?

LUMB: *I've been doing this about ten years so I have about twenty synthesizers and a full blown recording studio with a Soundcraft console, a twenty-four track Pro-Tools system and I run a bunch of different samplers. For my live show I run two or three samplers, I have a live drummer and a bunch of Roland digital synthesizers. But each remix is uniquely different. First I decide what kind of tone colour I want. If I want a really synthetic tone colour, I might pick two or three analogue synths and a sampler and do something really simple. Sometimes I find that I have so much equipment that I get lost. And maintaining that much equipment can be a pain.*

FRITZ: There has always been a dichotomy between the creative and the technical, a point at which the technology becomes more of a hindrance than a help to the creative process.

LUMB: *Yes. That definitely happened to me a couple of years ago. It was great leaning the technology down to the microprocessor level but once you've mastered it, you are* *left with pure expression. What's happened for me is that these electronic gizmos started out being musical instruments, then became pure technology, and now it's coming back around to being pure expression. For the Bob Marley remix I am working on I am using a Mac G3 in place of a sampler running a hard disc recorder and then I'll use something to take the digital edge off of it, like a Roland space echo or an analogue filter and maybe an old Juno. I may have a studio full of equipment but on one song I'll probably only use a computer, a couple of vintage effects processors and maybe two synths. That's all you really need. You can do a great remix with a four-track and a set of decks. In the end it comes down to you more than the gear. But the gear makes it a lot easier!*

FRITZ: What are the considerations when choosing software over hardware?

LUMB: *I don't think that the computer-based stuff is really there yet. When I'm remixing I use my computer for an interface with the samplers I already have. I use the computer to digitally load all the information that I need. The computer is supposed to do everything but in reality, it doesn't do one thing really well. I've also found that the more applications you are running on the computer, the more time you are going to spend making sure that the computer is still running. One of the biggest complaints that I hear is, "I'm a musician and not a computer technician," and people are spending a lot of time keeping their computers running. Things like cleaning off the hard drive, checking for viruses, updating and de-bugging software. There's a lot to be said for sitting down at a keyboard with a built in sequencer that works the same way every day and doesn't crash.*

There has always been a dichotomy between the creative and the technical, a point at which the technology becomes more of a hindrance than a help to the creative process.

FRITZ: What pieces of equipment would you recommend to someone who wants to start making tracks?

LUMB: *The first thing I tell people is look around and see what you've got because you may have what you need already. If you have a computer, you can go out and get* *freeware or shareware demo software and play with it. A computer may not be the most Hi Fi way to go but it's a good start. I started out with an old Ensoniq sampler with a built-in sequencer and I did loads of mixes and remixes on that alone. A good pair of headphones, a master keyboard that samples, and a desire to do it is all you really need. I did a mix last year for a movie called Pi, a track called Full Moon Generator. I was on tour and I did it in a hotel room with a K 2000, a Mackie 12-02 and a set of headphones and it turned out to be the best work I did that year.*

FRITZ: So it's the musical ideas that make the track rather than the technology?

LUMB: *Exactly. The technology will always be a component because even if you just sing into a microphone, you need a microphone, a pre-amp and a tape deck.*

FRITZ: Is there a trend towards using more organic sounds in electronic mixes?

LUMB: *We go out with field recorders and collect sounds. It's something that the computer is really good for. One of the things that has happened with electronic music is, people use samples and make a track, then the track gets sampled and so on until this audio is five or six generations down the road and it gets flat and loses its dynamic range. If you go back and listen to Dark Side of the Moon or some classical music, you are blown away by how much depth and detail there is in the recording. So you wonder how to get that depth back into your recordings and the answer is to get a microphone, record some stuff and put it into the background of your electronic track. That will create a depth and ambiance behind the beats and really helps to open it up.*

FRITZ: What are the most exciting new developments in electronic music technology?

LUMB: *Cheap hard disc recording. If you are using samplers, one of the big limitations is memory. Samplers really lend themselves to drums because a drum hit takes up a small portion of memory. A hard disc recorder can record a four-minute passage of music, like a slowly evolving synthesizer passage that's never the same twice. All of a sudden, a producer with an $899 Imac has the ability to record a studio quality vocal track, bass track or even a sound effects track. So it can take electronic music one step away from the loop and focus on arrangement and* *composition a little bit differently. I think that cheap hard disc recorders will bridge the gap between electronic music and so-called "real" music. The successful hybrid artists are the ones with access to high-end technology. Like the stuff from New York where they take a full orchestra and put minimal beats behind it. Everyone will be able to do that soon.*

THE HISTORY OF ELECTRONIC DANCE MUSIC

The electronic experiments of the sixties and seventies were mostly concerned with incorporating electronically generated sounds into existing musical forms. Musicians such as Klaus Shultz, Kraftwerk, Tangerine Dream, Brian Eno, Jean Michele Jarre and many others helped to pave the way for the electronic dance revolution. Although these experiments were extremely fruitful, it wasn't until the birth of house music, with its distinctive 4/4 rhythm and eight bar repeating cycle, that electronic dance music emerged as a unique musical genre and spawned a plethora of exciting variations.

House music began evolving from disco in the early eighties. A few years previously, disco music hit a crossroad and split into two distinct forms. One branch became the most commercial and superficial dance music available, personified by the fancy dress fashions of The Village People and the glamour and glitter of Saturday Night Fever. This trend eventually culminated in the 'disco sucks' campaign that went as far as staging public events in sports stadiums where disco records were actually burned on bonfires. The other road led to the underground where conditions were ripe for the evolution into house music. Rennie "Dubnut" Foster is a DJ and producer who is part of the Nu-Skool Samuraiz, a DJ

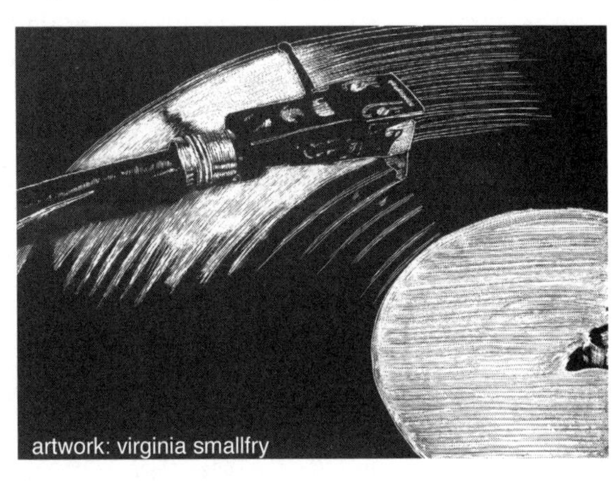

artwork: virginia smallfry

collective with a residency at Club Loop in Tokyo, Japan.

"Disco was just music that worked in a club, specifically made just to dance to. Disco people went to the disco to do disco drugs and disco things. Then it got commercial and whitewashed and eventually died. But it didn't really die, it went underground. Black people and gay people didn't relate to rock music so they created new forms out of what was left from disco."

DJ Rennie "Dubnut" Foster

photo: trent warlow

What was left was the heavy four-four dance rhythm. The disco beat remained but intensified, the vocals were minimized and eventually dropped out all together and the song structure gradually gave way to a repeating, never-ending cycle of sound.

At the time most DJs were playing records on two decks, cueing up one record and fading it in as the last record was ending, with the two sources primarily being used to create a smooth, seamless transition from one record to another. In the seventies, hip-hop DJ's in New York began to use the backspin capabilities of the Technics 1200s turntable to create scratching. They were also cutting back and forth between two copies of the same record creating an endless mix. DJs soon discovered that they could mix in the second source at any time, enhancing and layering records together. If a record had an instrumental passage, it could be selected and mixed in with an instrumental section from another record, thus giving the DJ the ability to "remix' the original recordings. Musicians began to respond to the mixing techniques used by the DJs and started to make records with longer instrumental sections or longer repeating vocal passages, creating the eight bar pattern distinctive to house. Records like Sinnamon's "Thanks To You" and D-Train's "You're The One For Me" began to use more synthesized sounds and dub effects creating a different sound. These developments were taking place as early as 1983 in dance clubs, and more specifically in the gay clubs of Chicago.

Terrence Parker, now a leading Detroit house producer and international DJ, was spinning hip-hop records at the age of thirteen and recorded his first track called The Question on a primitive six track recorder in his bedroom at three o'clock in the morning. It subsequently sold thirty to forty thousand copies in England and was on two platinum compilations. Parker witnessed the evolution of disco to house first hand. *"House was primarily happening with the gay scene which is where it developed. In fact, house gets its name from the gay scene. House is gay terminology for group or family. Gays would group together into "families" and members of the family would be called "children." In Chicago these family groups were called "houses" and the music they were playing took its name from that."*

You will sometimes hear from British ravers that house music was named after the warehouse parties that sprang up all over England in 1987, but people were dancing to house in Chicago well before the form migrated across the Atlantic to be embraced by the Brits. The British may have invented rave but Chicago is definitely the birthplace of house music. Another popular story is that house music took its name from the Warehouse Club in Chicago where resident DJ Frankie Knuckles became known as the godfather of house. Frankie was a gay DJ from New York so it's possible that it may have been a combination of the two influences. But it is no coincidence that house music evolved in the climate of freedom that characterizes gay clubs. Because of a long history of persecution, gay people had been forced to band together and form their own clubs and cliques where they could be free from the prejudices of a largely homophobic society. It was this atmosphere of autonomous liberty that provided the fertile ground for musical experimentation which led to a new style of disco and eventually house music. Even today, whether you're in London or Paris, Moscow or Iceland, if you want to hear cutting edge electronic dance music, you will find it in a gay club.

Even today, whether you're in London or Paris, Moscow or Iceland, if you want to hear cutting edge electronic dance music, you will find it in a gay club.

The next major development in the evolution of house came in the early eighties when DJs began to mix new-style disco records with electronic tracks from Europe. English electronic pop artists like Depeche Mode, Soft Cell and the new-style disco sounds of Giorgio Moroder, Klein and MBO were gaining in popularity in America and more specifically, New York and Chicago. Kraftwerk, the electronic group from Germany were also a major influence on the development of house in the early days. But it was an Italian electronic music label called Italo that was inspiring many of the club DJs in Chicago. Terrence Parker, once again, was on the scene. *"In late 1984 a producer called Don Was formed a group called Was Not Was and I heard a legendary Detroit DJ called King Collier mixing some of their tracks. I was under age at the time, but some friends smuggled me into a club called The Downstairs Pub and a DJ named King Collier was playing some incredible music. I recognized a lot of the disco records he was playing but he was mixing in these electronic records and then I noticed other DJs started mixing in these records at parties and other clubs and people were really liking it. The records were coming from Italy and there was a movement called Italo which was Italian disco. These were early records like Love and Music, Disco Magic, I Love the Piano and Alexander Robotnic. These records were being produced in Italy and were big club hits there. At the same time Jesse Saunders in Chicago produced a record called On and On that was a combination of Italo and the German style of Kraftwerk. That's how house music was first created. That was in early '85. After that, everybody started making house records.*

Although it is difficult to say which recording was the first house record, most people agree that it was made by Chicago musician Jessie Saunders for the Mitchell label in 1983. The new sound incorporated Kraftwerks heavily synthesized strings with a Eurobeat bassline and a simple, insistent rhythm of a drum machine. Things really started to take off when the music began to be played regularly to a wider audience. In Chicago, several clubs picked up on the new sound and the Windy City quickly became the breeding ground for a decade of new music. Among the most influential clubs in Chicago at that time were The Warehouse Club and The Music Box. These clubs, along with others like The Paradise Garage in New York, were not only responsible for introducing new music to a new generation of clubbers, but also broke down a lot of sexual and racial barriers in club land. Until this time, it was normal for clubs to be either black, Hispanic or white, or straight or gay with very little middle ground. Now the music became the focus and people of all stripes were coming together for the first time, a trend that would continue and become a defining feature of rave culture.

By 1986 it seemed like everybody in Chicago was making house music.

Frankie Knuckles had an enormous influence on the evolution and popularity of house music. But before moving to Chicago, Frankie had been inspired by Larry Levan at The Paradise Garage in New York and took the new sound to Chicago where he took the form one step further and helped to develop what is now known as Chicago house. The records coming out of New York were more mid or down tempo and the kids in Chicago were more attracted to the more upbeat European sound.

Another DJ from the gay scene, Ron Hardy, who began playing at The Music Box around the same time as Frankie Knuckles left The Warehouse, was pushing the envelope even further, setting the stage for the next leap forward in the evolution of house. Ron Hardy had a reputation for playing the wildest, newest, rawest tracks he could find and became the backbone of the Chicago club scene while establishing The Music Box as a testing ground for producers to introduce new recordings to the public. If it didn't fly at The Music Box it probably wouldn't make it anywhere else.

The popularity of house led to the creation of new record labels dedicated to the emerging musical form. As early as 1985, Larry Sherman had established a label called Trax Records which was responsible for many of the early house classics by Marshall Jefferson, Larry Heard, Frankie Knuckles and others. By 1986 it seemed like everybody in Chicago was making house music.

Ron Hardy is also credited with nurturing and giving exposure to one of the first of many variations on the house theme, acid house. This was a form of house characterized by high pitched screaming "acid sounds" created by a Roland 303. These new psychedelic sounds were particularly effective while under the influence of LSD, also known as acid. Acid house marked a new sensibility from the fashion-based club scene and heralded in a new age of psychedelic experimentation. The music had now moved far away from its song based disco roots and had evolved into an interactive musical form that created an irresistible momentum, transporting dancers on an inner journey. Psychedelic drugs such as LSD and magic mushrooms were a natural adjunct to this new form of musical meditation and their use in the club scene began to grow. When acid house hit England around 1986, the Brits embraced it with open arms. Up until then, only the more commercial forms of house had been available in England and the arrival of this new incarnation set off a whole new direction as "acid house parties" became the trend. This first generation of ravers quickly outgrew the club scene and sought out locations where they could be afforded more freedom. Parties sprang up in garages, farmer's fields, and abandoned warehouses as the rave scene kicked into high gear. By the summer of 1987 promoters started staging large, outdoor, all night events that could accommodate thousands of people.

ROLAND MC 303

When Chicago house with its characteristic galloping rhythm and smooth textured sound, migrated to Detroit, it took on a harder, more urban sound. At the same time, Detroit DJs were mixing in heavier doses of Italo records, Euro electobeat and other purely electronic tracks created in Germany and other European countries. The beat intensified and speeded up and the sounds being sampled were mostly technological. The vocal tracks and the last vestiges of song structure fell away and gave birth to a new sound called techno. Terrence Parker was already a seasoned Detroit DJ at the time. *"By late 1985 the house movement had really taken off and there had been a couple of big hits like Marshall Jefferson's The House National Anthem, also known as Move Your Body, J.M. Silk's, Jack Your Body and Jack The Bass by Farley Jack Master Funk. These were full-fledged underground hits that were coming out of Chicago and migrating to Detroit where the local scene was starting to develop its own music. By early 1986 the Detroit sound was happening with records like Nude Photo by Rhythm is Rhythm with Derrick May. That was a revolutionary record because even though it used the basic drum patterns of house music, the bass line and the whole vibe was different. That's when Detroit techno began to develop and if you listen to a lot of early Detroit techno records they sound like house music. This was before house went over to the UK in late 1986 and became really big. Records like Jack Your Body became massive hits in the UK and made the mainstream charts."*

Juan Atkins, a Detroit musician who had been recording electro-funk records under the name Cybotron since the early eighties became one of the early pioneers of techno along with Kevin Saunderson, Derrick May, Eddie Fowlkes and Blake Baxter. Techno was faster and harder and therefore more danceable than house, with a larger dose of European electrobeat. The last remnants of disco were gone and the electronic dance music revolution was now in full swing.

Ironically, the Paradise Garage, that had done so much for racial integration was finally closed down because of racial bigotry.

In New York, the center for new musical experimentation was The Paradise Garage Club. With a capacity for two thousand people, this groundbreaking club led the way in developing a distinctly New York sound. Pioneers such as Larry Levan, Tony Humphries, Timmy Regisford and Boyd Jarvis were busy delving into their rhythm and blues roots to create a deeper, more soulful sound that became known as Garage after the name of the club. DJ Terrence Parker was a frequent visitor to New York at the time. *"Garage came out of New York from a club called The Paradise Garage where guys like Larry Levan and Tony Humphries and a lot of different guys played. They were playing a lot of the same house music and Italo that was coming out of the Chicago clubs but mixed it in with records that were nothing to do with house or disco like, I Miss You by The Rolling Stones. You could hear Farley Jack Master Funk or a deep house tune mixed with Love and Music from Italy or even a Rod Stewart song. As long as it kept the same vibe it would work.*

Now, coming into the early nineties, house music had already been to the UK and made it on the charts as pop hits. As house started to grow and develop, some records were just tracks, no vocals, no changes and no song structure. Just a groove for the crowd to get into. Then you had what I call more traditional house records that stayed with the original format. Europeans love to label things and started to call it Garage because a lot of what was being played at The Paradise Garage had vocals, even though it wasn't all house. But it was mostly songs rather than tracks. If you went to the Warehouse Club and heard Frankie Knuckles spinning you would hear some songs but you would also hear a lot of tracks.

The New York scene wasn't as deep into house and techno during the late eighties. It wasn't until the early nineties that it started to get popular. In the late eighties we had big records from Chicago and Detroit that had gone over to the UK and became huge hits. We also saw house and techno records on the charts in France, Italy and Germany and they were all coming back as imports to the US through New York."

After eleven years as one of the most influential dance clubs in the world, the Paradise Garage threw its final party on September 26th, 1987. The owner, Michael Brody claimed that the club closed because of protests from the white Soho community who objected to a black club in the neighborhood. The resulting conflict eventually prevented his lease from being renewed. Ironically, the Paradise Garage, that had done so much for racial integration was finally closed down because of racial bigotry.

photo: tristan o'neill

Meanwhile in England, American house music, which had also originally made its debut in gay clubs, was catching on fast in mixed clubs and rave parties across the country. House tracks, originally created in Chicago and Detroit became huge commercial successes in Britain and inspired a new generation of British electronic musicians to produce variations on the original house formula. One of these variations, now known as old school, employed a break beat technique originally used in hip-hop, where a percussive phrase is sampled and repeated to create the rhythm track. The resulting beat created a more complex rhythmic form, quite distinct from house and techno where the bass drum emphasized every beat. This was also referred to as "rave music" by British ravers. This variation would later be speeded up and blended with techno sounds to become hardcore. In 1992 to1993 hardcore split into two rhythmic groups, one retaining a 3/4 time sampled break beat and the other, known as four-beat, went back to the four/four beat familiar to house and techno. If hardcore was speeded up and cartoony vocal samples added, it became happy hardcore. Add some hypnotic effects used in trance music and you have trancecore. Throw in some scary sound effects and samples lifted from horror movies and horrorcore is born.

As the original forms of house and techno spread around the world, each region produced more variations on the theme. The Dutch embraced the harder sounds of techno, but speeded it up to insane levels and called it gabber techno. Another branch of techno specializes in hypnotic repetitive sounds designed to put listeners into a trance state became known as trance. In Goa, India, trance became more complex and multi-layered and was renamed Goa or psy-trance. Chika of Solstice productions is a rave promoter and DJ from Tokyo, Japan, who specializes in Goa trance music. He has been to Goa many times and has helped to export the Goa scene back to Japan. *"In Goa they only mix DAT tapes because vinyl records melt in the sun and records are too heavy to travel around India with. It is limiting because you can't really beat mix DAT tape because you can't adjust the beats per minute. You can just fade out one source and fade in another. But Goa trance is not really designed to beat mix because it is too complicated. A lot of techno or house tracks are relatively simple and you need two sources playing at the same time to make a big sound, but Goa trance is more like classical music and is composed with a beginning and an end and is much more complicated, layered music."*

Break beat forms, and in particular jungle music, retained the under-siege philosophy of hip-hop culture rather than the peace and love ethos of rave culture.

Chicago house can be identified by its characteristic energetic, galloping rhythm. The smooth, ultra produced, soul-based sound from Philadelphia became known as Philadelphia house which in turn lead to deep house where the vocals are stripped away altogether and the bass line is emphasized, giving it a deep, rich sound built on subtle changes and extended soulful grooves. When musicians experiment with the house formula, taking it farther away from its disco roots, adding big builds and crescendos, it becomes progressive house. Slow it down, add a smattering of world beat or traditional primitive music, and it becomes tribal house or exotica. Mix in a few jazzy samples with acid house and you get acid jazz. So we see that every variation creates the need for new name in order to invent a language to describe and classify each new style.

One way that electronic music is classified is by its speed, which is measured in beats per minute (bpm). Electronic dance music can run anywhere from 115 bpm to 300 bpm, although most forms will be between 120 bpm and 140 bpm. Some ravers will tell you that they prefer 120 bpm because it simulates the sound of a heartbeat as heard by a fetus in the womb. By the same token, gabber techno, with breakneck speeds of up to 300 bpm might represent the heartbeat of an epileptic gerbil being mauled by a cat. At these speeds a dancer can do little more than vibrate on the spot.

While it is true that most electronic dance music is directly descended from house/techno origins with its "four on the floor" or 4/4 time sequence, there is another branch of the electronic family tree that has a distinctly different background.

In the early days of house, a lot of DJs were playing hip-hop, which was also incorporating sampled music. These DJs already had the mixing skills necessary to play house so it was inevitable that some cross over took place. Hip house was an early result of this musical marriage in which hip-hop MCs would rap over house records. Terrence Parker was one of the many young hip-hop DJs that got swept up in the house revolution. *"When I was a freshman in high school I was listening to, and playing hip-hop, but I was also into disco. That was 1978-79, which was the high point of disco. I watched disco birth one of the biggest rap records in history. That was Rapper Delight by the Sugarhill Gang, so I always made a connection between hip-hop and disco. At that time I was listening to Kano, Peter Brown, Sheik, Saturday Night Fever. I was really into Gary's Gang because of the percussion and rhythms."*

Rennie "Dubnut" Foster along with DJ Hiraku and other members of the Nu-Skool Samuraiz are dedicated to crossing the barrier between house and hip-hop by mixing house records with a hip-hop style and attitude, similar to The Mongoloids in New York. The style includes beat juggling, chopping up beats, two copy mixes and scratching. For Rennie, the divisions between house, techno and hip-hop are blurred. *"If you listen to a classic hip-hop track like Planet Rock by Afrika Bambata, it's close to 130 bpm so it's faster than house. It's a techno, electro record with chanting over the top. All the tones are electronic and it has a heavy 808 drum machine, so essentially, if we made the same record today it would be called techno. But since it was made at that time it's a hip-hop record."*

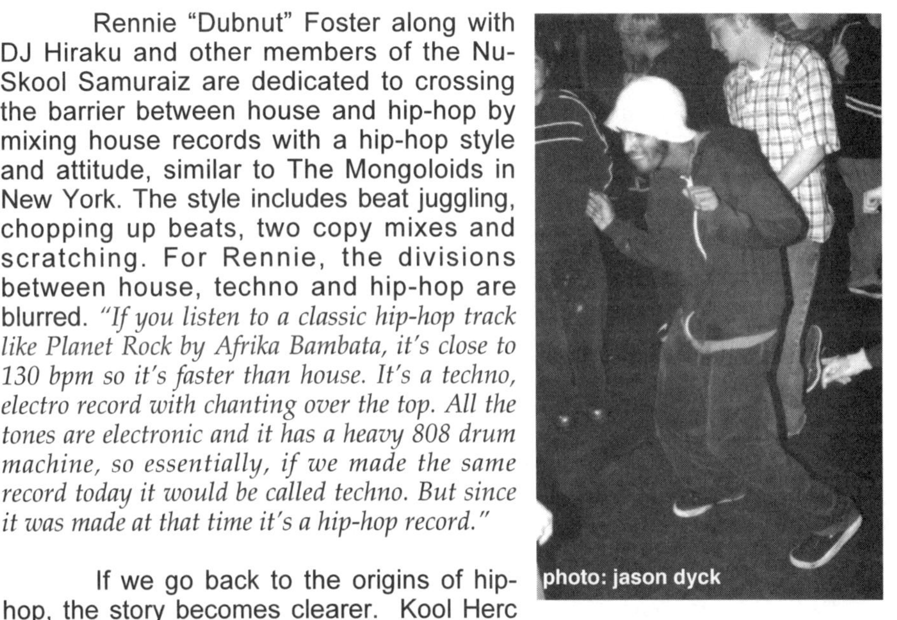
photo: jason dyck

If we go back to the origins of hip-hop, the story becomes clearer. Kool Herc was a DJ from Kingston, Jamaica who came to New York City in 1970. Herc came from the Jamaican tradition of rhyming over dub reggae records but quickly realized that reggae didn't go over too well with New Yorkers and instead took to playing old funk records like James Brown and the incredible Bongo Band. He began to stage block parties in the black neighborhoods, and before long discovered that by mixing two copies of the same record he could extend the percussive breaks - parts of the songs where everything drops out except the beat. This was the original break beat, which in turn gave rise to break dancing. The followers of this new musical form were known as break boys or b-boys, the form and the culture that developed around it became known as hip-hop. Cool Herc is also credited as the first person to rhyme over the break beats, creating the first rap. He eventually turned his attention to the complexities of DJing and let two friends, Coke La Rock and Clark Kent handle the microphone forming rap music's first MC team known as Kool Herc and the Herculoids.

All hip-hop and rap music today is still based on a break beat which gives the form its distinctive syncopated rhythm and sets it apart from the even 4/4 non-syncopated beats of house and techno. The break beat has now been indelibly assimilated into the electronic dance music family tree and now comes in a variety of forms, all of which stay true to their hip-hop roots. Hardcore was the first break beat form to evolve from techno and in London, England circa 1993, jungle music was born and in less than a year dominated the electronic music scene in England. Jungle took the energy of hardcore, mixed in sampled dub reggae bass lines or sampled break beats along with speeded up samples of other records used as rhythm tracks. Like hip-hop, jungle represented the voice of the urban black community. The dense, richly textured, industrial sounds layered on furious and fractured beats represented a completely different musical identity, one that reflected the frustrations of a militant sub society. In this way, the break beat forms, and in particular jungle music, retained the under-siege philosophy of hip-hop culture rather than the peace and love ethos of rave culture.

At a rave, the music creates a three-dimensional sound environment that we both react to and interact with.

When jungle caught on in England and then spread to the rest of the world, it too produced a number of variations. Drum and bass was the first incarnation, although it is difficult to say where jungle ends and drum and bass begins. As jungle became a little more sophisticated and perhaps a little less dense, emphasizing the drum and bass tracks, people began to call it drum and bass and the name stuck. Today, the name jungle is generally used to describe the earlier or "old school" tracks, while drum and bass is used for later recordings. Other variations on drum and bass include hard step, hard hop, tech step and jump up. (See: Musical Categories and Definitions.)

Yet another variation of hip-hop derivative electronica is known as trip hop. This is a slowed down syncopated rhythm blended with ambient music to create a relaxed, introspective mood. In the mid 1970s, Brian Eno coined the term "ambient" and released an album entitled, "Another Green World." Ambient has now become an established form of electronica and is often used in the "chill out lounges" or relaxation areas found at raves where people can cool down and take a break from the intense action of the main dance floor. Ambient music lacks the big beats of dance music and is designed to create a musical landscape or atmosphere. If it puts you to sleep it is known as Sombient. Illbient is sick and twisted ambient music. If the sounds become more intricate and thought provoking it can be described as Intelligent.

Now we can see that there are really only three distinct genres. The first group would contain house, techno, trance, and all the variations that use a 4/4 time signature. The second group would contain all the variations of hip-hop derived break beats, including old school, early hardcore, break beat, jungle, drum and bass, trip hop etc. And the third group would include the non-rhythmic variations of ambient, intelligent or other forms of down tempo, atmospheric music.

Electronica is such a breeding ground for new ideas and experimentation that it is virtually impossible to keep up with each new twist and turn. Variations on the many themes are endless. And with electronic music borrowing and sampling from every imaginable audio source the terminology used to describe the new mutations are as diverse as the music itself. A lot of the nomenclature in use today probably springs from the fertile imagination of magazine writers trying to review and describe new recordings that are being released faster than they can be categorized. It used to be easy to tell a blues song from a rock song from a folk song, but electronica is changing the way we classify music, blurring the boundaries between genres, forcing us to not only listen more closely but requiring that we develop new listening skills.

Whether you come from New York City or Namibia, drive a Daimler or a donkey, or pay homage to Kali the destroyer or the Great White Rabbit, you will hear something you can relate to in rave music.

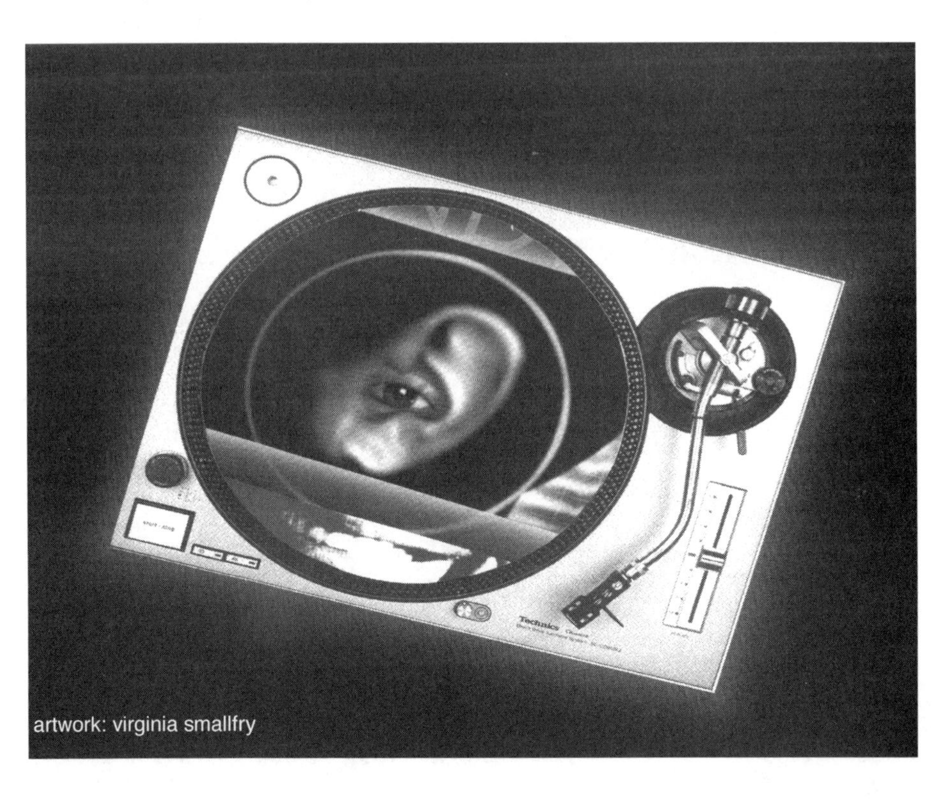

artwork: virginia smallfry

NEW SOUNDS AND NEW EARS

Although Electronica is as good a word as any to describe the extensive world of electronic music, for the purpose of this section, I am specifically talking about the experience of listening to electronic dance music at raves and so I will use the term rave music to describe any electronic music that might be played at a rave party.

Rave music is not just about creating new sounds. It is also about learning to listen to music in a different way. Popular music has long been dedicated to the form of the song, where a familiar musical structure of verse and chorus is remembered and recognized by the listener. The lyrics tell us what the song is about, conveying the point of view of the singer and the music sets the mood and dictates how we should react to the content. In this way, popular songs are very much an extension of our story-telling traditions, designed to give information, share experiences, teach lessons, entertain and so forth. Like stories, song structure has a beginning, middle and end, a structure that also serves to help interpret and shape the material to impart its intended meaning. Songs are neatly formatted into three or four minute sound packages that make them easy to listen to, and more importantly, easier to showcase and sell in commercial arenas such as radio and television.

Rave music is about a new and bright future. It is about spontaneity and change, emancipation and revolution, personal exploration and freedom.

To benefit from the full effect of rave music we are challenged to develop new listening skills. With conventional music we listen to the form and follow the lyrics, but with rave music there is no beginning or end. The music is cyclical and continuous and acts more as a catalyst for our own personal inner journey, more a transportation system than an end in itself. Rave music is specifically designed to make you move your body, whether you sway back and forth to your own internal groove or thrash around like a demented gymnast, the intended effect is to inspire a physical reaction. When we allow the music to influence our movements in this way it becomes a truly interactive adventure.

The experience of listening to electronic dance music is closer to the experience a musician has when creating music, in that it requires a certain level of concentration and focus. In this focused state the listener becomes closer to being a part of the musical process rather than a passive audience. At a rave, the music creates a three dimensional sound environment that we both react to and interact with. Our journey is not guided by the personality or agenda of the musicians but rather it is self-directed, providing a more personal perspective that can ultimately be more meaningful.

With conventional popular music we identify with the singer or musician and their personalities become the focus. Rave music on the other hand, is not concerned with the personalities of the musicians or singers involved. Like rave culture itself, it fosters an egoless or selfless approach. In fact, it is virtually impossible to even find out who the musician might be unless you are equipped with infrared night goggles and can read the label of a spinning record in the pitch dark. Even then, the track may be full of samples taken from several other recordings which themselves may have borrowed from various other sources. Even when we know the name of the musician it is likely to be one of many aliases used by the same artist. Authorship becomes obscure to the point of meaningless.

We are used to identifying music by the personality of the musician as presented by the vocals but here again, this can be a tricky business. The earlier forms of house music often retained some form of vocal chorus, a remnant of its disco ancestry. As the vocals and the verse/chorus song structure diminished, the instrumental breaks extended. House retained the odd vocal but only as an occasional repeating mantra with the human voice becoming just another instrumental element. Even when present, the singer's voice is often distorted or obscured to the point where the lyrics are unrecognizable as words. The singer remains anonymous and the meaning of the words is left to the listener's interpretation. When I hear a vocal phrase repeating at a party, I will often do a little on-the-spot survey and ask a few people what they hear. I am always amazed at the range of responses, with everyone hearing something different like a game of musical Chinese whispers. One person's "Feel the Beat" is another persons "Field of Beets." One friend of mine, a woman who has a background in the Hare Krishna movement, swears that she hears esoteric, Sanskrit phrases and chants in the music. Here again we get to participate in the meaning and intention of the music.

artwork: virginia smallfry

Another exciting aspect of this new music is the fact that it is borrowing sound samples from our past, present and future, creating an all-encompassing, universal perspective that crosses all cultural and social borders. Whether you come from New York City or Namibia, drive a Daimler or a donkey, or pay homage to Kali the destroyer or the Great White Rabbit, you will hear something you can relate to in rave music. The new sounds being produced by the next generation of electronic technology can be truly awe inspiring, arousing emotional effects that we are only just beginning to understand.

The repetitive nature of rave music is deceptively simple. Like the shaman's drum, it represents a symbolic beating heart.

We have long known that vibrations cause by sound waves can have a profound effect on our mental and emotional states. An interrogation technique used for brain-washing uses the effects of audio static known as white noise. Prisoners are blindfolded and subjected to the incessant crackle of white noise through a set of headphones for prolonged periods, creating a disorientating effect which eventually reduces the subject to a gibbering mess, unable to organize their thoughts enough to tell a lie. On a more positive note, recent developments in modern medicine are now employing sound waves to knit together damaged tissue and bone. It is certain that in the not too distant future as our knowledge grows in this area we will be using the vibratory qualities of sound waves for a wide variety of applications previously unimagined. Electronic musicians are already experimenting with sub-sonic and ultra-sonic sounds beyond our normal hearing range. These frequencies can vibrate through our bodies without being heard and may be partly responsible for the powerful emotional response people have when listening to rave music. The deep bass sound that seems to penetrate and reverberate deep within your core may be giving your heart a massage, or even stimulating some primitive genetic memory.

The repetitive nature of rave music is deceptively simple. Like the shaman's drum, it represents a symbolic beating heart, the first sound that we hear from inside the womb and one that confirms our very existence. The continual beat forces us to attune to our own rhythm and mood, acting as a bridge that connects us to ourselves and indirectly, to each other. When played at high volume, the music demands our whole attention, becoming an audio environment that supersedes any other stimulus. In this way, it provides a context for a personal journey that can take us anywhere we want to go.

A great deal of the power inherent in rave music comes from its continuous, cyclic form. In this respect, it can also be compared to the drumming and chanting techniques used throughout history for spiritual advancement. At a rave, the music never stops and can go on for up to twelve hours, creating an irresistible momentum that produces a trance state identical to those reached through such religious practices as Sufi dancing or the Kirtan dancing of Hare Krishna devotees. For most ravers, however, the trance state is non-denominational and rather than having a specific spiritual goal in mind, serves to fuel a more personal journey through the dancers own psyche that can ultimately prove to be equally rewarding for spiritual or psychological growth.

Finally, rave music is not about entertainment or information. It harbors no ambition to become top of the pop charts, win prizes or go platinum. It is not about musicians becoming stars or influencing a mass audience with a particular philosophy, opinion or viewpoint. And it does not compete or strive for money or power or status, or any of the other goals and ambitions of most contemporary popular music.

Rave music is about a new and bright future. It is about spontaneity and change, emancipation and revolution, personal exploration and freedom. Unlike the egocentric, pain-filled, opinionated voices of pop culture, rave is optimistic and enthusiastic about the future. The music does not seek to influence or manipulate but simply strives to create a musical environment designed to expand the mind, open the heart and inspire the soul. More a transportation system than a final destination, rave music is concerned with creating a musical momentum or journey. Where that journey leads is entirely up to the listener. For those with open minds, open hearts and a sense of adventure, the rewards can be enormous.

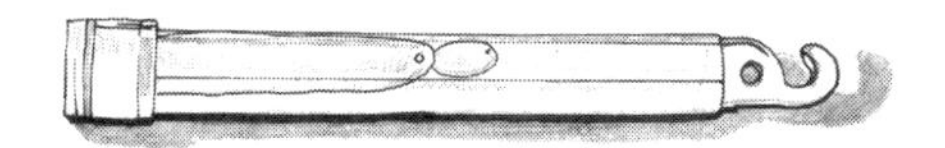

"People I used to play guitar with fifteen years ago say they can't stand electronic music and they can't hear anything in it. I used to feel the same way. It was just a banging in my head. Then all of a sudden something just merged and clicked in my head. I started dancing and danced like I've never danced in my life. It became the most wicked beat I'd ever heard. It was like my brain had just opened up to it and instead of just banging outside my head, my mind opened up and let it into my body."

- Jen Jen a.k.a. DJ Mis-Chief, Big Love, England.

"I enjoy dancing and I find electronic dance music to be deep, melodic and energetic with a high level of musicality. I love it when the overall energy of the music increases throughout the night, continuously building. It sweeps you away on an inner musical journey that can be very rewarding."

- Virginia SmallFry, artist, raver, Canada.

"The music excites something deep in me and makes my body start to scream for movement! I get so excited and experience a total natural high! What makes it special is the inherent positive feeling to it. It just sounds like you feel when you feel really, really good."

- Maya Berelowitz, student, raver, Cape Town, South Africa.

"The "untrained" ear thinks the music is so repetitive and lifeless. I agree it may be repetitive at times, but it is filled with LOTS of SOUL. The repetitiveness is useful for establishing a mind state or "tribalistic" feeling. A state which is conducive to dancing and trancing."

- Albert Mancuso a.k.a. DJ Science, Florida, USA.

"The qualities in this music that effect people so deeply are the energy and the melody. It's uplifting and spiritual. There's a lot of soul in it and it really is about the feeling. It's similar to soul music in that you listen to it from an emotional standpoint."

- Paul Oakenfold, DJ, London, England.

"The music is very dynamic and easy to dance to. When I am at a rave I feel like I am in the clouds. I close my eyes and feel like I am traveling through clouds and mountains. I feel great. My soul is filled with happiness. And I do not use any drugs. "

- Ivan Arar, raver, Zagreb, Croatia.

"Electronic dance music extracts from every music that there has ever been. Nothing is taboo."

- J, The Trip Factory, Saltspring Island, Canada.

"The music has a completely different "soul" than any other music. It is not created to make money, it is created with, by, and for the spirit. I have not found the energy it releases and creates in any other kind of music. It makes me want to get up and move around, smile, laugh, hug someone, dance, or just exist."

- Fredrik Larsson, electronic musician, Stockholm, Sweden.

"I have a special appreciation for the music as a music major because I have studied all forms of music. I listen very intently to all forms of music to try to figure out about the person that created it. People say that I "zone" when I listen to music, more so with techno than with any other form of music. I get to the point where I can't even dance. I just have to stand there and listen."

- Nicole A. Tobias, festival director, raver, New Jersey, USA.

"Music has been a form off expression from the times of Paleolithic man. Music is about communication. Trance music speaks to you - like telling you a story and taking you to places that you never been before. I think that this music can teach us a lot and make us more sensitive to little things. It makes you more friendly and gives you a very big open mind."

- Foka, administrator, DJ, raver, Alverca, Portugal.

"If you listen to trance music you'll hear a lot of emotion and feeling in it. If you are on a dance floor with six or seven hundred other people and you hear those lush strings and beautiful melodies it has a euphoric effect and there's nothing wrong with a bit of euphoria. That's what it does for me. These tracks really take you somewhere and a good DJ puts these elements together and creates a journey."

- Dave Ralph, DJ, Liverpool, England.

"The music is pure energy and emotion. The music makes my day, it keeps me going and is my energy. I just plug in to the music and let it sway my emotions back and forth."

- Jari Nousiainen a.k.a. Super attaK, psychology student, raver, Helsinki, Finland.

"Rave or techno music is something special because it creates molds and gives you an unforgettable feeling of being different. You feel like somebody better. Above all, it makes you move without realizing it."

- Tomasz Wileński, media planner, electronic musician, Warsaw, Poland.

"I've listened to plenty of other genres of music in my time and absolutely nothing apart from a rare few tunes have taken me to intense levels that this music does and hold it there. There is nothing like it in the world, it is like reaching a orgasm when a good dark powerful tune comes in and you just let the music control your body to its full physical abilities."

- Lloyd Morgan, musician, DJ, Cardiff, South Wales, United Kingdom.

"When I was 14, I met a guy on the ferry from Rijeka to Split who wanted me to listen to some "cool music". At that time I listened to Guns'n'Roses. When I heard "Hypnotic ST8", a track from Altern8, and then some other stuff, everything changed. I could NEVER listen to any non-techno music EVER AGAIN!!!!"

- Petar Mimica, student, raver, Mimice, Croatia.

"For me, every track is a feeling. A "song" is a story about something and the sound that comes out is what it feels like to experience that. That's why I like Goa trance, because that is the most "happy" techno in the world. The music gives me an opportunity to experience something. Sometimes I start to cry when listening to Goa because it is so beautiful."

- Veny Veronika Vere, secretary, raver, Oslo, Norway.

"It's the feeling that spreads into every part of your body while listening and dancing to that music that makes it special. In a way it is also a sort of intoxication."

- Sebastian Zillinger, soldier, raver, Amstetten, Austria.

"With rave music, a synergism is created that appears to connect to both the collective unconscious and higher forms of intelligence and synchronicity."

- Pappa Smurf, rave promoter, Kind Gatherings,
Toronto, Canada.

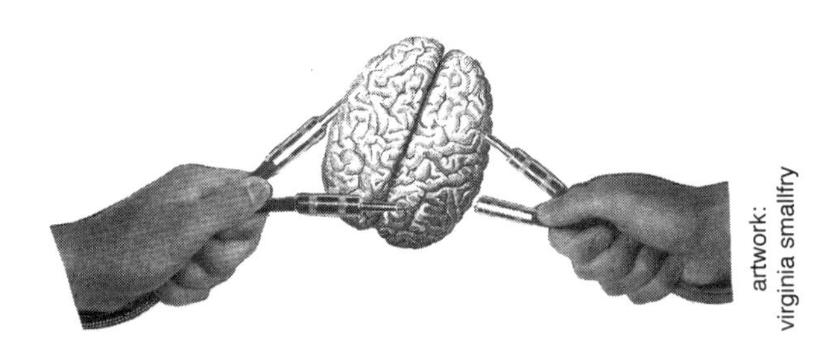

artwork: virginia smallfry

"I was really into New Order and the alternative stuff like Bauhaus, but at the same time I was also into soul and funk and then later electro and hip-hop. As new stuff came along I was reading magazines and always trying to stay on top of things. I can remember when all the early DJ International stuff and the Chicago tracks started coming to the UK. That's when I started thinking that things were really stepping up a peg or two. The kick drums and everything were just so in-your-face and that's when house music really grabbed a hold of me."

- John Digweed, DJ, producer, Hastings, England.

"Electronic dance music is a new way of presenting sound. I think that part of the attraction is that some of the new sounds I'm hearing, I recognize from sounds I've generated in my own head before I ever went to a party or tried ecstasy. It's like I'm listening to my own brain wave patterns."

- Leandre, raver, Victoria, Canada.

"There are very few vocals which means that the music is the focus and the identity or ego of the track is less. The sounds create effects within your body, affecting different chakras and feelings."

- Katherine Wheatley, raver, Melbourne, Australia.

"Most of the dance music started in Detroit, Chicago and New York. It came out of disco in the gay clubs and migrated to England and Europe where people like Malcolm McLaren, Eno, Kraftwerk, and Steve Hillage were doing a lot of experimental electronic music. Somewhere along the line we started to get a melange of the new disco with the new electronic music. It found a niche in the music market and created a sound of its own. When it went back to the States it had become a full-blown musical genre."

- Tim Laughlin, The Vibe Crew, England.

"For myself, as audience and a DJ, I would like to see house music treated in the same way that jazz and other "intelligent" music is treated. House music is the soul of the twenty-first century in the same way that jazz was the soul of the twentieth century."

- Jussi Mononen a.k.a. DJ Athens, Espoo, Finland.

"House is more melodic and based on traditional song structures with a chorus and a bridge and so on. Techno has no song structure, it's just a track that may go through three or four changes but the changes may have nothing to do with the melody. House is something that my parents could listen to and understand where it's going because it has vocals. Techno has no vocals, it's instrumental and uses more electronic sounds. Another big difference is that house was trying to emulate disco and techno just wanted to be techno and was a completely different vibe altogether. It took house and went to the future with it."

- Terrence Parker, producer and DJ, Detroit, USA.

"Electronic dance music is a brand new, cool musical genre, very progressive and modern. It is a new step of human musical progression and I think it is the music of the future. It represents a varied and serious culture and not just some crazy ecstasy junkies."

- Alex Martyshev, student, raver, Moscow, Russia.

"I first heard electronic dance music in 1991. It was a bit of a rude awakening and took some getting used to. It was totally different and it made me want to go out and see what it was all about. I loved a track called The Dominator with a classic keyboard sample. I remember a night at The Echo Club in Loughborough with a DJ called Mister E. The music was very impressive and exciting, but a little intimidating."

- Rob Blackburn a.k.a. DJ Robynod, Nottingham, England.

"The first time I went to a Goa trance party was in a small club in England and it was totally amazing. The room was filled with fluorescent decorations and everyone was dancing really freely. I think that techno and house music is really influenced by western culture, but Goa trance evolved more out of eastern traditions and a more spiritual philosophy. Goa trance is not just electronic sounds. It uses more tribal instruments and natural sounds."

- Chika, Solstice DJ, Tokyo, Japan.

"I went to my first rave in Los Angeles in January of '92. I was completely blown away. There were so many different kinds of people there and a really good vibe. I felt like I could completely let go. It was very tribal. The music for me is about feeling. I'm channeling the music from an inner place and feeling it out as I go. I don't think of records as different songs so much as different vibes or feelings and I'm using these tools to create my own music."

- Daniel, Moontribe DJ, Los Angeles, USA.

"It's got to be the bass and the rhythm that does it for me. I know when it's a good night when I get on the dance floor and just don't leave for hours, locked into the groove, not caring about anything else but the pure joy of the music."

- Alan, raver, Buckingham, England.

"There's a whole lot of different genres of music. There's a lot of very warm, organic sounding music that hits you right in the heart chakra. It's a core sound, the tones of the earth and sounds that we all vibrate on. There is so much that people can tap into. I think that the music sets the dancer up to fully let go, to allow the body do the magic and let the mind create an epiphany of group dynamics. Everyone becomes a sea of rhythm and that creates a phenomenal feeling of being one, which is the essence of our being. It's about realizing and remembering that we are not separate."

- Gena Womack, founding member of The Moontribe Collective, Los Angeles, USA.

"When I hear people say that rave music is just a lot of electronic noise I know that they haven't listened to it. They only hear the beat and that's it. They miss all the layers and depth and subtleties. As far as I'm concerned, the best rave music has all the depth and texture as the best classical music."

- Tim Laughlin, The Vibe Crew, England.

"When people first listen to rave music they say it all sounds the same. All they can hear is the repetitive heavy, backbeat common to all genres of electronic dance music. After some exposure at raves, they begin to listen to all the other sounds and they discover that there's a lot more going on. It's the difference between listening and not listening."

- Michael Elenwonibi, musician, rave promoter, Canada.

"The repetition is primarily important - it is hypnotic and addictive. With a proper sound system the music is so loud you can feel it in every part of your body. The low bass notes connect you to the earth and remind us how physical and animal we all are. The melodies and higher frequencies extend us up out of ourselves into a higher state of consciousness. It is an embracing of both earth and sky. Its effect is the most liberating ecstasy possible."

- Vix, music major, rave promoter, London, England.

"The music is technology based and so it will progress as far and as fast as technology does. And technology is moving at an astronomical rate. It's impossible to know where it will go from here but the possibilities are very exciting."

- Topher, underground rave promoter, Canada.

"The first time I heard house music was on a radio station called Q103 in Manchester. The first track I heard was Mr. Finger's Washing Machine. This was very early stuff around '86 or '87. I loved it immediately, thought it was amazing and had to go all the way to London to about four shops to find the records. There was an old woman that must have been around seventy who worked at Groove Records who totally understood house music. She had Traxx records that were pressed on second hand vinyl. They used to take old K-Tel LPs and re-press right on top of them. They always sounded bloody terrible. But you had the music.

- Dave Ralph, DJ, Liverpool, England.

"The music is not about a middle eight and a chorus or three and a half minutes and a fade, which is what we're used to with songs on the radio. Electronic dance music is about creating a continuous mix that is played for a lot of people. It's like one long record that lasts from five to twelve hours. It's different every time, even if you use the same records, the mix is always different and new."

- Rob Blackburn a.k.a. DJ Robynod, Nottingham, England.

"One of the things that makes the music so unique and special is that people will go to any lengths to be together with other people to listen to it. It brings people together in a tribal sense. It takes you on a journey, elevates your level of consciousness and releases your musical instincts. It's not just dance music. You can sit and listen to it, drive to it, swim to it, make love to it. Music is the driving force that fuels the rave movement."

- Logan, a.k.a. Beats Off, The Vibe Tribe, Canada.

"Electronic music is definitely the future of music. The new technology and the new sounds that are being created are generating more diversity and stimulating more creativity."

- Troy Roberts, DJ, Platinum Records, Seattle, USA.

"A lot of friendships have been made out of this music and people have shared great nights together. People have a lot of fond memories from going out and listening to the music. It's very powerful. Electronic music is playing a massive part in a lot of the films being made today as well. You'll be watching a scene in a film and an Underworld track will come on and send shivers up your spine."

- John Digweed, DJ, producer, England.

"Rave music is less intimidating than a lot of popular music that has lyrics. You don't have to understand the language in rave music because you can make it up yourself. It's just, Zimmer, zimmer, zim... it's what ever you want it to be. It's a universal language."

- Surfer Bob, The Vibe Tribe, Canada.

"Music is harmony, harmony is perfection, perfection is our dream, and our dream is heaven."

-Henri Frederic Amiel, Swiss poet and philosopher, 1821-1881

MUSICAL CATEGORIES AND DEFINITIONS

House, Acid House, Progressive House, Deep House, Happy House, Hard House, Chicago House, Oriental House, Hip House, Diva House, Amyl House, Techno, Gabba Techno, Ragga Techno, Trance, Happy Trance, Hard Trance, Acid Trance, Goa/Psy Trance, Hardcore, Happy Hardcore, Horrorcore, Trancecore, Punkcore, Handbag, Hardbag, Hardstep, Old School, Minimal, Bubblegum, Industrial, Jungle, Ragga Jungle, Drum and Bass, Trip Hop, Tech step, Hard Step, Jump Up, Ibiza, Anthem, Ambient, Sombient, Illbient, Intelligent, Electra, Down Beat, Break Beat, Funky Breaks, Funky House, Garage, Speed Garage, Raggage, Hi-NRG, Nu-NRG, Darkside, Tribal, Euro, Dub, Funk, Acid Jazz, Experimental, Banghara, Chutney Soca....

HOUSE

The original electronic incarnation from disco. House typically runs around 120 beats per minute (bpm) and uses a 4/4 time sequence and an eight bar repeating cycle. The beat is maintained by a heavy kick drum that alternates in a 1-3 pattern with a high hat accent. Like its disco roots, house often features vocal choruses, real instrumentation and a more traditional song structure.

ACID HOUSE

An evolution of house characterized by high-pitched screaming "acid sounds" created by a Roland 303 bassline machine. These new psychedelic sounds were found to be particularly effective while under the influence of acid or LSD. The hard, uncompromising, tweaking samples are designed to produce a hypnotic effect.

PROGRESSIVE HOUSE

Originating in the United Kingdom, progressive was originally a blend of German trance and house. More electronic sounds are used in progressive house, like analog synths, which brings it closer to techno than the more soulful house. Generally faster than house, progressive is also known for its big dramatic builds, crescendos and breakdowns.

DEEP HOUSE

Also known as deep disco, deep house is one of the earliest incarnations of house music originating in Philadelphia and New York. When you strip away the vocals and organ sounds of traditional house music, you are left with the deep soulful, extended grooves of deep house. Driven by a deep throbbing bass line, deep house is firmly rooted in the black American soul tradition.

HARD HOUSE

Hard house, also known as pumping house, is an ambiguous, umbrella label that can include everything from progressive, trance and techno, to vocal-led "beaty" house and even Nu-NRG. Originally used as a term to distinguish the "underground" dance floor friendly, faster house tunes from the more commercial sounding handbag that swamped British night clubs at the time. Hard house is basically any kind of house music that emphasizes a heavy dance beat.

FUNKY HOUSE

This became popular in England around 1994. Funky house is quite distinct from other house forms in that it employs the broken beat of old school rather than the familiar 4/4 time signature of house. Add a funky bass line and an electric rhythm guitar and you have funky house.

CHICAGO HOUSE

The original house sound created in Chicago around 1984. Chicago house features simple bass lines, driving four-on-the-floor percussion with a high hat accent and textured keyboard lines. It is also recognizable by its characteristic galloping rhythm.

ORIENTAL HOUSE

A South East Asian spin on the house formula. This is high energy house music with a heavy dose of samples featuring traditional Asian instruments or vocals culled from Asian folk or classical music.

HIP HOUSE

An early fusion of house and hip-hop featuring hip-hop MCs rapping over house records.

DIVA HOUSE

A form of house music popular in gay clubs. Diva house is dramatic, campy house music built around operatic vocal samples.

AMYL HOUSE

An English variation on the house theme aimed at the users of Amyl nitrate, a nasty, speedy, pharmaceutical inhalant used by people who don't know any better. Amyl house is a fast, frantic and unfocused form of house.

TECHNO

An electronic evolution of house developed in Detroit. Techno uses the 4/4 beat structure and eight bar repeating structure of house to build predominantly percussive tracks that use purely electronic sounds. Originally influenced by the European electro sounds of Kraftwerk and electronic tracks from the Italo label in Italy.

GABBA TECHNO

Originated in Holland, gabba means "buddy" in Dutch. Gabba is Dutch, four-beat hardcore. Hard as hell and fast, fast, fast, featuring distorted 240 beats per minute kick drums and big bass drum sounds. Its popularity has waned in recent years but it is still popular in Holland and Belgium.

TRANCE

Trance is an evolution from progressive house and techno. Trance is designed to take the listener on an inner journey and so features extended journey motifs with repeating and cyclic hypnotic elements. Trance also tends to be more densely layered and intense than techno.

HAPPY TRANCE

Trance music can get a little serious for some, so happy trance retains all of the hypnotic qualities but adds some uplifting, light-hearted, melodic elements designed to make you smile on your inner journey. It is also a little faster than regular trance.

HARD TRANCE

Trance music with a heavier emphasis on the beat and a less layered or dense sound.

ACID TRANCE

Trance music that uses the squelchy, acid sounds generated by the Roland 303, also known as The Acid Box. The same sounds that define acid house blended with the hypnotic elements and journey motifs of trance.

GOA/PSY TRANCE

Goa or psy trance takes its name from Goa, India. An incarnation of trance music with a more complex texture of psychedelic sounds woven into a kaleidoscopic tapestry. Goa tracks tend to be finished, complete pieces of music and are therefore less conducive to beat mixing. The beat is a steady 4/4 kick but is often buried in layers of analog sounds. The drug of choice for Goa trance fans is LSD.

HARDCORE

Hardcore is a devolution of techno developed in England. The original form used high speed, 3/4 time, sampled break beats as its rhythmic base and was also known as UK break beat. In 1992/93 another form called four-beat used a four/four rhythm. Hardcore is dense, fast and aggressive and often features a characteristic 909 kick drum through a distortion pedal. Mostly listened to in England, Belgium and some eastern bloc countries.

HAPPY HARDCORE

This is fast and furious four-beat hardcore with wacky, speeded-up, cartoony vocals added. The chipmunks on meth-amphetamine.

HORRORCORE

Horrorcore is very dark and ominous hardcore. It incorporates a lot of eerie, moody, pitched-down effects and gets its name from using scary, distorted samples from horror or science fiction films.

TRANCECORE

A fairly recent development of the hardcore family that incorporates all the hypnotic elements of trance layered over dense hardcore. Trancecore is still mostly unique to the United Kingdom.

PUNKCORE

Fast and furious, anarchistic hardcore blended with samples lifted from punk rock records. (Punk music from the eighties was also known as hardcore but has no relation with the modern electronic dance form.)

HANDBAG

Named after the groups of girls who danced around their handbags in the clubs of Northern England. Handbag is heavily influenced by the disco of the seventies and is up-tempo, commercial house music with a cheesy but happy feel to it. Handbag also features squealy, happy vocal samples.

HARDBAG

The same roots as handbag but less commercial and cheesy. Similar to hard house, hardbag has a much heavier beat than handbag and there are generally no vocals.

OLD SCHOOL/OLD SKOOL

This is the original break beat form from England that led to hardcore. Old school features a 3/4 time sampled break beat as the main rhythm track. Though old school is distinctly different rhythmically, it retains many of the other original elements of house. This form was popular in England in the late eighties and has since disappeared.

MINIMAL

Used to denote a striped-down form of techno originating in Detroit. Sometimes called Detroit minimal, this form is basically just a simple persistent percussion track with very little embellishment.

BUBBLEGUM

Similar to handbag, bubblegum is a term used to describe the most blatantly commercial form of house music played in clubs.

INDUSTRIAL

Industrial music is an early development of electronic music and one of the influences that led to the development of house and techno. Industrial is characterized by deep and densely layered mixes that use samples of machine noises and industrial sounds.

JUNGLE

Originated in London, England by black urban musicians, jungle merges a syncopated hip-hop rhythm with dub reggae bass lines and sampled break beats. As with hardcore, speeded up samples of other records are also incorporated for the rhythm tracks, giving jungle a dense and complicated rhythmic base.

HARD STEP or HARDSTEPPER

This is an evolution of jungle with a strong, heavy, offbeat bassline. The main percussive beat is also emphasized and made sparser and heavier making it more danceable than conventional jungle.

DARKSIDE

Also known as dark jungle, this is an evolution of jungle music that uses dark, eerie, ominous samples and deep and creepy bass sounds.

DRUM AND BASS

This is a direct progression from jungle. Today the term is mainly used for later recordings while jungle is used to describe older recordings. Generally speaking, drum and bass tends to be less complex rhythmically than jungle with more of an emphasis on the drum and bass tracks.

TRIP HOP

This is very slowed down, instrumental version of hip-hop. The syncopated beat is slowed down to less than 90 bpm and layered with the electronic, spacey sounds usually associated with ambient music. Made popular by musicians like Tricky and Massive Attack, trip hop has been described as hip-hop in a flotation tank.

TECH STEP

Tech step is dark jungle music that uses techno style sounds. Could also be described as a cross between drum and bass and techno.

HARDSTEP

Very close to tech step but the beats are sparser and heavier.

JUMP UP

Jump Up is a high-energy form of jungle designed to be more danceable. This Jamaican influenced form often features hip-hop and ragga samples.

IBIZA

Also known as Balearic beat, this up-tempo club house was made famous at Club Amnesia in Ibiza in the late eighties. Ibiza is characterized by powerful grooves mixed with Spanish influenced themes. Ibiza tunes are easy to remember and often feature builds with high-end synth sounds designed to get the dance floor jumping.

ANTHEM

Anthem is the name given to a series of massive house hits that swept across England in the late eighties. They are anthemic house classics that were instantly recognizable and loved by a huge number of ravers and clubbers in the United Kingdom.

AMBIENT

This is essentially electronic atmosphere music designed to relax the listener with its soothing vibes. Generally under 90 bpm or totally beatless, ambient music takes you on a relaxing or thoughtful journey using a variety of sounds, from wind and whale sound samples, to richly textured electronic landscapes.

SOMBIENT

This is ambient music with a somber flavor, specifically designed to bring you down and put you to sleep.

ILLBIENT

Illbient is the darker, evil side of ambient music with a jungle influence. The melodies are warped and twisted and sick and horrifying sounds are used to disturb and shock. Perfect for the chill out lounge at a gabba or end of the world party.

INTELLIGENT

Intelligent is a term that is used more to describe an approach to music rather than a specific genre. There is intelligent techno, intelligent ambient, intelligent trip top etc. A term used to describe music that is a little more complex or ambitious that may require more listening, understanding and attention.

ELECTRO

Popular in the early eighties in New York, electro is an early form of hip-hop that marries syncopated rhythms with more techno type sounds. Electro runs around 120 bpm and features the kick drum and electronic snare sounds made by the Roland 808.

BREAK BEAT

Originally invented by DJ Kool Herc by isolating percussive breaks from soul records to form the basis of hip-hop and rap. In recent years however, electronic musicians have re-invented the concept by isolating "breaks" from house and techno tracks, creating something quite different. The syncopated rhythmic breaks are speeded up and the bass drum emphasizing the 4/4 beat is dropped completely.

FUNKY BREAKS

A form of break beat with a soul flavour, driven by a funky bass line.

DOWN BEAT

A term used to denote any kind of music that is slowed down to 120 bpms or less. Down beat house, down beat hip-hop, down beat breaks etc.

GARAGE

Named after the Paradise Garage club in New York, garage is the Big Apple's answer to Chicago house. Predominantly vocal-oriented house music, garage was the blending of house records with a wide variety of other sources including, techno tracks, soul records and even rock songs, resulting in a unique blend also known as the Jersey Sound where many of the artists and producers came from.

SPEED GARAGE

Despite the name, speed garage actually has very little relation to garage except the fact that it is a form of house with vocal samples. Unlike garage, speed garage is based on a 4/4/ time break beat and is characterized by a distinctive reggae influenced, jumpy, synthesized bass line and time stretched, phased or flanged samples.

RAGGA

Ragga is a blend of house music, traditional Indian music and reggae that was originally developed by the Indian community in Jamaica. Ragga became a popular form in Jamaican dance halls and uses distorted reggae bass lines and reggae influenced vocal verses intertwined with an East Indian flavour.

RAGGAGE

As the name suggests, raggage is a hybrid of speed garage and ragga.

HI-NRG

Hi-NRG is an early evolution of new-style disco. Simple, fast, danceable early house where the bass often takes the place of the high hat. Considered to be a cheesy, obsolete form of house by underground fans but still played in some of the more commercial clubs.

NU-NRG

Nu-NRG is the next generation of Hi-NRG and a harder, faster version of commercial European-style house. Nu-NRG uses a hard techno-based 4/4 bass beat with heavy pumping bass lines. Melodies tend to be anthemic with epic build-ups and breakdowns. The predominately female vocals are usually on the breathless and corny side.

TRIBAL

Tribal is a form of house that incorporates samples from third world cultures. A heavy primal tribal beat is layered with sounds and flavors from the world's indigenous people.

EURO

A European style blend of pop, techno and house, very similar to Hi-NRG. Euro is popular in the more commercial clubs in Europe.

DUB

Dub music is a synthesis of early electronic experiments and reggae that began in Jamaica in the late sixties. Though often ignored, dub has had an enormous influence on the evolution of electronic dance music. These early experiments with echo, reverb, delay and other electronic effects by Jamaican reggae and ska musicians were groundbreaking and served to inspire the next generation of electronic experimentation.

FUNK

This is basically any house music with a heavy dose of black American funk music characterized and driven by a funky bass line and/or an electric rhythm guitar.

ACID JAZZ

This is acid house music that incorporates improvised jazz melodies and chords. Often features a Hammond organ.

EXPERIMENTAL

Experimental is a term used for any electronic music that falls outside of present definitions. Music that intentionally breaks the rules or goes into a new area of exploration where anything goes.

BANGHARA

Banghara meshes traditional Punjabi folk songs and drumming with electronic house rhythms.

CHUTNEY SOCA

Chutney Soca comes from Trinidad and mixes Indian style melodies with a fast electronic calypso beat.

AN INTERVIEW WITH BRENT CARMICHAEL...

DJ Brent Carmichael

photo: trent warlow

Brent Carmichael is a veteran West Coast DJ with Phatt Phunk Records and the resident DJ at Storm and Lush at the Limit nightclub in Victoria, Canada. Brent is well known for presenting two of the best club nights around which also serve as a showcase for both local talent and top DJs from all over the world.

Brent has been spinning vinyl for several decades and has seen many musical genres come and go in the club scene. From disco to wave to house and trance, Brent has adapted to the changing times maintaining a well-deserved reputation for excellence throughout.

I warm up by outlining my three-musical-revolutions-per-century-theory. Brent disagrees.

BRENT: *I think that to split up the history of music into just three categories is to exclude movements that have been just as influential, like disco in the seventies, which I think was bigger than the sixties movement. Rock and roll in the fifties fueled the sixties and in the eighties, wave was very influential.*

Each musical development added to the next scene, so I see it as more of a continuous progression than separate movements. People demand freshness, so one scene dies out and another begins. I hear people complaining at the parties now about the music and the parties getting too big and attracting the wrong crowd. At the beginning of all the movements I've been a part of, they wanted people to come in, but after a time the scene slows down and something else comes along to take its place.

FRITZ: When I first heard that house music evolved from disco, I had a hard time reconciling the two. I could only remember when disco sucked. I had no idea that it had such an illustrious underground history. How did we get from the most commercial superficial musical form to the hippest new underground sound of house?

BRENT: *Disco and house are almost the same thing. Seventies disco has a few more vocals but it's basically house. When people think of disco, they think of eighties disco, but just like now you can get pop-techno or pop-house you had pop-disco. Disco was one of the first musical forms that separated itself from live instruments. It always had those long instrumental eight bar phrases like house music today. All the house and techno music today came directly from seventies disco.*

(Brent plays me a track to illustrate the evolution of house from disco. He describes the track as an early eighties cross over of acid house and disco. The rhythm is definitely disco based, the vocals are heavily processed and the instrumentation is made up of high-end synth sounds. He describes it as early house/acid house, or early techno/late disco.)

BRENT: *I can play that at parties and people will ask me where I bought that new track, not realizing that it's fifteen years old. A lot of DJs are discovering old tracks and playing them again. There is a long evolution of house music, a lot of turns and new directions as it tried to find its way. A lot of those experiments just died off.*

FRITZ: Like what?

BRENT: *Like Rotterdam, for example. It was big for about a year and then died out right across the world. It was really, really fast. I don't know how anyone could have danced to it.*

FRITZ: Was that an evolution from British hardcore?

BRENT: *Yes, that's part of the influence for it. Rotterdam was even faster and had very little musicality. Most of the people who were into Rotterdam moved over to jungle and drum and bass when it died out. Jungle and drum and bass are not as insane as Rotterdam but they have a similar energy. Once you start listening to all the forms you can hear that they all influence each other.*

FRITZ: How would you define house music today?

BRENT: *House is a culturally based music rather than industry based. So it has geographical centers. New York house has real instruments and vocal choruses, Detroit house is much more electronic, and it's really Detroit techno. Chicago house has that galloping rhythm most people associate with house music today.*

FRITZ: What's the relationship between house and techno?

BRENT: *To trace the musical evolution, you have to hear the music in a certain time period. If you listen to Inner City, who pioneered the Detroit techno sound, you might think that it sounds like disco but the instrumentation is different. The original techno wasn't meant to be something heavy and fast or dark and evil, it was a very musically correct form. It's only much later that it re-animated as a darker form.*

Stacy Pullen, who is the new school of Detroit techno, will tell you that it's the only intelligent form of techno. Most people think that the harder, faster, less musical forms of techno, void of melodies is pure techno. Other people would say it's acid trance or gabba techno. But someone who listens to gabba might call it house.

FRITZ: There seems to be some confusion with the difference between progressive house and trance.

BRENT: *Trance started out being anything that could trance you out. Now it's become a different form, influenced by people like Sasha and Paul Van Dyk and BT. It crosses back and forth with progressive house. In fact, now - if they're silly enough to try and classify the music - you'll see on the flyers, progressive house/trance because they're so close.*

FRITZ: While we're on the thorny subject of classification, is there an identifiable difference between jungle and drum and bass?

BRENT: *Jungle is an old form. The early stuff was just speeded up breaks with vocals and as it developed they replaced the sampled vocals with ragga rap and took the bass beat out of it. There are maybe a few tracks where you can say, this is jungle or this is drum and bass but mostly you'll have a hard time finding two DJs that will agree on exactly where one ends and the other begins. The term jungle started to become unfashionable and so people started to call it drum and bass. I find that most of the new drum and bass has begun to use really beautiful harmonies and melodies and sometimes they'll even have live MCs rapping over it.*

FRITZ: What's the most popular electronic musical form at the moment?

BRENT: *It depends on where you live. In Toronto, you'll here a lot of jungle and drum and bass in the clubs. On the West Coast you hear mostly progressive, trance and breaks. In San Francisco they're playing a lot of deep house that is a sparser form of house. In Los Angeles now, because of the influence of people like Moontribe, you will hear a lot of hard trance that* *they are starting to call desert trance or Mojave.*

FRITZ: I've heard some people classify electronic dance music by the beats-per-minute. For instance house is anything between 125 bpm to 140 bpm and trance is anything faster than 140 bpm but not above 170 bpm. What about classifying by bpms?

BRENT: *You might be able to get away with that, but there are lots of examples that don't follow that description. You can take a really clean breaks song and if you slow it down enough it becomes hip-hop or trip hop and if you speed it up enough it becomes drum and bass or jungle. The speed does relate to it, but no more than the harmonies or any other elements of the music.*

FRITZ: How would you classify yourself as a DJ?

BRENT: *Some people say I'm a trance DJ, some people say I'm a techno DJ or a breaks DJ. It's whatever they hear in the music.*

FRITZ: Do you pre-plan your sets?

BRENT: *No. A lot of people do, but I like to work in a more esoteric way. I like to figure out the energy in the room. When I've got a bad crowd, something about it feeds back to me and gives me less energy and makes me feel really drained. If that happens I will try to shift the music to connect with the crowd. If I'm on a build that is not working, I might do three short songs that will vary in style, gauge the reaction to give me some idea where the crowd it at and begin the build again. If I work a whole night like that, struggling to connect with the crowd, I go home totally drained of energy. But normally I can figure it out and make it work.*

You can be a good technical DJ and program your nights, and if you are playing at a party where everyone likes your music, you will do great. But if you always do that, you can become too egocentric and the music is not allowed to grow the way it's supposed to grow. The person who originally taught me was DJ Mindkind from Toronto and he would never let me program my nights. He would never let me repeat a mix either and if I did, he would threaten to fire me.

Every record should have more energy than the one before it. You can do that with speed or freshness and it doesn't necessarily have to be a nice long mix, sometimes a complete, dead drop out with a new sound coming up underneath will increase the energy. I try to follow the patterns that I've seen music take over the years. It comes in waves with one thing trailing off and another new sound coming up at the same time.

FRITZ: Do you still go to parties to just have fun?

BRENT: *I often go to parties for fun. I tend to avoid the parties where every one is talking about the drugs more than the music. I don't have a moral judgment against ecstasy but I do disagree with the drugs being more important than the music being played. If you can't go to a party without* *doing drugs, you may be starting on a slippery slope that could eventually bring about the destruction of the scene. So I choose parties for the music.*

FRITZ: Have you ever had any religious experiences or deep insights on ecstasy?

BRENT: *I think that people do have religious experiences and insights when they are on drugs, not just ecstasy, but many other drugs. But I think that it's a little like cheating because when they come down, they can't put it into practice. They could, but I don't think that most people do. That experience you have has obligations that come with it. If you see something that's wrong or something that needs changing you have to act on it when you come down. If you only get insights when you are on a drug then you have to keep taking the drug and that can become a problem.*

FRITZ: Do you think that the rave scene will have a lasting value or is it just another fad or fashion?

BRENT: *Fashion to me is a form of ego and I don't think that the rave scene is that. I think that the rave scene is a continuation of the growth of music. I don't see it as any different than the early tribal drumming. It has the same energy as any primitive musical form. It might be drifting back to those early roots. There's a specific attraction we have to circular beats and rhythms that has always been around. These types of rhythms were originally associated with religious music like early pagan music or nature-based religions and they are resurfacing in the music now.*

I think that if the rave scene wasn't so regulated it would have greater benefits for society. If people could dance off their energies there would be less problems. People end up blocking their energies and create a kind of build up that can be unhealthy. When the bars close at 2 a.m., a lot of people have energy to burn and they don't know what to do with it. Even in the rock and roll bars, if they could party until 5 a.m., they would be too tired to fight.

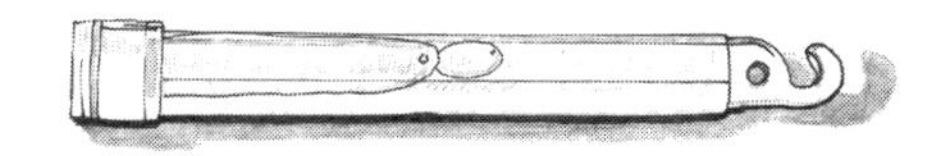

CHAPTER 7:

THE BUSINESS OF RAVE

- the underground
- the midground
- the overground
- events and clubs, facts and figures
- sample budget
- the business of music
- the art of flyers

artwork: virginia smallfry

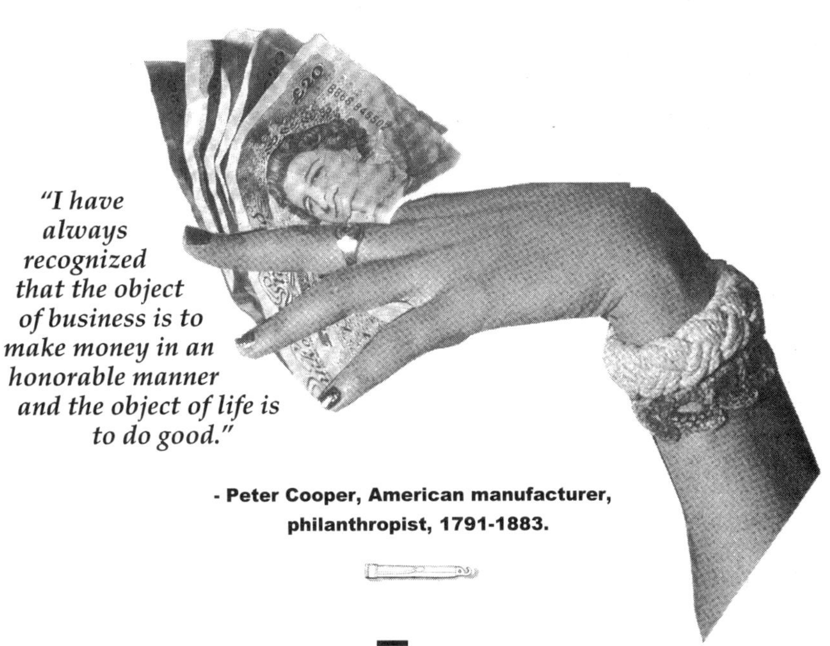

"I have always recognized that the object of business is to make money in an honorable manner and the object of life is to do good."

- Peter Cooper, American manufacturer, philanthropist, 1791-1883.

7
THE BUSINESS OF RAVE

Generally speaking, ravers don't take business very seriously. The stuffed shirts and formality of the conventional business world are the antithesis of the freedom and fun loving rave mentality. Ravers shun the traditional models of hierarchical power systems, profit margins and projections in favor of a more spontaneous group effort. Like laid-back worker ants, they often appear to operate in a haphazard, casual fashion flitting this way and that, one minute solving a financial problem, the next, patiently listening to someone's theory on DMT hypnotherapy while at the same time maintaining a complete and unshakable faith that everything will come together in the end. Superficially, ravers may appear unorganized or unfocused. But they get things done. Big things. Complicated things.

I arrived early for one party and the set up crew was still wandering around solving sound and lighting problems. One of the speaker stacks was mysteriously shorting out and some powerful lighting units had blown a fuse somewhere in the building so the projectors were not working. Ravers were now flooding into the place and hanging around patiently while the set up crew were still perched on ladders hanging screens for projected images. But no one seemed particularly concerned about the situation. The organizers stood around nonchalantly smoking cigarettes and cracking jokes. At one point, someone who appeared to be a head technician strolled by with a coil of cable over one shoulder and someone called over and asked him what the problem was. He paused, scratched his head and casually said, "Don't worry, man, everything will work out. It always works out."

And sure enough within the next half-hour, hundreds of ravers were dancing to crystal clear music in a sea of pulsing light. The story not only illustrates the relaxed approach to getting things done but also the unflagging faith that everything will work out in the end. In New Age philosophy this is known as positive manifestation. The belief that matter is thought form made manifest; the more we believe that something will happen, the more likely it is to happen. And although ravers may not formally subscribe to, or expound this philosophy, it is very much evident in the way they do things and comments on the spirit with which they approach business.

Rave culture's attitude towards business is analogous to the hippie's perspective on government. Like the foundations of a true democracy, ravers believe that if it is not "for the people" and "by the people," then it is of little use to the people. Like the hippies before them, ravers harbour a healthy distrust of those who are purely motivated by money and reject any philosophy that puts profits before the needs of people.

He paused, scratched his head and casually said, "Don't worry, man, everything will work out. It always works out."

In fact many ravers believe that it is almost immoral to make money from raves. The old adage, "never mix business and pleasure", comes to mind. With so much pleasure being generated at raves it's hard to reconcile the fact that for some people, i.e. the organizers and investors, it is also a business venture with potentially huge overheads and high risks.

Although you will often hear ravers complaining about all the money that promoters are racking in, the truth is, all but a very few promoters actually see any real profits at all. This is borne out by the fact that very few rave outfits last more than a year or two. Only the larger arena events have any real potential of producing significant profits and they come with an equal potential for financial disaster.

One of the reasons the rave movement has managed to remain underground, despite its massive popularity, is due to its rejection of over-commercialization. Throughout rave culture there is a pervading anti-commercial sentiment; an underlying fear that if the scene becomes too commercial or mainstream, its vital elements of innovation and freedom will be diluted, a fact borne out by a long history of other fringe movements that have been absorbed and neutralized through popularization.

The fear is a valid one. I recently heard an instrumental "muzak" version of John Lennon's Revolution playing in an elevator. The once rasping and raw vocals had been replaced with a sanitized and saccharine string section. What was once a powerful and cynical warning about social change had been reduced to insipid and empty background music. Many great musical innovators and cultural icons of the sixties are now being used to sell products and services to people who once bought their records as an endorsement of their revolutionary philosophies. Bob Dylan's The Times They Are A Changing, once a potent anthem for a generation in flux, is now being used to advertise a commercial bank. Janis Joplin was being satirical when she sang a song praying for God to buy her a Mercedes Benz. Today, she would be spinning in her grave if she knew that the same song was now being used by Mercedes in a national television advertising campaign to sell the elitist cars to her former fans. In these examples the original meanings are not only diluted or obscured, they are completely reversed. In a culture obsessed with advertising and mass-markets, where the bottom line is valued above all else, it is easy to see that there is no place for anti-establishment messages. Like the Borg of Star Trek, elements that smack of individualism are assimilated and become the standardized property of mass culture. This is the reason that rave culture has traditionally shunned commercial advertising of any kind. You will not see raves advertised in the local newspaper, on TV or radio. Traditionally, rave parties have been exclusively advertised by word of mouth or with flyers passed from hand to hand. In the past few years, however, there has been a move towards bigger and bigger events involving thousands, or even hundreds of thousands of ravers. These massive undertakings can cost a fortune to put on and we are now seeing these mega events sponsored by the likes of Coca-Cola, Nike, Camel Cigarettes and IBM.

Like the Borg of Star Trek, elements that smack of individualism are assimilated and become the standardized property of mass culture.

For many old school ravers, corporate sponsors and their ulterior motives go against the underlying spirit of the movement. For others, the chance to see a huge line-up of international DJs, mind-blowing visuals and extravagant light shows along with tens of thousands of like-minded people can be an exciting prospect. Luckily, one does not have to rule out the other and nowadays both extremes, from small intimate gatherings to giant arena events and everything in between are available. At the base of this inverted pyramid and what many ravers would call the heart and soul of the movement, is the underground scene.

THE UNDERGROUND

Rave is essentially a revolutionary movement and from its inception has passionately demanded the right to dance all night, even if this means circumnavigating the regular channels of permits and permission. Underground parties are generally smaller events attended by fifty to five hundred people. They are produced without the permission or knowledge of local authorities in locations that are usually not officially zoned for this type of activity. In the early days of rave, break-in parties or hit-and-run parties were the norm and promoters would actually break-in to unoccupied or abandoned buildings to stage an event. Nowadays these types of events are rare, and even the most subversive promoter will have some sort of arrangement with the manager or owner of the location.

photo: tristan o'neill

An underground promoter will generally not be a registered company or have a business license and will operate on a cash only basis as part of a purely underground economy. This does not necessarily mean however, that this type of promoter is totally irresponsible. They may lack respect for a set of rules imposed by a system that they see as irrelevant to their lifestyles but they generally have a healthy respect for the welfare of their fellow ravers. Stories of promoters turning up the heat in overcrowded locations in order to sell bottled water at inflated prices might make good copy in the local newspaper but are more likely to be fiction than fact. Most underground promoters will impose their own limits on capacity to avoid overcrowding, provide "in-house" security, make free fresh water available and take other measures to ensure the safety and comfort of those attending. After all, a good number of those attending will probably know the promoter personally and if there were any obvious underhanded tactics the people responsible would not be too hard to find.

Topher is a consummate underground rave promoter from the West Coast of Canada and echoes the views of many underground promoters that small is beautiful. *"I don't want to promote the big parties with thousands of people. Two or three hundred people parties are the perfect size. It creates a more intimate environment. You get to meet the people you want, rather than seeing someone go by for a few minutes and then disappear into a sea of people, never to be seen again. Large parties can be fun but that's not what attracted me to this movement. At smaller parties you have an opportunity to really meet people and have a meaningful interaction."*

Intimate and meaningful connections are at the heart of rave culture for many people and the reason why smaller parties will always be an essential part of the scene. Smaller events are usually organized by an individual or group of ravers whose only goal is to provide a venue for music and celebration. The underground promoter has little or no chance of making any profits and more often than not will actually lose money or go into debt to produce a party. I know of many promoters who repeatedly produce small underground parties that lose money but repeatedly bounce back to put on another event. Their reasons for doing this are a testimony to the spirit of the movement itself. Little or no regard is given to the commercial success of the venture or the considerable time and effort involved in organizing and setting up a party. Success is measured exclusively by the quality of the event itself. If the music is hot and everyone goes off, all the effort is well worth it. If the promoter breaks even it's an added bonus. If they lose their shirts - and pants and underwear - then their only problem is where to find new clothes. Although underground organizers will try and defer payments until after the event and solicit as much free labour and services as possible, there are still a significant amount of hard costs that have to be covered. Sound and lighting equipment can be very expensive, the venue will usually want money up front and any out-of-town DJs will need transportation costs and will also often require non-refundable deposits. Costs can range from a few hundred to a few thousand dollars. But apart from hard financial costs, there is a considerable amount of time and energy involved to produce a successful underground rave. A small army of dedicated volunteers working long hours under impossible conditions with limited resources is often required. Setting up lighting, sound systems and decorations for inside events can be a tremendous amount of

artwork: virginia smallfry

work and in the summer, outdoor parties pose their own unique set of problems.

Outdoor events are becoming more and more popular with the underground promoter because there are no location costs and no space limitations. The trick is to find a place far enough from civilization to avoid noise complaints but close enough to be assessable. All the equipment and supplies must be carried in, sometimes requiring a major trek over difficult terrain. I have seen outside set-ups go on for days with a huge crew of ravers carrying equipment through the woods or down steep, muddy slopes to remote beaches. Wayne Grimwood, mentioned in the introduction, spent one summer with a collective known as The Vibe Tribe, a committed group of ravers including Surfer Bob, DJ Davie and Beats Off, whose lives revolved around producing small impromptu, outside raves on the isolated beaches and virgin forests of British Columbia, Canada. Their feats of strength and endurance that summer were truly inspiring. One party, on a beach only accessible only by sea, required bringing in a large sound system in a small boat. Due to the choppy water and lack of docking facilities, the speaker stacks and other equipment had to be carried from the boat to the beach. This meant wading through the freezing water, neck deep, carrying heavy speaker stacks and other equipment up over their heads! The last waterlogged trip was made at one a.m. in the pitch dark amid cheers from the small but enthusiastic group of ravers waiting patiently on the beach. By two a.m., the system was finally set up and the party went ahead. The Vibe Tribe is typical of many loose-knit rave collectives around the world who make a lifestyle out of producing small, often free parties, with little or no consideration for financial gain. These groups of friends are motivated only by a desire to share their positive experiences of rave culture with others by constantly re-creating the conditions necessary to achieve the rave experience.

Stories of promoters turning up the heat in overcrowded locations in order to sell bottled water at inflated prices might make good copy in the local newspaper but are more likely to be fiction than fact.

Transportation is sometimes a problem for raves set in remote locations so shuttle buses are often used to ferry people to and from out-of-the-way places. But even in cases when transportation is not supplied and the location is in the middle-of-nowhere, crowds of loyal ravers will inevitably show up. The now legendary Moontribe parties in the Mojave Desert are a good example of how dedicated ravers are to find the party, despite the obstacles. Moontribe are a collective from Los Angeles who began holding spiritually orientated full-moon parties in remote areas of the desert to avoid contact with authorities. Although the group never produced a flyer or any other form of advertising, and the only source of information was word of mouth, the parties eventually attracted up to three thousand people. (See: The Moontribe Collective.)

I remember an outdoor party staged in a remote location that was virtually impossible to find. With little or no directions available, the general area was relayed by word of mouth only and crude piles of rocks and twig arrows left at the side of the road were the only indication of where to turn. By midnight only about a dozen people had made the impossible journey. But sure enough, by one o'clock in the morning, ravers began flooding in across a muddy field, appearing like magic out of the pitch black night into the pulsing lights of the party like techno elves, complete with plastic backpacks, silver eyelashes and feather boas.

Quiet music just doesn't cut the mustard at a rave.

The most disappointing scenario for the promoter and raver alike, and one of the most common problems with underground parties is the inherent risk of getting shut down. While it is often possible to talk the management of community halls, or the owners of warehouses, into giving their permission for an all night event without the necessary assembly permits, fire inspections and other requirements of city councils, there is a fairly good chance the party will not go ahead at all or be shut down sometime before dawn. In this case, the strategy of the promoter is to stall the closure for as long as possible. If the authorities show up and ask for a fire inspection permit, a business license, or any other non-existent paperwork, the organizer will often be extremely hard to find. Once found, they will stall for time by promising the documents, then promptly disappear again to find them. This game of cat and mouse might continue for hours. Meanwhile, the party continues.

Because these events are taking place in the middle of the night and the location information is only available hours before the party begins, spot-checks for things like business licenses or assembly permits are rare. The most common reason for the police to show up is noise complaints. Quiet music just doesn't cut the mustard at a rave. The sound must be loud and clear and if anyone is living nearby, the chances of someone complaining about the noise is extremely high. If this happens, the promoter will promise to turn the music down and reassure the officers that the party is just wrapping up anyway. The police will usually issue a warning the first time and the party continues. When they come back, the promoter once again apologizes profusely and the same story is given. If the police become sufficiently annoyed they will issue a ticket which is a small price to pay for the party to continue. If things do not go well, as a last resort, the promoter will not be above begging and pleading with the authorities to let the party continue. Sometimes they are successful. The outcome of this time-honored ritual will usually result in the party being closed and several hundred ravers wandering off into the night looking for an "after party."

Ravers and organizers alike accept closures as an unfortunate fact of life. Even if the ticket price is relatively high, it is rare to find anyone requesting a refund or demanding to see the management. The game is understood by all involved and the inherent hazards are accepted as part and parcel of the adventure. Whether the party goes off or not is everything to the underground promoter and as with gambling, the thrill of a big win can far outweigh the disappointment of a few losses.

THE MIDGROUND

I'll call the next level of rave party the midground. These are parties for five hundred to two or three thousand people that are *mostly* legal. It is difficult to keep parties of this size a secret and the financial risks involved with this type of event are much higher than with the purely underground affair. Here, there is too much money involved to take a complete loss so the promoter has to take measures to ensure a profit margin or at least break even. This type of event can cost anywhere from five thousand to sixty thousand dollars, depending on the line up and production values.

photo: tristan o'neill

With this kind of operation, numbers are everything. To be successful the event may need as many as five hundred or a thousand people just to break even. This means that the organizers must do everything they can to guarantee a large turn out. They will need to circulate a high quality flyer well in advance of the party and get it to all the right outlets. Once they have attracted the eye with an impressive flyer, the most important factor in attracting large numbers is the DJ line up. Events that need a large turn out have to include well-known DJs and some of these "stars" are paid huge amounts of money because they can guarantee a big turn out. Ravers develop loyalties to certain DJs and will usually decide which parties to attend by who is playing. In England, DJs develop "posses," crowds of faithful fans that follow their favorite DJs from gig to gig all over the country. A midground event will usually feature at least one international headliner and sometimes even two or three. The rest of the line up will typically be made up of a couple of secondary out-of-town celebrities and a selection of local talent. International DJs will require return airfares, accommodation, work visas and will often ask for a non-refundable deposit. Some will even demand that the promoter purchase a brand new pair of turntables for them to use or other expensive requests. If the line up includes several out of town, or out-of-country DJs, the budget can go up significantly. International headliners will usually cost anywhere from one to five thousand dollars or more for a two hour set but in recent years, some DJ's fees have gone through the roof with reports of up to $15,000 being paid for a two hour set.

Many ravers, particularly those that have been involved in the scene for a few years, still believe that big commercial raves or massives go against the philosophical grain of the movement.

Lighting and sound systems that can fill a large hall or arena can also run into many thousands of dollars. Lighting equipment can include computer controlled, intelligent lighting systems, Mk3 Goldenscans, Flower strobes, massive overhead projection screens, video projectors, panoramic visuals, UV back drops and a host of other very expensive high-tech visual and audio gadgetry.

Because of the increased production values and generally higher costs involved in a larger event, the midground promoter has to do everything in their power to safeguard against anything that might cause the party to be shut down. The location will generally be an approved venue with the appropriate licenses and permits for this kind of event, and promoters will often seek advance support from City Hall or the police department in an effort to minimize any problems. Having said this, I am always amazed at the amount of midrange promoters that lay out huge amounts of their own and other people's money, to promote big parties that often end up being canceled or shut down because they have neglected to take care of the legal details. This says something about ravers incorrigible optimism and their attitude towards business in general. Even when the stakes are high and the pitfalls proven, they will continue in the belief that everything will turn out in the end. And when it doesn't, they will walk away, shrug it off and live to rave another day.

J.C. is a self-employed private businessman in his forties who has been promoting raves for the past two years. As a father of two young adults, he became aware that venues for young people were few and far between, and as a child of the sixties he was no stranger to wild parties and new music. His experience with rave promotion is a common one. *"I lost my shirt on the first party I promoted, broke even on the second one and did a little better than break even on the next two. I may have made a couple of thousand dollars profit but that's not much considering the huge amount of work involved. If something goes wrong with a big party like this, people are pissed off to lose their thirty dollars, but I stand to lose thirty thousand. There is no such thing as a 100% bust-free party. Things can go wrong with any party. People think that promoters are making hundreds and thousands of dollars but the only people who are making money on my parties are the people I hire. No one is making any big money here."*

photo: tristan o'neill

Some midrange promoters operate their businesses legally and take care of details like business licenses, wage deductions, insurance, etc. They may even keep their books up to date and file tax returns. But many do not and, like underground promoters, operate as part of an underground economy or a combination of both. While it is true that some rave companies in this range do well and make a reasonable living, most do not. Even with the best planning, these larger parties often do not make any significant profits for the amount of work involved and many promoters have other forms of income, promoting raves as a sideline or a labour of love.

THE OVERGROUND

In recent years there have been a growing number of huge, extravagant events all over the world that speak volumes about the mass appeal of rave parties. These affairs can attract anywhere from tens of thousands to hundreds of thousands of ravers. An annual rave event in Berlin, Germany, known as The Love Parade, attracted over one million people this year, making it the largest cultural event of any kind in Europe. During the three-day event there were eighty-eight full scale, all-night raves held in and around Berlin. A techno parade in Zurich, Switzerland, now in its seventh year, boasted a crowd of four hundred and fifty thousand. Next year there are similar events scheduled for Paris, Vienna and even Croatia. In Germany, gabba techno events regularly attract crowds of twenty thousand or more and even in South Africa and Brazil promoters are staging rave events that attract crowds in the tens of thousands.

photo: daniel kinderman

An annual rave event in Berlin, Germany, known as The Love Parade, attracted over one million people this year.

The budgets involved in staging these kinds of events can mushroom to astronomical proportions but at this level of involvement, the rewards can also be enormous. Events like this can cost anywhere from a hundred thousand to five hundred thousand dollars and require a well-financed, sophisticated organization to pull them off. Like large sporting events, organizers are turning to sponsorship and it is increasingly common to see companies like Coca-Cola, Sony, Nike and many other large corporations sponsoring such events all over the world. In the Eastern Bloc countries and South East Asia, most of the large parties are sponsored by cigarette companies like Camel and Lucky Strike who actually send reps to hand out free cigarettes.

Needless to say, with so much at stake, these huge events are totally legal affairs with every last detail taken care of. The venues used are usually large sports centers and arenas. Wembley soccer stadium in London, England is home to an enormous annual New Year's Eve party and last year the World Trade Centre in Toronto, Canada was rented for a rave. Tickets for these massive parties can run anywhere from twenty-five to fifty dollars and an average turn out of ten thousand people would put the income for the night at a quarter to a half a million dollars. With an expensive international line up and the highest production values there is a lot of money to be made, but even at this level, things can go wrong. A party scheduled for the same night in the same city can split the crowd and adversely affect both parties. Also, rumors and gossip travel at lightning speed through the rave community and any promoter who gets a bad reputation is libel to pay the price. If there are any reports of the organizers mistreating DJs, breaking promises, or any other kind of underhanded dealings, ravers, with their keen sense of justice, are likely to respond by boycotting the party.

"Rave culture is about belonging to a family. You have the feeling that you know these people."

Many ravers, particularly those that have been involved in the scene for a few years, still believe that big commercial raves or "massives" go against the philosophical grain of the movement. DJ 608 a.k.a. Michael Angelo is a Los Angeles DJ who believes that big events lack the intimacy necessary for people to connect. "Giant parties with corporate sponsors are like rock concerts. They lack the intimate qualities of the small parties where the focus isn't so much on money but bringing people together. There are a lot of promoters in LA who are very young and new to the scene who can only see the dollar signs and the popularity. But that's not what it's all about. It's about the music and opening up and connecting with a lot of different kinds of people. Rave culture is about belonging to a family. You have the feeling that you know these people."

Other veteran ravers, like Tim Laughlin of England's Vibe Tribe believe that there is room for all types of events. *"I think that the commercial aspects of the rave scene are important because it's an expensive undertaking to stage a large rave and you need the income to cover the expenses. If people want to pay for big, glossy, massive raves then let them do it. It's no different than going to a big rock concert, and big rock bands are getting more money than any DJs. There is still plenty of possibilities for smaller parties or free parties, I think that one feeds the other. But I do object to bringing in the big sponsors like Pepsi or Coca-Cola because of what they stand for. They are only interested in dance music to sell drinks. In 1993, the dance music industry in England was worth 1.3 billion pounds, which was five times more than the film industry. And that's only the legal side of the rave scene."*

Surfer Bob of Canada's Vibe Tribe has this to say about corporate sponsors. *"I don't think there's anything wrong with big commercial parties. There may be some thing wrong with a big corporation sponsoring the party if they have sweatshops in Taiwan or whatever. But someone who is throwing a big party and doing a good job and everyone is having a great time, there's nothing wrong with that promoter making some money. It's a big risk to do a big party. If you put everything you have into it and everybody leaves with a smile on their faces, you did a good job and deserve to make some money."*

With so much money on the line, bigger and bigger companies are becoming involved in producing rave events and over the next few years we will doubtless see this trend continue. And while rave culture will probably always foster an underground scene, it seems likely that the new generation of mega-raves will continue to be successful ventures for the promoters and ravers alike, serving to introduce more and more people to the culture of rave.

10,000 people at a World Dance event in the U.K.

photo: tristan o'neill

"We have to look at the underground because that's where it all started. What's exciting about this music is that the underground is always changing and so it's always important to keep abreast of what's going on. But the underground is also becoming much more overground and becoming bigger and bigger. We are now seeing these rave events taking place in concert venues like The South Jersey Convention Centre. It just shows that it's gone from an underground entity to these big commercial events."

- Dave Jurman, senior director of dance music, Columbia Records/SONY.

EVENTS AND CLUBS, FACTS AND FIGURES

THE LOVE PARADE

An annual, carnival-style, techno parade in Berlin, Germany. Began in 1989 by DJ Dr.Motte (a.k.a. Matthias Roenigh) with 150 people. Within a few years the crowd swelled to a 100,000 and last year in 1998, an estimated one and a half million people attended The Love Parade, now the biggest cultural event in Europe.

RAVELATION

Ravelation is produced by Strictly Underground and Naughty But Nice at Wembley Stadium in London, England. This annual New Year's Eve party attracted 14,000 people in 1996 and featured 200,000 watts of sound, 14 hours of music and 30 DJs. The cost of the event was $450,000.00. Ticket price: $70

LABYRINTH

The Club Labyrinth in London, England, features five levels and ten rooms with a large tree garden for a chill out.

FANTASY ISLAND

Fantasy Island in Skegness, England is a $50,000,000 facility with nine arenas. Regular weekly events can attract up to 10,000 people.

MAYDAY

Mayday began in 1991 and is one of the biggest events in the German techno calendar regularly attracting 25,000 or more to its indoor events. This party is sponsored by Sony, Camel Cigarettes, VIVA TV and various clothing companies and magazines.

THE SANCTUARY

The Sanctuary Warehouse in Milton Keynes is a rave club that regularly attracts up to 8,000 people. Tickets for their last New Year's Eve party were $70

CONNECTED

In 1998, Dose, a rave promotion company from Canada, celebrated their five-year anniversary with a rave called Connected. This was an international event featuring six large parties in Toronto, Denver, Atlanta, Seattle, Vancouver and Montreal. Each event was linked to every other with large screen projections via the Internet, creating a "North American Celebration."

UNIVERSE AND TRIBAL GATHERINGS

Universe is an organization that started producing underground warehouse parties in the south of England in 1989. In 1992 they produced "Mind, Body, Soul and the Universe," attended by 10,000 people and voted party of the year by Mixmag. In 1993 they produced the first Tribal Gathering party and attracted a capacity crowd of 25,000 in Warminster, Wiltshire. Since then, Tribal Gatherings have been held every year and continue to get bigger and better.

WORLD DANCE

World Dance is one of the biggest rave promoters in Britain and have produced many huge parties including events at The London Docklands Arena, a venue licensed for 11,000 people. World Dance are renowned for their impressive line-ups and big budget productions.

GABBA EVENTS

European gabba techno events in Germany, Holland and Belgium regularly attract crowds of more than 20,000.

THE STREET PARADE

Now in its seventh year, The Street Parade in Zurich, Switzerland, has gone from 2,000 people in its first year to a staggering 450,000 in 1998, making it the biggest cultural event in the country. Over 40 all-night parties take place before and after the parade.

MINISTRY OF SOUND

Last year The Ministry of Sound, one of London, England's leading rave clubs hooked up with clubs in Manchester and New York for a live simulcast of the evenings entertainment that was also broadcast live on Britain's leading radio station.

HELTER SKELTER

Established in 1989, this mega rave outfit from Britain has a reputation for producing massive parties at the Denbeigh Leisure Complex in Milton Keynes, now known as the dance capitol of the United Kingdom. Early parties attracted up to 2,000 people but in recent years the parties have gotten bigger and bigger. Their last event, entitled Human Nature, featured 100,000 square feet of musical and leisure environments with four arenas, 43 DJs, 13 MCs, a free midway fair with state of the art rides, a market place, a video game area, a cinema, a cafe, a relaxation area or chill out lounge and two licensed bars.

THE BOWLERS

A club in Manchester, England with a dance floor that holds three thousand people.

ENERGY

Energy is an annual party held in Zurich, Switzerland. Energy '98 featured ten dance floors in four buildings, an open-air concert stage, a fun park area, two chill out gardens and a techno village. 23,000 people from all over Europe attended the event.

DANCE VALLEY

An annual outdoor rave event in Holland which regularly attracts up to 20,000 people.

THE LAKOTA

Located in Birmingham, England, The Lakota was the first club outside London to be granted a 24hr license. It is still one of the only four clubs in the country to hold this license.

EARTHDANCE

An event originated in Melbourne, Australia dedicated to planetary peace and the freedom of the Tibetan people. Over thirty countries now participate in this global rave event. All the parties are linked by video broadcasts via the Internet in an effort to create a global dance floor.

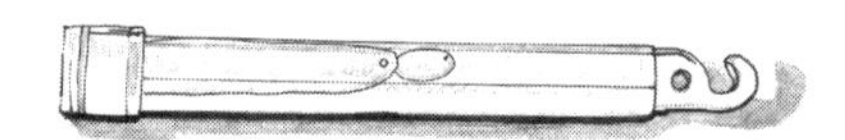

A SAMPLE BUDGET FOR A LOW BUDGET ARENA RAVE FOR ONE TO THREE THOUSAND PEOPLE

(Prices in American dollars)

ARENA COSTS	
Building Rental	1500
Security	1300
2 special duty police x 9hrs	1300
Power (metered)	450
SOUND/LIGHTS	
Sound system	3,000
Lighting	4,000
Projections/lasers	2,500
Decks /Mixer	300
STAFF	
Sound Technician	200
Lighting Technician	200
Set-up/Set deck crew	
$10 hr x 6 hrs x 6	360
Ticket/Door person	100
Juice/Water bar X 3 @ 125	375
Clean up crew	
$10 hr x 4 hrs x 6	240
DJs	
Headliner 1	1500
Headliner 2	1000
Headliner 3	500

Local DJ 1	200
Local DJ 2	200

TRAVEL/ACCOMMODATION

DJ Headliner 1	1000
DJ Headliner 2	1000
DJ Headliner 3	600
Work permits	300

MISCELLANEOUS

Insurance	600
Phone answering service	100
Cell rental/service	200
Printing flyer	2000
Printing tickets	200
Decorations	500
Contingency	500
Total	**$26,225**

PROFIT/LOSS PROJECTIONS

Total Costs $26,225

(At $25 per ticket)
Break even point = 1,049 tickets @ $25 = $26,225

1500 @ $25 = $37,500 Profit = $11,275
2000 @ $25 = $50,000 Profit = $23,775
2500 @ $25 = $62,500 Profit = $36,275
3000 @ $25 = $75,000 Profit = $48,775

At $25 a ticket there are profits to be made, but this event will still need over a thousand people to break even. Another event on or near the same date could easily spell disaster. If there are several partners sharing the profits, even two thousand people will not make anyone rich considering the huge amount of time and energy involved in organizing the event. At twenty-five dollars a ticket, the headliners will have to have the reputation to draw a big crowd and this may mean paying more for the main act. A large turn out is more likely with a lower ticket price. But at fifteen dollars a ticket you will need 1,748 people just to break even. With 2,500 people at $15 a head, a big crowd for most cities, our sample budget would still only produce an $11,275 profit. Split between four partners this would realize less than $3,000 profit each for an event that can take months to produce.

The real money kicks in when the attendance reaches three to ten thousand. The costs are higher at this level but ten thousand tickets at twenty dollars each would yield two hundred thousand dollars income for the night. This is fine in theory but attendance can never be guaranteed. I have seen spectacular flyers advertising the worlds best DJs produce poor turnouts and massive losses for the organizers. In a worst case scenario, putting on a large party can turn into a major financial catastrophe.

Typically, big profits on parties are rare so it takes a lot of nerve to put your own or someone else's money on the line. The rave promoter not only faces the risks inherent in any business venture but may also have the added uncertainty of unsympathetic or even hostile opposition from the community, city hall and the local police. It is also not uncommon to see large, well-organized events booked into legal venues, canceled at the last minute because of bad press. An irresponsible or uninformed reporter writing an article on the horrors of raving for the local newspaper can wreak havoc for anyone involved in the business of rave parties.

It is sometimes difficult to completely understand why people do what they do and rave promoters are no exception.

Rave promoters are a rare breed who are willing to risk a lot to give people the experience of a lifetime. It is sometimes difficult to completely understand why people do what they do and rave promoters are no exception. But whether motivated by love or loot, one thing is sure; to produce a quality event takes a lot of hard work and dedication, nerves of steel, and a belief in rave culture that transcends conventional business concerns. If not for the courage and vision of these new age entrepreneurs, rave culture could not have achieved the mass appeal that it enjoys today.

"If you want to make money, the last thing you should do is promote raves."

- Damien a.k.a. DJ K-Rad of The Alien Mental Association, Canada.

THE BUSINESS OF MUSIC

The music industry has had a somewhat rocky relationship with electronic dance music over the past decade. In the late eighties, when the first house tracks became commercial hits in Europe, North American record companies began to sit up and take notice. By the early nineties they were signing up the new talent as fast as they could find it. Kevin Sanderson was the first house music artist to sign with a major label but many more followed close behind. Terrence Parker was just starting to produce house music at the time and saw a lot of people getting signed up. *"In the early nineties the big labels saw some potential with house music. Frankie Knuckles signed with Virgin Records, Little Lewis signed with a major label and Jack Master Funk had a deal with Warner. But they put this music out and they didn't know how to market it and the sales were not what they expected so all the house artists got dropped. Now, going into the late nineties, the majors are putting their hand back into the pot. Why? Because now they see the money and they know how to market it. Now you have a real purist like Goldie turning down an offer to do an album with Madonna."*

After producing several successful house tracks of his own, Parker was signed by Sony and shipped off to England. The experience ended up being a disappointment when Sony reps tried to convince him to produce more commercial music. They actually took him on a tour of the London clubs, explaining as they went which sounds they were after. Parker did what he could to satisfy their demands but in the end gave up and left the company frustrated. *"I couldn't understand why they didn't want me to do what I had been doing. They had liked it enough to sign me and then wanted me to change everything. I had always wanted a deal with a major so I tried to do it, but my heart wasn't in it and I had to let it go."*

Electronic musicians are deeply involved and committed to electronic dance music as an art form and have never been motivated by making money.

Parker's experience with Sony illustrates the breakdown of communication and understanding that is common between electronic music artists and the major record companies. Electronic musicians are deeply involved and committed to electronic dance music as an art form and have never been motivated by making money. As such, they have more of a personal relationship with what they are doing and feel they have a right be involved in every aspect of the production, from cover art to marketing. This kind of attitude does not go over big with record companies whose prime concern is the bottom line. *"At the very beginning it was important for musicians to be involved in the process, how the music was going to be represented, who's going to design the cover art, the logos for the labels.*

Everyone who was involved in making music in the early days were very passionate about it," remembers Parker.

The record companies failure to successfully market electronic dance music was mostly due to the fact that, they had focused on expanding and maximizing its commercial appeal, as they had with other musical forms. But rave music's appeal lies in its non-commercial format. The music is exciting because it conjures up the irrepressible spirit of the underground, untamed and unpredictable. Its mission is to break out of existing molds and defy commercial formats and concerns. Ravers don't rush out and immediately buy what they see advertised on MTV. Discriminating and perceptive, they will shy away at the slightest indication of being hyped and instinctively reject the manipulating ways of conventional business.

Consequently, there is a proliferation of smaller independent labels that are sympathetic to the underground sensibilities of the electronic dance musician. Many of these small labels are run by DJs and producers who are happy to sacrifice mega-sales for more freedom, and this is where cutting edge music is to be found. New advances and cheaper equipment are also giving way to a new generation of do-it-yourself producers who are churning out tracks in basements and bedrooms all over the world with total freedom from commercial concerns. And with Internet technology now poised to handle large sound files with relative ease at hyper speeds, it is likely that within the next few years the record industry as we know it will be completely transformed, transferring the power back to the musicians. Already there are hundreds of web sites worldwide promoting and selling electronic music to computer savvy ravers.

Chris Cowie is an extremely talented electronic musician who operates the Hook/Bellboy labels in Scotland. He produces his own music under various aliases including X Cabs, Vegas Soul, Scan Carriers, Bulkhead and Stonemaker. Hook/Bellboy also represent about twenty other artists including Christopher Lawrence, Sandra Collins, Chris McSpadum and Frankie Bones. *"The biggest threat to major record companies is the Internet. One guy could basically set up his own label in his house, make music and download it to anyone anywhere. That's a few years away but it's a scenario that will definitely happen. The technology is not quite fast enough yet. The guy in his basement burning a few CDs is not really going to bother the major record labels at all. But the Internet will be a problem for the record stores. If a label like ourselves were able to bypass our distribution and sell direct to the public we'd make a lot more money."*

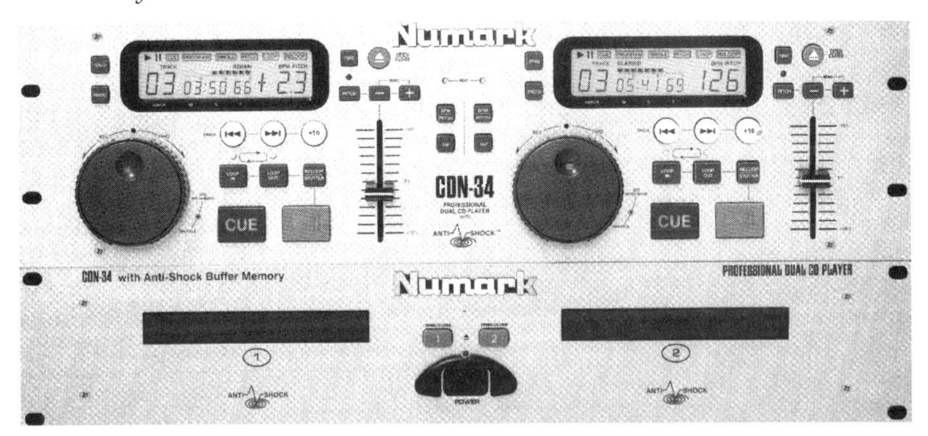

I also asked Chris Cowie to comment on the advantages and disadvantages of signing with a major label rather than an independent. *"It's an advantage to sign with a major if you can get a good advance. If they give you loads of money up front then that's great. But at the end of the day they can sink you. The advances for indie bands are still far more than the advances that dance artists get. Even the majors won't really splash out that much money. The disadvantage is, take a guy that has done a couple of tracks and signs with a major, there's a ninety per cent chance that he'll never be heard of again because he won't have had enough time to develop. And when he gets dropped he thinks there something wrong with him and gets writer's block or something. I experienced this with the very first label I signed with. It depends what you are looking for. Are you looking for a lot of money or do you want to get your music out there and survive for a long time? I'm not saying that everybody who signs to a major label will be a disaster but what tends to happen is the smaller labels get the guys first and then the majors come in and buy their contract. They're better off going to a small label first because these labels are more likely to look after their artists and be a bit more friendly as well."*

In England, where electronic dance music first proved that it could be commercially viable, the market continues to grow and many electronic tracks are being edited down to a more commercial length to be compiled on CD collections. These short remixes are promoted through the club scene and marketed with music videos. DJ Robynod held residencies at the Echo Club and The Union Club in Loughborough, England in the late nineties. *"In England there is always two or three or four dance tracks in the charts because the club scene is so big. People are used to going out to a club after the pub, but now the club is a house music club so they end up buying a mix CD."*

For now, the big record labels are still attractive to many musicians because of their potential to sell huge amounts of product but these days it is fairly common to see an artist recording with a major label under one name while producing records for a small independent company under an alias. This is perhaps the best of both worlds and ensures that the artist can make a good living while retaining a high degree of artistic freedom in creating cutting edge, new music.

I asked Dave Jurman, senior director of dance music at Columbia/Sony if they would have a problem with one of their artists releasing underground tracks under an alias. *"No, not at all. As a matter of fact I think that it can help because as this music gets bigger and bigger I think it's important to never lose sight of the underground roots. Mainstream success comes and goes and there is no guarantee that it will continue at all, but when you have a strong underground following, it can continue for a long time and actually sustain careers. We have an artist now called Mousse T with a hit called Horny that has been a huge smash and has now been released in the United States. But as big as he's become, he doesn't want to lose the underground following that has supported him from the beginning, so he also releases underground records and I think that is very smart of him."*

Junior Vasquez, a top New York DJ, built a song around a telephone message left on his answering machine by Madonna.

Another way that electronic music and rave culture in general is challenging our existing systems is in the area of copyright, a thorny issue in many areas of the arts. Because rave is a "sampling" culture, borrowing from anywhere and everywhere, the issue of ownership can become almost impossible to prove one way or another. A so-called "original track" will often contain snippets of sound from a wide variety of other sources. The musician might sample a drum pattern from another track, an excerpt from a TV show or movie soundtrack, or a vocal passage from a current record. In fact, any source of sound information is fair game for today's electronic musician. Junior Vasquez, a top New York DJ, built a song around a telephone message left on his answering machine by Madonna. Junior had repeatedly failed to return calls requesting that he mix one of the pop diva's latest recordings. Unaccustomed to such shoddy treatment she left her angry rantings on tape which were then used as the vocal track for a dance mix. And it does not end there. This "original" recording can then be used by other DJs to make mix tapes, where a whole collection of other people's music is remixed and released in another form. This remix might then be sampled in part by another musician in the creation of yet another track. This process can go on indefinitely until the music becomes a collaboration between a large group of musicians who may never have even heard of each other. The legal ramifications of sampling have posed a major problem for copyright law since hip-hop musicians began the practice in the seventies. Today it is virtually impossible to control, although many performing rights organizations around the world are working to create laws that can effectively enforce ownership. Meanwhile, rave culture, for the most part unknowingly, seems to be questioning the whole notion of copyright and ownership. To rave culture, sounds vibrating in the air belong to everyone and therefore represent a kind of group ownership. If the borrowed sounds lead to a new musical innovation or just a great track then even the registered owner of the original source is likely to stand up and applaud the effort.

THE ART OF

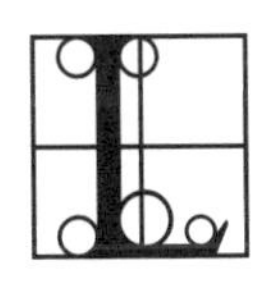

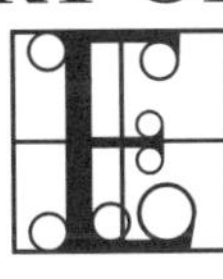

Flyer art is a major feature of rave culture, and in many ways reflects the artistic spirit of the movement. Flyers are designed not only to give all the relevant information about the rave but also capture the flavor of the event. If the party features hard and dark techno music, then the imagery will reflect that ambience. If the event is held outdoors on a sunny weekend with happy house music, the flyer may include fairies and elves dancing in a forest glen. Like rave music, the imagery used for flyers simultaneously celebrates modern technology while embracing the natural and organic world. Computer-generated, technological imagery with 3D graphics featuring space age designs will often be blended with natural elements or environments like forests and waterfalls or flowers and trees. Primitive, archaic, or religious imagery is sometimes incorporated, creating a seamless and harmonious fusion of past, present and future.
Here are a few examples of flyer art...

Kamal of Velvet and Digniti Productions had Prototype Designs realize his ideas for a rave called Salvation.

The Philosophers of Phunk had LA designers Valerian produce this flyer for a party featuring Frankie Knuckles.

V.I.B.E. Productions produced this flyer for a party called Emotion celebrating their five-year anniversary.

This flyer is for a Goa trance party produced by Japanese DJs, Chika and Taka of Solstice Productions. Japanese Equinox artist, K.C, created the original artwork.

Although larger events will often be advertised in rave publications or other underground magazines, most raves are still advertised by passing flyers from hand to hand. An appealing flyer, put out well in advance of the rave, is still an essential tool for attracting a large crowd. A print run of a few thousand high quality, double-sided, full colour flyers can be a major expense and one of the hard, up-front costs. Some flyers come in elaborate shapes or high-tech plastic finishes and can range from business card size to two-foot square posters. Generally speaking, if the flyer has high production values then there is a good chance that the party itself will be a higher quality event. Of course this is not always true, but the promoter who promises the earth and does not deliver will very quickly lose the support of the notoriously ethical-minded ravers. The party promoter's reputation is often the deciding factor in rave attendance; rave promoters live and die on their reputations. If the location is too small or overcrowded, if a DJ doesn't show up, if the sound or lighting is inadequate, or even if the party gets shut down, the promoter is held responsible and ravers may be reluctant to buy tickets for their next event.

Sometimes a pre-flyer will be circulated to create some advance spin. This will be a lower budget flyer with some, but not all, of the information and a promise of more to come. For larger events there may even be a series of flyers, each one different, each one bigger and better than the last, building anticipation for the event. The flyer will tell you everything you need to know about the event including who the DJs are, where they are from and what kind of music they play. Details of the lighting and sound systems might also be included, as well as the whereabouts of ticket outlets, and an info line number which can be called on the day of the event to find out the party's location.

The Alien Mental Association is an informal collective of rave promoters and DJs from the West Coast of Canada, an area famous for its vibrant rave scene. This group has a well-earned reputation for producing some of best events, and some of the most imaginative flyers. Nigel Tasko is the leader of the collective, who also produces parties under the name Noble House. Nigel has been promoting raves since 1992. *"I had been promoting alternative live bands for five years before I discovered rave music. The first parties I produced were crossover events with alternative DJs or bands up to midnight then rave music till four a.m. After a few parties like that I managed an after-hours club for a year then started promoting raves. I started with budgets of $6,500 and worked up to budgets of $45,000."*

Nigel works with Alien Mental associate Damien (a.k.a. The Professor a.k.a. DJ K-Rad) to produce the flyers for their high-powered events. In keeping with the sampling traditions of rave, The Alien Mental Association is not above borrowing corporate logos and designs - as long as it's fun. *"Alien Mental Association is just another way to have fun. Whenever we do rip-offs, we try and make them as playful and witty as we can and have as much fun with them as possible," says Nigel.*

Ideas can come from anywhere. One morning, after a particularly heavy night of ecstatic celebration, Nigel awoke and staggered into the bathroom, wondering whether he was fit enough to start the day or should go straight back to bed. The first thing that caught his attention was a Crest toothpaste box lying by the sink. Through blurry eyes, he read the front panel of the box as, "?rest", which he took it to mean: "Why Rest." Good question. So instead of going back to bed, he started work on the flyer for his next party, now entitled "?rest" and based the flyer on the Crest toothpaste box. Here are the results:

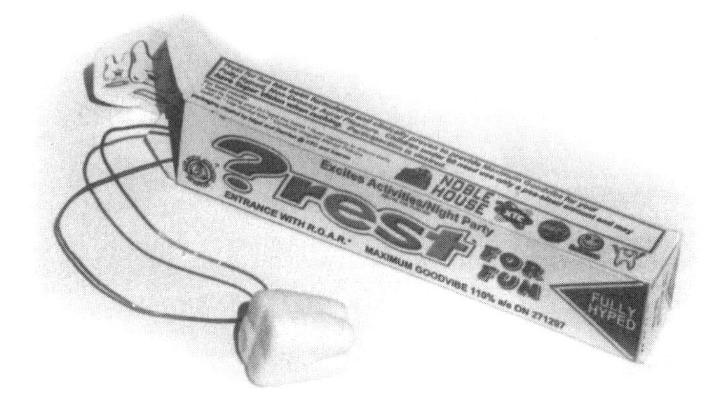

The first few hundred flyer/boxes also contained a plastic tooth necklace.

Nigel also produces club nights to showcase international DJs at the Sonar Club in Vancouver and the Limit in Victoria. These club nights are called Launch, and Nigel was approached by Raevn of RV Designs with a novel idea for the flyer. Raevn wanted to do something interactive, something that people would have to figure out and then want to keep. She came up with the idea of a do-it-yourself rocket ship, which is an excellent example of the playful creativity and sheer inventiveness that is a defining characteristic of rave culture. When cut out, the flyer assembles into a model of a rocket ship, and is designed to be placed over a bottle rocket and launched into space!

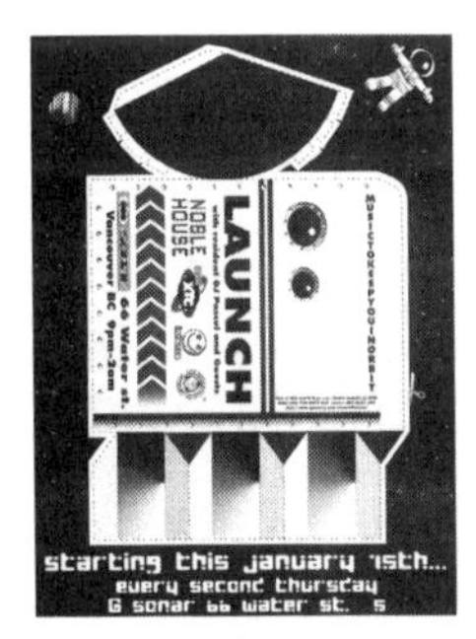

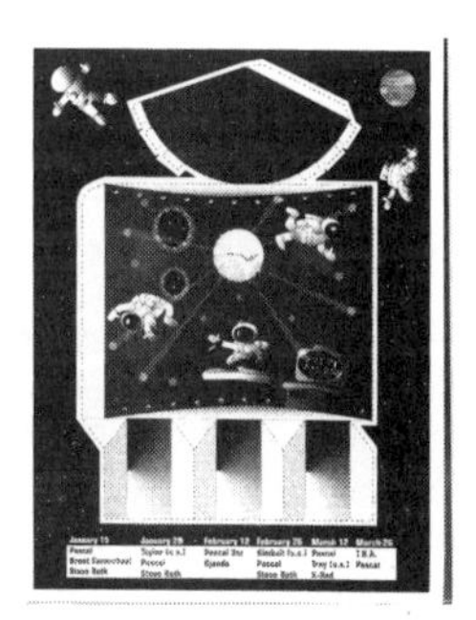

A flyer that turns into a rocket ship complete with a DJ and partying spacemen onboard.

It is interesting to note that when the rocket is assembled you can no longer see the raving astronauts inside, but you know they are there. This in itself is a telling comment on the underground nature of rave culture and its tendencies towards obscurity. Another example of this enigmatic tendency is the lettering on flyers, which is often buried and blended with the imagery to the point where it becomes obscure and difficult to read. The idea here is not to make it more difficult to get the information but to make it more interesting and fun.

Underground rave promoter, Topher of Dai∂'lectic Productions is also known for a playful imagination when it comes to flyer design. He produced these sticker/flyers which were designed to stick onto individual packets of sugar and distributed in local raver hangouts.

Front and Back stickers for existing packet of sugar.

One of Topher's other parties was called Shag and he stuck the flyers onto pieces of shag carpet.

Shag carpter fyler designed by Topher

The appropriation and re-working of corporate logos is a common pastime with flyer and clothes designers. This is another example of rave culture's attitude towards a corporate mentality that puts profits before people. Like music, logos are sampled and recycled into something new.

Two more examples from those playful plunderers at The Alien Mental Association. Control Lost, based on a Castrol Oil can and Summer School, based on a school crossing sign.

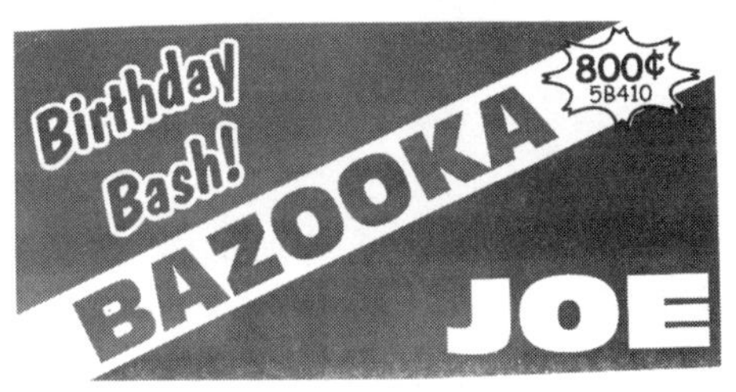

Above: A party called Bazooka Joe from Rust & Rouge's Soapbox.

Left: A flyer based on the Shake and Bake box by Fi-ance Productions.

Again, the notion of ownership is being challenged in a whimsical way. But although lighthearted, there is a larger political statement being made. These symbols represent the amount of corporate control or influence that a company commands in the market place. The more familiar a logo, the more powerful an influence a company has with its customers. By stealing and reusing these potent symbols, ravers are doing more than merely thumbing their noses at big corporations. They are challenging the power and authority of these mega businesses by showing the corporations may have less power than they would like us to believe. By blatantly flaunting their illegal handiwork in the faces of corporations they perceive as the antithesis of rave philosophy, ravers are demonstrating that these companies are in fact powerless to stop obvious copyright infringement. For now, it seems big business is willing to turn a blind eye. It would be both time consuming and costly for companies to sue the individuals responsible and in the end might prove more trouble than it is worth. But the message is out there, and it is influencing a whole new generation to re-think the concept of absolute corporate control.

A party staged by Etheric Link and Unity Productions playfully appropriates the Pepsi Logo.

"Mainly it's a playful thing, but I think there is something being said. Originally rave was a very underground thing and that drew us together. In that sense it's a kind of mockery to take a major product name and appropriate it to advertise a rave. The statement is that, like major brand advertising, we are everywhere and have an influence too."

- Damien a.k.a. DJ K-Rad, The Alien Mental Association, Canada.

CHAPTER 8:

DRUGS, DRUGS, DRUGS.

- mdma
- the psychedelic experience
- the healing qualities of ecstasy
- a rave as a healthy environment
- buyer beware: ecstasy buying tips
- additives sometimes found in ecstasy
- other drugs used in rave culture
- a profile of MAPS

artwork: virginia smallfry

"I have argued that every human being is born with an innate drive to experience altered states of consciousness periodically - in particular to learn how to get away from ordinary ego-centered consciousness. I have also explained that this drive is a most important factor in our evolution, both as individuals and as a species. Non-ordinary experiences are vital to us because they are expressions of our unconscious minds, and the integration of conscious and unconscious experience is the key to life, health, and spiritual development, and fullest use of our nervous systems."

- Andrew Weil, M.D., author, Arizona, USA.

8.
DRUGS, DRUGS, DRUGS...

Drugs are by far the most contentious issue of rave culture and their use at raves are the most touted aspect of the scene and the one most likely to be reported by sensation seeking media. Drugs have always been good copy. Now more than ever, with the US leading the never-ending war on drugs, it seems we must suffer yet another myopic and misguided campaign against one of mankind's most innate and fundamental drives; to expand our consciousness and explore our own psyches.

For thousands of years, human beings have been ingesting various substances to explore the subconscious realms, bring us closer to God, gain insight into the world around us, or to provide relaxation and pleasure. Throughout our long and illustrious history of experimentation there have been relatively few casualties. Until now.

There are many good arguments to support the fact that most of our current problems with drugs, from the crime infested crack houses of Los Angeles to thieving junkies overdosing on bad heroin, are caused by prohibition itself. We have only to study the results of alcohol prohibition in America to know that simply banning a drug does not solve the problems that may be associated with its use, or more accurately, its misuse. Despite Nancy Reagan's best intentions, just saying no to a symptom does not address the underlying cause. The problems associated with misuse of drugs are always symptomatic of larger social issues.

I believe that most, if not all, of our social ills can be attributed to the breakdown of the family and the isolation of the individual from society as a whole. We have lost our connection to others and therefore, to ourselves. Many people in today's society feel isolated, lost, left out and left behind. Human beings have a fundamental need to feel connected, first to our mothers, then to our families and then to society as a whole. When these connections are fractured or lost all together our lives can quickly become empty and meaningless. We no longer care what happens to others or ourselves. This negative state of mind can soon lead to self-hating and self-destructive behavior.

Drugs are usually not the problem but the symptom. When people lose their way and become desperate they will look for a way out. When no illegal drugs are available, people with problems will drink themselves into oblivion. This is amply demonstrated each and every Saturday night in any city center in the so-called civilized world. If alcohol is not available people will drink after-shave, sniff glue or even guzzle gasoline. These people are displaying aberrant behavior because they have very real psychological problems. When desperate souls can take no more and leap to their death, we do not make tall buildings illegal. If you look into the background of anyone with a drug problem you will invariably find that their dilemma began with a breakdown of some sort in their family or community.

Mainstream society has been brainwashed into thinking that any drug that is not approved or sanctioned by their government must be harmful. But when we take a look at a “soft” or benign drug such as marijuana and compare it to alcohol or tobacco it is like throwing Minnie Mouse in the ring with Mike Tyson. We obviously have some discrepancies in our attitudes and policies towards drugs, and it is about time that we replaced mass hysteria with informed decision-making and begin learning how to use drugs responsibly to enhance and enrich our lives.

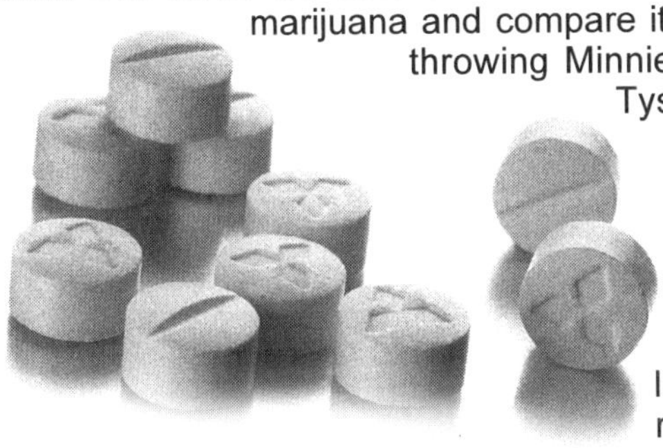

Another important thing to keep in mind when dealing with the subject of drugs is what we mean when we use the word “drugs.” This word has been bandied about far too freely, and through over use has become virtually meaningless. It is time we learned to be more specific. No one would argue that penicillin is interchangeable with crack cocaine or that we consider strychnine in the same category as coffee. Why then do we use the word “drug” to encompass any substance that may have an effect on our body or mind? The word itself has become synonymous with bad or harmful and is no longer useful as a descriptive term. And while we are on the subject of bad or harmful drugs, let’s not forget societies most available and most used drugs: tobacco and alcohol. These two legal drugs alone are responsible for more sickness, deaths and social ills than all other illegal drugs combined. Recent official Government figures from England report that over one thousand British children under fifteen years of age are hospitalized each year suffering from acute alcohol poisoning and over one hundred and fifty a year die directly from alcohol poisoning. The report also states that twelve per cent of all male deaths in Britain are directly related to alcohol consumption. One wonders what the reaction would be if the same could be said of ecstasy use. Similar figures around the world have confirmed time and time again that alcohol is without doubt one of the most dangerous and destructive drugs on the planet. But when was the last time you heard anyone calling for a total ban of alcohol? The statistics on tobacco are even worse. The World Health Organization now estimates that up to four million people a year die from tobacco-related diseases!

This is not to say that the psychedelic drugs sometimes used at raves are completely harmless. Any doctor will confirm that drugs are tools and must be used appropriately and responsibly. Thousands upon thousands of people are killed by cars every year but if used properly, an automobile can be a wonderful tool. When misused, it can very quickly be transformed into an instrument of death and destruction. Power tools are completely legal but used improperly can cause some very serious injuries. Our world is full of tools that can be useful or harmful. It is our job as responsible human beings to learn to use tools in a beneficial, rather than a detrimental, way.

> When we take a look at a "soft" or benign drug such as marijuana and compare it to alcohol or tobacco it is like throwing Minnie Mouse in the ring with Mike Tyson.

After decades of dealing - or not dealing - with this issue, it is still difficult to find a public forum in which to exchange ideas on the subject of recreational drug use. You will not find any stories in the newspapers or on television news shows about the positive effects of psychedelic drug use, although the vast majority of users will testify that psychedelics have had extremely positive effects on the quality of their lives. In most societies today it is acceptable to use drugs to relieve pain or mask the symptoms of disease. It is okay to use drugs to wake us up or put us to sleep. We even sanction the use of anti-psychotic drugs that improve the mood and temperament of the mentally ill. Prozac, a drug not so distantly related to ecstasy, is now one of the most commonly prescribed drugs in North America.

But there are also significant risks involved with prescription drugs. Many people die every year from adverse reactions to drugs prescribed by their doctor, or problems caused when taking combinations of drugs. For instance, hundreds of people in America die each and every year from allergic reactions to paracetamol. Next time your doctor prescribes a drug for you, ask to see the information from the manufacturer and read the list of possible side effects. Prescription drugs are tested by undergoing a thorough process of double blind studies, and are often approved for public consumption when it has been shown that the benefits outweigh the harmful side effects, which in some cases can be appalling. One look at the recipients of chemotherapy, with its dreadfully low, twenty per cent success rate, will tell you that sometimes the side effects can be far greater than the benefits. In comparison, a drug like ecstasy, which produces a child-like wonder of the world and a feeling of universal love with negligible side effects is still a class A illegal drug. It is ironic that in a society where the majority of ordinary citizens take drugs for one reason or another, to use a drug to induce pleasure is still considered taboo.

Most problems associated with recreational drugs are caused by irresponsible use, i.e. taking them too frequently or in too high a dose. There are no drugs, legal or otherwise, that can be taken in unlimited amounts. All drugs have a correct dosage that, if exceeded, can cause adverse reactions or toxic effects and the recreational drugs used in the rave scene are no exception. It should be noted that users of psychedelics generally consider them to be special occasion drugs and it would be rare to find anyone taking ecstasy, LSD or magic mushrooms on a daily basis. When used with the right attitude and consumed at the correct dosage and frequency, they can be as safe and enjoyable as a camping trip with the family.

In England alone it is estimated that since 1992, one million doses of ecstasy are consumed each and every week. If we multiply this figure to take into consideration the amount being used by the world population, we have an extremely large sample group. From a group this large there has been only a handful of negative reports. In fact, most of the problems that have been attributed to ecstasy use are usually due to other causes such as overheating caused by insufficient ventilation or overcrowding, dehydration due to the unavailability of water, or problems associated with other, more harmful drugs. One incident in England where a young woman's death was linked to ecstasy was eventually credited to the over-consumption of water, a phenomenon where the blood is diluted and causes tissue cells to swell, creating pressure in the skull. These are all problems that could occur without ecstasy use.

At any large event attended by thousands of people the law of averages will ensure at least a few health problems. People drop dead from heart attacks, heat prostration, strokes and a variety of other reasons at sporting events every year but we do not hear concerned citizens calling for a total ban of football or baseball. The violence at English soccer matches is a good example of our double standards when it comes to how much risk we are willing to tolerate. Every Saturday afternoon in dozens of cities around England there are appalling incidences of soccer violence. Serious injuries and even deaths are common as opposing armies of soccer supporters battle each other in the stadiums and in the streets. The trains used to transport the fans are routinely destroyed and the neighborhoods and towns where the games take place are regularly ransacked. A recent incidence of soccer violence involving English fans at a game in Belgium resulted in forty-two deaths! This madness presumably continues because the pleasure that the majority of soccer fans get from the game supersedes the injuries and deaths caused by a minority of irresponsible hooligans. If we apply the same logic to raves we would see that the risk factor is negligible in comparison while the enjoyment quota is equal, if not higher. Again, there are no city councils in England calling for a ban of soccer matches.

In England alone it is estimated that since 1992, one million doses of ecstasy are consumed each and every week.

Perhaps the English government should rate soccer with their own recently developed system of determining risk factors. If we use the current statistical estimates of consumption from England, the risk of death from ecstasy would be 1 in 6.8 million. In comparison, parachuting kills 3 people in 1000 each year, and skiing kills 1 in 500,000. And if you think that it would be safer to stay at home, think again. The risk of being killed due to an accident in the home is 1 in 26,000 a year. That's over two hundred and fifty times more dangerous than taking a dose of ecstasy. According to the British system, ecstasy use rates the same risk factor as an afternoon of fishing. With dangerous sports like skiing, hang gliding and motor sports, we understand that the inherent risks involved can be extremely high, but at the same time, for some people, the benefits of the excitement and enjoyment outweigh the potential danger. The point is, every activity or drug comes with a risk and we must learn to weigh the risks with the benefits. As anyone who has experienced ecstasy will tell you, the benefits far outweigh the minimal risks.

Recently there has been a growing feeling among the leaders of the world that the war on drugs has been lost and a mountain of statistics from around the globe supports this stance. A United Nations General Assembly Special Session on Drugs was held on June 8-10, 1998 in New York City with an agenda to introduce new strategies to intensify the war on drugs. A petition recommending decriminalization, the introduction of harm reduction policies and other measures to end the war on drugs was sent to The Secretary General of the United Nations, Mr. Kofi Annan. The petition was presented to the assembly on the eve of the meeting and also published in a full-page ad in The New York Times. Signed by over six hundred prominent people from forty-one countries, the impressive list included presidents, cabinet ministers, lords, senators, lawyers, ministers, bishops and judges. Even the ex-head of Scotland Yard in England is now publicly calling for the legalization of all drugs, citing the many years of pain and misery he witnessed in the drug squad, which he now sees as a direct effect of prohibition. We can only hope this is a trend which will eventually lead to the end of the persecution

Even the ex-head of Scotland Yard in England is now publicly calling for the legalization of all drugs.

and criminalization of recreational drug users, an increase in harm reduction policies and the initiation of programs that address the underlying causes of addiction and other forms of drug abuse.

Rave culture seeks to heal social ills by strengthening our connections to others and therefore ourselves. It is about understanding ourselves so we may better understand others. It is about expanding our hearts and consciousness to see beyond our differences. Rave culture endeavors to promote tolerance and acceptance and the creation of a more positive world. The responsible use of drugs are part of that equation.

"Our generation is the first, ever, to have made the search for self-awareness a crime."

- Alexander Shulgin, Ph.D., biochemist and "Stepfather" of MDMA.

"No drug, not even alcohol, causes the fundamental ills of society. If we're looking for the sources of our troubles, we shouldn't test people for drugs, we should test them for stupidity, ignorance, greed and love of power."

- P.J. O'Rourke, American author.

There are as many different drugs used at raves as there are at any other venue where people gather for celebration or entertainment, but by far the most prevalent and significant is MDMA, more commonly known as ecstasy or E.

Ecstasy was first patented in 1913 by the German pharmaceutical company Merck. Its early use is not well documented and it didn't surface again until 1953, when it was supposedly tested by the US army. In the early eighties, a Ph.D. biochemist from the University of California at Berkeley named Alexander Shulgin began to experiment with mescaline and later, MDMA. In 1984 ecstasy leaked onto the dance scene in Texas and shortly thereafter it was outlawed as an illegal drug. The disciples of the Indian guru, Bhagwan Rajneesh, are credited with bringing ecstasy to Europe in 1985 and by 1986 the drug was being widely used in all-night dance parties on the island of Ibiza. The parties caught on in England and quickly spread to other parts of the world. The rest, as they say, is history.

For a comprehensive and in-depth look at the use, effects, research and history of ecstasy, I can highly recommend the following books: "E for Ecstasy," "Dance, Trance and Transformation," and "Ecstasy Reconsidered are all by Nicholas Saunders and "The MDMA Story" is by Bruce Eisner. Another great source of information on this subject is Nicholas Saunder's web site at www.ecstacy.org

Because the issue is so contentious - and illegal - many people in involved with rave culture tend to underplay the use of ecstasy, and in an effort to protect the scene will tend to misrepresent how many people are using the drug. When interviewed or put on the spot by a reporter, a raver is likely to say that the use of ecstasy is vastly exaggerated. They may tell you that its use is declining and it is becoming less and less important to the scene, and to many veteran ravers this is true. Once familiar and practiced with the ecstasy experience, the music becomes a hypnotic trigger and one can actually feel the effects of ecstasy without consuming the drug. But the truth is that ecstasy remains a key element in the rave experience and is still used extensively at parties.

Ecstasy is to rave what LSD was to the psychedelic movement of the sixties. But whereas the sixties were about opening our minds, rave culture is about opening our hearts. With LSD, we may *think* about the nature of love but with ecstasy we are more inclined to feel it as a direct experience. The sixties were a time of massive philosophical upheaval that required people to comprehend and take a stand on a variety of complicated social issues. The civil rights movement, race relations, gender issues and the war in Vietnam all required a mindful approach to deal with these complex new realities. LSD helped to give people a new perspective on themselves and inspired a generation of young people to change the world. We are still feeling the effects of the social changes that took place thirty years ago. Today we have different problems to solve and the cerebral perspective gained from the use of LSD has been replaced by the heart-centered effects of the ecstasy experience. It seems that many of our problems stem from a lack of empathy in that we fail to understand and relate to the problems of others. When we hear about children starving to death in far-off places, we feel powerless to act and inclined to retreat to the safety of our own insular world. The ecstasy experience helps us to relate to other people more directly, enabling us to transcend our prejudices and see ourselves in others.

Most ravers will testify that ecstasy has improved the quality of their lives and transformed them into more compassionate and loving individuals.

The positive and empathetic effects of ecstasy can also remain with us long after the drug has worn off. Most ravers will testify that ecstasy has improved the quality of their lives and transformed them into more compassionate and loving individuals. Introverts tend to come out of their shells and learn to relate to other people in new and satisfying ways. Ravers report that their relationships improve, they become more self-assured and enthusiastic, less critical and judgmental or more understanding and patient.

Here are some experiences and observations from ravers around the world:

"Ecstasy took me back to place where I was before adolescence. When the world seemed new and I wasn't limited by my immediate past. It made me think about what I wanted to do and what was important in life. It reminded me of when I was a child and didn't feel guilty or ashamed or anxious about anything."

- J, The Trip Factory, Saltspring Island, Canada.

"A lot of people grow up living a certain way and they go to a rave where a lot of different kinds of people are getting along and experience a whole different mind-set. They may take ecstasy and have revelations and open their minds to other possibilities. Many people end up being closer to their friends or become more understanding. They question things that they may have done their whole life."

- Dennis Barton, Skylab200, Los Angeles, USA.

"I'm clean. Music is my dope. I think we don't need ecstasy, but I'm okay with anybody else using it."

- Sonic Intervention, Tallinn, Estonia.

"Doing E responsibly gives you a beautiful feeling and sense of clarity. It expands your mind like most psychedelic drugs and takes you into different realms of thought. Things get blocked out in your regular life and E can help you to sort things out and give you a new focus."

- Surfer Bob, The Vibe Tribe, Canada.

"Ecstasy has made me more peaceful with myself and has taught me the extent to which love can be experienced. I never thought that I could feel that much love and positive affection. It's made me a lot closer with my friends and a lot more aware of my relationships. It also opened me up to emotions that I wasn't really in touch with. The bonds I've made with other people in the rave scene are so much stronger than usual. "

- Raevn Lunah Teak, raver, designer, Brisbane, Australia.

"Ecstasy has helped me to explore my feelings more and overcome my insecurities. I can express my feelings to other people more easily now and feel more confident about who I am as a person. I've seen hardcore rockers do ecstasy for the first time and in a few days go from a full-blown, alcohol loving, aggressive rocker to an outwardly caring person who seems to enjoy life a lot more. I know that I'm a better person for taking ecstasy."

- Nigel Tasko, rave promoter, The Alien Mental Association, Canada.

"People tend to exaggerate the importance and presence of drugs at raves. I will not deny that drugs exists and make a difference in the rave scene, however, it is not the drug itself that is important, it is the pleasure and joy it brings to not only the user but to his or her whole surrounding. Why not do something that makes you feel good, why not do something that makes you and everybody else happy?"

- Fredrik Larsson, electronic musician, Stockholm, Sweden

"E makes you feel like everyone around you is a trusted friend who will take you as you are with no judgment. You become more accepting and open to other people."

- DJ Billy, Victoria, Canada.

"I tried ecstasy for the first time on Halloween. I was dancing to a tribal house mix of K.D. Lang's Lifted by Love and it sounded like a voice coming down from heaven. I was smiling from one side of my face to the other and remember screaming for about four hours. I had never felt anything like that before. From that point on everything changed for me. It gave me a whole new outlook and I started listening to music in a whole new light."

- Troy Roberts, DJ, Platinum Records, Seattle, USA.

"The first time I did ecstasy was life changing. I felt like I became the music. It was so amazing, I could go up to anyone and hug them. It inspired me to buy more music and start to push the boundaries of my musical knowledge. Ecstasy helps to let thing out and help you to become who you are."

- Daniel, Moontribe DJ, Los Angeles, USA.

"As a DJ, ecstasy helps me expand my perception of sound. It has also helped me to enhance my relationships with other people. I try to be happy and fun loving anyway but E has made me 110% more so. Even when I'm not on E, I feel the positive effects."

- DJ Davie, The Vibe Tribe, Canada.

"Ecstasy makes you feel like you love the world! When you see thousands of smiling faces in love with the world, it's an indescribable feeling. It gives you an idea of what our world would be like if we were as accepting of everything as we are when we are one."

- Frank Zelaya a.k.a. DJ SoR, Los Angeles, USA.

"Drug taking is as much a part of rave as any other group of people who get together for recreation. But the focus is the music, not the drugs. I always encourage people who rave with drugs to also be able to rave without drugs so they can see that the magic is still there."

- Kim Stanford, The Toronto Raver Information Project, Canada.

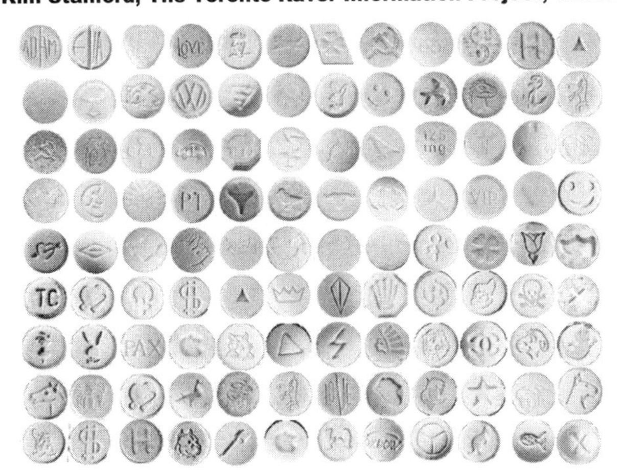

THE PSYCHEDELIC EXPERIENCE

Although ecstasy is sometimes classified as a psychedelic amphetamine, there is no amphetamine in MDMA and no real consensus to the use of the word psychedelic in relation to other drugs. Dan Merkur is a research reader in the Center for the Study of Religion at the University of Toronto. He is the author of "Gnosis: An Esoteric Tradition of Mystical Visions and Unions" and more recently has published, "The Ecstatic Imagination: Psychedelic Experiences and the Psychoanalysis of Self-Actualization." I asked him for a definition of the term psychedelic.

"The term psychedelic was originally invented to mean mind-manifesting. There is no agreed usage of the term, which is not intended to be as broad as psychoactive, but has not achieved any clear definition, much less one that a consensus has agreed on. In my book, I start by saying that I will use the term as a synonym for drugs that produce pseudo-hallucinations (you know you are hallucinating while you are doing so) rather than hallucinations (you think it is objectively real, and not merely a hallucination.) I then limit my book to LSD, psilocybin & mescaline."

Although sometimes classified as a psychedelic, ecstasy is not hallucinogenic, pseudo or otherwise. Saying that ecstasy has the ability to expand our consciousness may be a more useful definition for the purposes of this book. Other drugs in this category might include LSD, psilocybin, mescaline, peyote, marijuana, ketamine, DMT and 2CB. These are all drugs that open up subconscious channels that can subtly or drastically effect the way we see ourselves and the world around us. If used responsibly, these drugs can provide valuable insights into our own psychology that might otherwise never come to light. Psychedelics affect us on a deeper subconscious level and, like hypnosis can alter or "reprogram" our subconscious mind that in turn can profoundly affect our lives on a conscious level. Rather than being a distortion of our everyday perception of the world, they show us an expanded version of reality and give us a waking experience of an extended reality we only usually glimpse in a sleeping or dream state. In fact, some cultures make no distinction at all between waking and dream states. To the Australian aborigine, "The Dreamtime" represents the totality of reality. They believe the "real" world" is being dreamed, a notion consistent with the mystical view that reality is thought form manifest. In other words, reality is first created as a thought form which in turn leads to a physical manifestation.

The psychedelic experience has been an integral part of human being's search for meaning for thousands of years and reflects our innate desire to see beyond our everyday experience.

The psychedelic experience has been an integral part of human being's search for meaning for thousands of years and reflects our innate desire to see beyond our everyday experience. Throughout history this type of mind expansion has consistently enriched our experience and awareness of both ourselves and the world we live in. Stretching the envelope of our consciousness makes our minds more fluid and creative which in turn makes us better able to solve our problems and think creatively. A fluid mind that has seen beyond its own boundaries can tap into an infinite imagination, or what Carl Jung, the father of psychoanalysis and successor to Sigmund Freud, called the collective unconscious. It is no coincidence that many of the greatest and most innovative works of art were inspired by psychedelic experiences and that many of the great minds of history were enlivened and energized with psychedelic substances.

Psychedelics can be powerful tools, providing a gateway to self-awareness and a deeper understanding of ourselves and our place in the world. They can show us parts of our own psyche that may otherwise remain hidden and have the power to change our belief systems by offering a direct experience of another reality, one that can give us a brand new perspective.

The psychedelic experience has been well documented over the years. Timothy Leary, Aldous Huxley, Ken Kesey and many others have had the courage to openly expound the virtues of psychedelics and their powerful influence in transforming peoples lives. But the majority of people still reject the psychedelic experience as dangerous, frivolous or irresponsible, despite centuries of evidence to the contrary. What are we afraid of? Why do we still fail to see the benefits of expanding our minds?

Some therapists have claimed that they can achieve more with a few sessions using ecstasy than years of more conventional types of therapy.

Generally, we fear most that which we do not understand and there is much that we do not understand about our own minds. The psychedelic experience can open the doors of perception to areas that we never knew existed and show us parts of ourselves that we may not want to see. To some people this can be a daunting proposition. Many people have very set ideas about the world. They have spent a lifetime deciding what they believe and even in the face of facts that prove otherwise, will still cling to old and familiar ideas. This is why psychedelics are mainly embraced by the young who have not yet fully formed their opinions and mind-sets about everything and are still open to the influence of new experiences.

photo: tristan o'neill

Psychedelic drugs are not for everyone. Many people are not yet ready to step outside of their well-developed belief systems. Many people will never be ready. However, let's not be too quick to condemn people who are ready. Most importantly, we should be wary of condemning an experience we have never had ourselves. People who have learned to use psychedelics responsibly will, without exception, extol their virtues. Whenever someone begins a tirade against the dangers of psychedelic drugs, you can almost guarantee they have never tried them.

"Since wars begin in the minds of men, it is in the minds of men that the defenses of peace must be constructed."

- UNESCO Charter.

THE HEALING QUALITIES OF ECSTASY

Since most of the information that comes to us about ecstasy tends to be extremely negative reports from a paranoid or ignorant press, I would like to represent the other side of the coin in the interests of a more balanced approach.

When used responsibly, ecstasy has been shown to have many healing qualities, both physical and psychological. Despite its illegal status since 1985, many psychologists and psychiatrists across North America and around the world regularly use ecstasy as a therapeutic aid. They have found the drug is extremely effective in short form therapy, as it allows the client to feel safe, secure and relaxed while giving them the ability to look at their problems objectively from a positive perspective. Coupled with an increased facility for communication, ecstasy may be one of the most useful counseling aids around and some therapists have claimed that they can achieve more with a few sessions using ecstasy than years of more conventional types of therapy.

One of the few formal studies that has been undertaken with ecstasy was conducted with terminally ill cancer patients. The drug was used to help people come to terms with their situation, to deal with their pain and to cope with the fear of death. Ecstasy is well known for its ability to produce a profound sense of well being by suppressing the anxiety centers in the brain. It is also an effective pain reliever. With their pain and fear eliminated, the patients were able to see their situation in a larger context and came to terms with their own mortality, enabling them to die more peacefully and with more awareness.

Most health professionals now recognize stress as a major factor in health care, some practitioner claim that stress may be the underlying cause of all "dis-ease" in the body. If these claims are true, then any agent that relieves stress will be beneficial. Ecstasy, especially when taken in a rave setting, has proven to be a powerful tool in stress reduction. It is virtually impossible to feel any stress or pressure while under its influence and many people find that they remain stress free, limber, and relaxed for several days afterwards.

The deep emotional calm experienced by ecstasy users can help remove and remedy chronic emotional blocks, which can result in powerful psychological healing.

During the hundreds of interviews conducted for this book, I have heard numerous stories of people who have had physical healing take place while on ecstasy. Many people have described the experience of coming down with a cold or flu, which would normally have slowed them down or laid them out for a few days only to discover the symptoms had completely disappeared the morning after a rave. One raver remembered limping to a party with a painful corn on the sole of his foot. He expected the ecstasy to deal with the pain temporarily and was prepared to pay the price the next day. As it turned out, the pain never returned at all. These kinds of stories are common among ravers and it seems likely that there may be other health benefits and applications for ecstasy that we have yet to discover. Only when more research is funded will we know the full potential and best uses for this versatile new drug.

A RAVE AS A HEALTHY ENVIRONMENT

Let's take a look at the potential health benefits of a rave. First, ravers get in a positive state of mind as they anticipate the approaching event. A positive attitude is the cornerstone of many self-improvement techniques. The more positive we feel about something, the more likely we are to have a positive outcome. On the day of the event it is common for ravers to avoid fatty foods - they have been shown to reduce the effectiveness of ecstasy - and choose instead to eat fresh fruits and vegetables, a high fiber, low fat diet which has been proven to reduce the risk of cancer and widely accepted as the healthiest way to eat. Many ravers choose a healthy diet and it is not uncommon to find a fresh vegetable and fruit juice stand at parties. These "smart bars" also feature health supplements such as spirulina or ginseng that are added to fresh fruit or vegetable juices to boost their nutritional value.

On arrival at the party friends greet each other warmly, and more positive, healing vibes are generated and passed around. When the party gets started, ravers dance for hours on end, gaining all the benefits of an incredible aerobic workout coupled with the stress-reducing effects of really letting go. Vigorous exercise of this kind has also been shown to be beneficial for immune responses by stimulating the lymph system. (Lymph is a liquid that is moved around the body by muscle movement and helps to carry away toxins and other waste products from the body.)

As the dancing intensifies, a trance state is attained, creating increased alpha wave activity. These brain waves are also produced in deep states of meditation and have been shown to increase healing rates by as much as four hundred per cent, while increasing concentration and mental clarity. Dancing in a trance state can yield many of the health benefits associated with a Yoga or meditation practice.

As the ecstasy begins to take full effect, a profound sense of love and compassion is experienced. In this state, we are able to forgive our enemies and openly show our deepest feelings towards our friends and family. The deep emotional calm experienced by ecstasy users can help remove and remedy chronic emotional blocks, which can result in powerful psychological healing. The next day – after a good sleep - ravers often feel renewed, exhilarated, toned and tuned up. And all for a fraction of the cost of a full-service health club.

BUYER BEWARE: ECSTASY BUYING TIPS

Ecstasy basically comes in two forms: as a powder or pressed tablet. The powder is usually white or off-white but can be almost any colour including beige, brown, yellow or even purple. The powder can come loose or packaged in gel caps.

Tablets come in so many forms that it is impossible to tell very much from their physical appearance. Some people claim that pills are safer because they are harder to cut or tamper with. But this is only true if the pills are being pressed at the lab where the MDMA is produced. Some people will buy powder from a lab, cut it with who-knows-what and then make it into pressed pills. Another potential problem with pills is that whenever a lab produces a superior product and puts it out in a tablet form, there are usually imitations that follow. A white pill with a Nike swoosh may be high quality this month but the adulterated and identical version that appears the following month may have half the MDMA and twice the additives.

A survey of ecstasy was recently undertaken by The Multidisciplinary Association For Psychedelic Studies (MAPS). Samples of ecstasy in pill form and gel caps from all over North America and England were tested for additives and amounts of MDMA. The results showed that nearly all the samples contained MDMA although most had fairly low doses. Many had one or more of the additives listed below

MDMA molecule

but none of the samples had toxic additives or heroin or broken glass as is sometimes reported in the press.

The most important thing is to ascertain exactly what you are buying and the best way to find out is to establish a relationship with a seller you can trust. The best sellers will tell you if it is a bit speedy or whatever and they can often give you a first hand report on the batch they are selling. They may have tried it themselves or will have reports from other customers. If all the reports are good and you are satisfied that it is pure MDMA, buy as much as you can afford then you won't have to hunt around again for a while.

It is never a good idea to buy ecstasy from a complete stranger, or at a rave. The chances of getting busted are much higher at a party and it is too easy to make a hasty decision on a dimly lit dance floor. It is far better to buy before the party and take it with you. Apart from any safety concerns, it is disappointing to be at a party where a good source of ecstasy is unavailable and even more disappointing to get ripped off completely.

Sellers will often have more than one kind of ecstasy and will sometimes try and sell their B-grade stuff first. Ask what is available and choose the best from all available options. Some people feel safer buying tablets rather than gel caps because they are harder to cut. Even though this is a logical argument, in my experience, caps have generally proven to be a better bet, although this is probably more true of North America than Europe where most of the best ecstasy comes in pill form.

In Amsterdam there are now ecstasy testing stations where you can take a sample and find out exactly what it contains. If you live elsewhere and are really serious about knowing what you are taking, ecstasy-testing kits are now available in Britain. The kits were developed by the Green Party's Drug Action Group who also give out drug awareness information at rave events. The basic kit contains a micrometer - to measure the size of the pills - a chemical called the marquis reagent and a list of laboratory results detailing the chemical composition of pills. The micrometer allows the pill to be accurately measured so that it can be compared with pills already tested in the same area. There is less chance of a pill being a look-alike if the precise dimensions match. The marquis reagent is a clear liquid that is put on a white saucer and a small scraping of a pill is dropped onto it. The liquid turns yellow/orange in the presence of amphetamines, and purple/black for MDMA and related compounds. When no colour appears, the pill is a dud.

To buy a kit that will test between 100 and 150 pills, send £15 (includes postage and packing) for the basic kit or £30 for the Advanced kit with a check or postal order made out to: Green Party Drugs Group, 1a Waterloo Road, London N19 5NJ, England. For more information, phone 0171 737 0100.

Another kit sold in head shops in Europe is called E-Z Test. It contains a patented reagent formula that tests up to 15 pills for seven substances. The kit costs £4.95 +50p postage and packing. International orders are accepted. The E-Z Test Kit is available from: E-Z Test LTD, Unit

503, 91 Western Road, Brighton, East Sussex, England, BN1 2NW.
Tel: +44 (0) 1273-241082 or email: e-z@mistral.co.uk

"The difference between a medicine and a poison is in the dosage."
- Paracelsus, German physician, chemist. 1493-1541.

ADDITIVES SOMETIMES FOUND IN ECSTASY

EPHEDRINE

A stimulant found in many plant sources that is used as a decongestant in over the counter remedies such as Sudafed. Ephedrine's effects are similar to that of adrenaline and should not be used by people with high blood pressure or heart problems. Not recommended to take with ecstasy.

PHENYLPROPANOLAMINE

A decongestant and mild stimulant found in cold medicines as well as diets aids.

DEXTROMETHORPHAN

An ingredient found in cough suppressants that in higher doses can produce a ketamine-like psychoactive effect.

CAFFEINE

The buzz in coffee.

MDEA, MDE, EVE.

A psychedelic amphetamine and chemical cousin to MDMA. MDEA has some of ecstasy's euphoric effects, less of its communicative qualities and acts as more of a sedative than a stimulant. Connoisseurs invariably prefer MDMA because of its empathetic qualities. The effects of MDEA last for 3-5 hours rather than the 4-6 hours of MDMA.

GLYCERYL GUIAICOLATE

A compound that dries sinuses and is used as an expectorant.

ATROPINE

A chemical found in belladonna that is used by modern eye doctors to dilate the pupils for retinal examinations. Also found in mandrake root and henbane. Used as a medicine for asthmatics and prescribed by doctors as Lomotil for the relaxation of muscles lining the intestine. It is also used to relieve cramps and irritable bowel syndrome.

artwork: virginia smallfry

OTHER DRUGS USED IN RAVE CULTURE

MARIJUANA, CANNABIS, POT, DOPE, SPLIF, WEED.

Widely used in the rave scene and throughout society in general. Produces mild euphoric effects increased awareness and warm fuzzy feelings. After thirty years of government testing marijuana has proven to be one of the safest drugs available.

MAGIC MUSHROOMS, PSILOCYBIN, SHROOMS.

Magic mushrooms are organic hallucinogens that have been used safely for thousands of years. They contain the mind-altering chemicals psilocybin and psilocin as well as traces of related chemicals similar in structure to seratonin, a chemical in your brain that is also affected by ecstasy and LSD. The effects usually last around six hours and are similar to LSD but are often described as more natural or organic. Mushrooms have low toxicity on the body with no physical after effects. Recommended dose is one to four grams.

LSD, LYSERGIC ACID DIETHALYMIDE, ACID.

One of the most potent mind-altering chemicals known. Effects last 8-12 hours and include a rush of thoughts, wild free association and visual hallucinations. An unstable mental state or environment can cause anxiety and result in a bad trip or extreme paranoia. If the conditions are right, the experience can be extremely inspiring, ecstatic and even life changing. LSD is completely non-toxic to the body.

MDA

Similar to MDMA but without the empathetic qualities, MDA was known as the love drug and used extensively in the sixties and seventies. MDA lasts twice as long as MDMA (8-12 hours) and has a rather more amphetamine-like effect. The usual dose is between 80 and 160 mg.

PCP, PHENCYCLIDINE, ANGEL DUST, OZONE, WACK.

First developed in 1959 as an intravenous anesthetic and later used in veterinary medicine as a powerful tranquilizer. It can be swallowed, smoked, sniffed, or injected and has very similar effects to ketamine.

METHAMPHETIMINE, CRYSTAL METH, SPEED, ICE, CRANK.

One of the most potent forms of speed. Has serious long-term effects and is very hard on your body. The effects last four to six hours, usually followed by an unpleasant come down that may include chills, nervous twitching, sweats and fatigue. Long term use can cause depression and paranoia. Not recommended.

AMPHETAMINE SULFATE, SPEED.

A form of speed common in England, likened to very strong cocaine. Highly addictive and very hard on both the body and the mind.

2CB, NEXUS, N, 4-BROMO-2, 5-DMPEA.

A phenylethylamine analog of DOB first synthesized by Alexander Shulgin in the 1970s. 2CB has been described as somewhere between ecstasy and LSD. 2CB is more body-oriented than LSD and more hallucinogenic than ecstasy. It is stronger than MDMA with mild visual effects and fewer of the amphetamine-type side effects. Also reported to be an erotic stimulant. Taking too much may result in LSD- type bad trips. A safe dose is 10-30mg and effects last about 8 hours.

KETAMINE, KETALAR, KET, SPECIAL K, VITAMIN K.

Though most psychedelics are in Schedule 1, Ketamine is an exception. A substance used for transpersonal psychotherapy that is also used in veterinary surgery as an anesthetic. In doses 6-10 times lower than used in surgery it can induce profound experiences which last 30 - 45 minutes. Adverse physical effects can include loss of motor control, temporary memory loss, numbness, drowsiness and nausea. It is extremely dangerous to mix ketamine with respiratory depressants such as alcohol, Valium or other barbiturates

GHB, GAMMA-HYDROXYBUTYRATE, LIQUID E, FANTASY.

Used in Europe as a general anesthetic, a prescription for insomnia and a treatment for alcoholism, GHB induces a pleasant state of relaxation, tranquillity, emotional warmth, drowsiness, sensuality and a tendency to verbalize. Extremely dose sensitive with higher doses causing nausea, sluggishness, dizziness, respiratory difficulties and loss of consciousness. When taken with alcohol, GHB can induce “forced sleep,” causing the user to collapse and remain unconscious for 4-6 hours.

DMT, 5-METHOXY-DMT.

A powerful, short-acting hallucinogenic tryptamine found in the human body, brain, spinal fluid, urine and blood with similar effects to LSD. It is also shown to be present in many plants including Acacia, Anandenanthera, Mimosa, Piptadenia and Virola. Dosage is 50-70mg

DOB, BROMO-STP.

This drug first appeared in England in the summer of 1973. It is a stronger version of the famous 1960s drug DOM a.k.a. STP and was often sold as an LSD substitute. Since it is so potent, DOB commonly appears as drops on blotting paper like LSD. DOB is not toxic and considered safe at the correct dosage level of less than 1 mg.

NITROUS OXIDE, N2O, LAUGHING GAS.

Nitrous oxide is a gas used for anesthetic purposes. Usually inhaled from balloons filled from a tank, it produces a variety of physical effects including disorientation, fixated vision, throbbing or pulsating auditory and visual hallucinations, increased pain threshold and deeper mental connections. Effects are fleeting and repeated use is necessary to maintain the high. Side effects can include oxygen deprivation, loss of motor control and nausea. Everyday risks include frostbite from the release of the pressurized gas.

A PROFILE OF THE MULTIDISCIPLINARY ASSOCIATION FOR PSYCHEDELIC STUDIES *(MAPS)*

The Multidisciplinary Association for Psychedelic Studies (MAPS) is membership-based research and educational organization founded in 1986. MAPS focuses on the development of beneficial, socially sanctioned uses of psychedelic drugs and marijuana. Such uses may include psychotherapy, treatment of addiction, brain physiology research and related scientific inquiries.

MAPS pursues its mission by helping scientific researchers design, obtain governmental approval for, fund, conduct and report on psychedelic and marijuana research in human volunteers. MAPS' core mission is to make MDMA an FDA-approved prescription medicine. Not coincidentally, MAPS was founded one year after the Drug Enforcement Administration (DEA) made MDMA a Schedule 1 drug and criminalized both its recreational and therapeutic uses.

Due to MDMA's uniquely gentle yet profound effects, the medical use of MDMA is more likely to be integrated into psychiatry before other more powerful, longer-lasting and more psychologically challenging psychedelics like LSD, psilocybin or mescaline. In addition to MDMA research, MAPS actively supports research with other psychedelics, each of which has its own therapeutic potential and risk profile. MAPS is currently the only organization in North America funding research into ecstasy.

A focus on altered states of consciousness requires MAPS to deal with deep-seated cultural and individual ambivalence toward religious experiences, the exploration of the unconscious mind, fear of death and loss of control, and powerful emotional states. If you can even faintly imagine a cultural reintegration of the use of psychedelics and the states of mind they engender, consider joining MAPS in supporting the expansion of scientific knowledge in this area. MAPS offers access to all its past newsletters on-line, searchable by keyword at: www.maps.org. Donations to MAPS are tax-deductible.

For more information, contact:

MAPS
2121 Commonwealth Avenue, Suite 220
Charlotte, NC 28205USA
Email: info@maps.com
Phone: 704-334-1798
Fax: 704-334-1799

"No man that does not see visions will ever realize any high hope or undertake any high enterprise."

- Woodrow Wilson, twenty-eighth president of the USA, 1913-1921.

"The subject of drugs at raves is very controversial. One wonders whether the rave scene would have been more easily accepted by the public had the presence of drugs not been so high. Of course, many others wonder how raves could have ever come about without them."

-Brian Behlendorf, founder of SFRaves and Hyperreal.com, San Francisco, USA.

"Some people are afraid to take a drug without knowing what's in it. But many people do this with prescription drugs and some die from bad reactions. Regardless of whether it's legal or not, any drug can be used responsibly or carelessly."

- Nicole Makin, raver, writer, Canada.

"The association of a drug and a music style or sub-culture happens but it has nothing to do with the experience of the music. I never use drugs and don't need them. I experience the music probably in an even bigger way."

- Dominique, raver, NT system administrator, Steendorp, Belgium.

"We get the young crowd before midnight, then the crowd changes at midnight with the real ravers, and then at 2am to 3am you get the bar crowd. If you have any problems at all, it's always with the bar crowd. We don't have any problems from ravers doing drugs. It's alcohol that causes the problems. We've had several big parties now and we've had no problems related to drugs."

- J.C., rave promoter, Sideline Productions, Canada.

"I believe that E is very important to a lot of people. I used to think that there was no meaning in going to a rave without taking E. But now I never take drugs anymore and I still go to parties and have the greatest time anyway. In one way, I can say that it means nothing, but still I would not have experienced rave if I did not take E in the first place."

- Veny Veronika Vere, raver, secretary, Oslo, Norway.

"I've seen ecstasy open people up and inspire them. They become more creative and sensitive. I think for men, it opens up their feminine side. American society is very male dominated so it's a good influence for men to experience their yin side. Women become more creative too. I see them getting in touch with their creativity, starting to sing or write poetry or whatever."

- Daniel, Moontribe DJ, Los Angeles, USA.

"Ecstasy helps people to understand their true being. It gives people a new perspective on the way they usually think and act and lets them see who they really are!"

- Amit K., electronic engineer, raver, Haifa, Israel.

"There is a lot less naiveté about drugs in rave culture. People know what they are doing and what the effects will be. The research has been done and the information is readily available. In the sixties, I think there was a lot more consumption of drugs by uninformed people. If you try to pass off some unknown funky orange pill to a raver, they are likely to say no thanks."

- J, The Trip Factory, Saltspring Island, Canada.

"Ecstasy is very important to the rave scene as it opens people up immediately to the experience. It has changed the way I communicate. With all that reinforcement, I find it progressively easier to communicate more intimately in every day interactions. But I also think that people who stay in the scene usually end up taking smaller quantities as they learn to find the same state of mind without the drug."

- DJ Sylk, Hobart, Tasmania.

"I don't think that enough people realize the powerful ability of psychedelic drugs to be used as a tool for self-discovery. This is obviously taboo in today's society, but it's interesting how many intelligent people I know who realize the value of altered states of perception and observation to discovering internal energy and feelings."

- DJ Drenalin, Salinas, California, USA.

"It's so obvious that the rave scene couldn't have existed without ecstasy."

- Pyc, electronic musician, student, Belgrade, Yugoslavia.

"I like to create an environment at my parties that's as much fun for people who are not on drugs as people who are, so the music has to be the focal point. We try and attract an older crowd that is a little bit more educated about the music and know why they are there."

- Nigel Tasko, rave promoter, Noble House, The Alien Mental Association, Canada.

"Psychedelics can help you to break down the barriers that our society forces us to put up with. Some people can get socially addicted to ecstasy but most people who go through a phase where they feel they have to do ecstasy to have a good time and bond with people, usually come to a point where they stop doing it. I've never seen any real negative effects of ecstasy."

- DJ 608 a.k.a. Michael Angelo, Los Angeles, USA.

"Ecstasy is important for some rave freaks but not for me. If I'm tired, I use energy drinks and go to the chill out zone."

- Peter, student, raver, Lodz, Poland.

"Most people were doing acid and speed at the early parties in England but when ecstasy came along, it transformed the whole scene and the music."

- Wayne Grimwood, raver, London, England.

"Ecstasy is a catalyst for the rave experience, once you're tuned in you should be able to go off without it. I've never had a bad experience with ecstasy."

- DJ Billy, Victoria, Canada.

"If the party is crap, there's no help. No matter how many E's you take..."

- Marko Vajagic a.k.a. DJ Mark Wee, architect, Belgrade, Yugoslavia.

"Now, I don't do as much ecstasy and the music acts as a trigger. I think we need more information on proper drug use. I'm not interested in just another Saturday night party experience. If you have a good ecstasy experience you can remember that moment when you loved everyone in that room and how good that felt. When you've had a good clean ecstasy experience, you go away with something that effects your life forever."

- Michael Elenwonibi, musician, rave promoter, Canada.

"My first ecstasy experience made me really love life for about a week after. I felt really open to the world. I think everyone has a very intense high their first time. It shows you your potential for absolute joy."

- Olivia, DJ, trader, Auckland, New Zealand.

"In Holland, the law is one of the easiest, if not the easiest in the whole world. It is legal to buy and smoke marijuana whenever you want and to use XTC at parties, as long as you don't sell it. The government even organizes XTC testing at raves so you can test it for the amount of MDMA and other substances. Not because the government likes good XTC but because they don't want people selling bad pills, and risking people's lives."

- NoRuleZ, web designer, raver, Nijverdal, Netherlands.

"After about half an hour the E started to kick in, and after that I slowly but surely started to realize the whole purpose of raving. The music I couldn't normally bear to listen to began to sound extremely inviting in its rhythm and beautiful energizing soundscapes. A wide smile spread across my face and the people I was with felt like brothers and sisters. I wanted to hug, to kiss, to smile, to let everybody know I felt warm and caring towards them. But these feelings are in no way dependent on MDMA. They are omnipresent in the universe, I just needed that first pill to open my eyes to them and to make me more sensitive to feel them."

- Hannele, raver, student, Helsinki, Finland.

"Here in Mexico, ecstasy is very important to the rave scene. If you don't have ecstasy, you don't go to a rave. But I never use any drugs and I have the time of my life at every party."

- Marco Antonio Pimentel a.k.a. DJ Marcore, Mexico City, Mexico.

"I think that ecstasy and psychedelic drugs like LSD are an important element in the rave scene because they get you connected to another world beyond your normal state of being to another, more spiritual world. I know special people in San Francisco and Los Angeles who make and sell pure MDMA and have a Tibetan Llama bless it."

- Gena Womack, founding member of Moontribe, Los Angeles, USA.

"In 1990 ecstasy was around twenty-five pounds in the clubs ($60US). I've heard that when the rave scene first started in England ecstasy was as much as forty-five pounds each in London ($110US). The quality was much higher then. We used to do red and yellow gel caps called rhubarb and custards that were the best. They were intense and very clean and made you feel totally loved-up. I don't think there has been anything to touch them since."

- Tim Laughlin, The Vibe Crew, England.

"I tend to be very introverted but on ecstasy I found myself going around introducing myself to people at parties. I thought that was a fabulous thing. It was a big change in my life to get into a scene where I felt accepted. Now it feels like family. I found myself being a lot more friendly and more accepting to people outside the scene too. Ecstasy isn't the central focus of the scene for me anymore but I'm still an extrovert!"

- Damien, a.k.a. DK K-Rad, The Alien Mental Association, Canada

"I've been to plenty of events where I've been straight and it's been wicked! The music has to get you there on its own. E is merely (or should be) a catalyst. I see drugs as a source of information that I then have to take away with me and use in my everyday life. Every time I use ecstasy or LSD, I make sure to take time out for myself to ponder. If used responsibly ecstasy can alter the way you view life, issues and people."

- Jo Fruitybits, raver, magazine editor, Melbourne, Australia.

"Rave scene would surely be as good without E as with it (if not better)."
- Petr Nejedly, economics student, raver, Hradec Kralove, Czech Republic.

"Ecstasy helps you to get past the repetitiveness of the music, but after you've experienced the music in that way, you don't necessarily need the drug. I've been to raves countless times without ecstasy and I can easily repeat that first-time experience. The music takes you back to that place."

- Topher, underground rave promoter, Canada.

"It is not essential that everyone is on ecstasy at a rave to make it a success, but I think it was the introduction of ecstasy that introduced the concept of Peace, Love, Unity and Respect, as that is exactly how you feel on ecstasy. It is almost as if you were allowed a glimpse of the far greater picture and this allows you to get a new perspective on things. I have accepted myself a lot more and I now realize that I am capable of doing and feeling all the things I feel on ecstasy, without it."

- Maya Berelowitz, student, raver, Cape Town, South Africa.

"Ecstasy is an important part of the puzzle but you need all the elements to make it work. The setting, the energy of the people around you and the music all work together to create the experience."

- DJ 608 a.k.a. Michael Angelo, Los Angeles, USA.

"I don't think that ecstasy is essential to the rave experience and I think that people can reach the same level without it. But, what is does do, is show people the way. It shows them that the place they reach with ecstasy exists, so it may be necessary the first time but, after that, I don't think it's essential at all."

- Kim Stanford, The Toronto Raver Information Project.

"I know but one freedom and that is the freedom of the mind."
-Antoine de Saint-Exupéry, French writer and aviation pioneer, 1900-1944.

"E goes in. Ego's out!"
- Leandre, raver, Victoria, Canada.

CHAPTER 9: SEXUALITY

artwork: virginia smallfry

"There's a greater acceptance of sexuality within rave culture which goes hand in hand with the philosophy of peace, love, unity and respect. There is more understanding between people and less preconceived notions."

- Anne Marie, raver, nurse, Victoria, Canada.

9 SEXUALITY

Like all revolutionary pursuits, rave is about personal freedom and this is nowhere more apparent than in the area of sexuality. Every social revolution has brought with it a transformation in the way we express and view ourselves sexually and rave is no exception.

Previous to the 1920s, even to talk openly about sex would have sent people into a state of shock and outrage. A bare thigh in 1922 might provoke the same response as a full frontal display at the local mall today. The androgynous flappers with their provocative clothes and suggestive dancing and the suffragettes with their political demands did much to change the repressive attitudes of the day. But it wasn't until the sixties that the doors of sexual expression were finally flung wide open. The peace and love generation, personified by the hippie movement, advocated and openly practiced free love and open relationships. Sex was brought out in to the open both metaphorically and literally with young people openly celebrating their sexuality. Hordes of hippies could be seen frolicking stark naked and even fornicating in public places as private parts became public property. The sixties also marked the beginning of the gay rights movement that demanded equal rights and acceptance of gay life styles that up until then had been relegated to the status of a secret underground society. For heterosexuals, sex was no longer confined to the exclusive domain of committed relationships or marriage and the parameters of sexual relationships widened to include a number of options and alternative models. Separating sex from committed relationships redefined the way we thought about relationships in general and represented an expansion and maturing of sexual identities.

photo: tristan o'neill

As with the development of music during the seventies and eighties, sexuality for the most part followed a trail blazed by the sexual revolution of the sixties. The advent of AIDS changed many people's attitudes towards open and free sexual relations. Sex became a dangerous and potentially deadly game, especially among the gay and bisexual population. A lot of people were forced to rethink their attitudes towards sex during this time, questioning and re-evaluating the benefits and pleasures of casual sex in light of the new risks. To the rave generation, which grew up with this reality, the inherent risks of sex translated into a more mature attitude towards sex in general.

For teenagers in the nineties, sex is not quite so much of a problem as it has been to past generations. Teenagers today are far more relaxed about intimate relations and no longer see sex as the point of no return, inevitably leading to the inherent responsibilities of a committed relationship. Even while involved in a relationship, the pressures of success are less today than ever before. This is the generation where record breaking divorce rates and single parent families are almost as prevalent as traditional family models. For teens today, the myth of white weddings, picket fences and perfect, life long partnerships have become the stuff of pure fantasy. But in reality, this seemingly negative state of affairs may end up having some positive benefits after all. With some of the pressures around relationships and sexuality lifted, young people now have the opportunity to evaluate their situations from a more objective standpoint. There is a good case to be made that the pressures and expectations around sex and relationships are precisely the reason that many of them fail so miserably. When the expectations are removed, the relationship is allowed to unfold and develop in a more natural way, either leading to a closer and more meaningful relationship in the case of a compatible couple, or an amicable drifting apart in the case of non-compatibility. With either outcome, the level of conflict is far less for everybody involved and in the long run may prove to create the foundation for a longer lasting relationship.

Hordes of hippies could be seen frolicking stark naked and even fornicating in public places as private parts became public property.

This maturing of sexual attitudes is increasingly prevalent among teenagers in general and even more apparent among ravers, where it is common for ex-lovers and partners to remain friends long after their intimate relationships have officially ended. Because of a more relaxed attitude towards sex and less inclination towards possessiveness and jealousy around sexual relationships, ravers can turn their attention to other, perhaps more important, aspects of a relationship. When the pressures of sexual politics are diminished, more emphasis can be given to communication, friendship and sensuality, qualities that if developed are more likely to result in both longer lasting and more meaningful relationships.

Safe sex and the use of condoms is another area where ravers are proving to be more mature and responsible than previous generations. In general, the statistics available today on teenagers practicing safe sex are pretty dismal. But ravers, with their tendencies towards natural foods and fitness, tend to be more health conscious than most and so more likely to practice safe sex than your average teen. With increased awareness comes increased freedom to make decisions. It is interesting to note that some ravers I have talked to have opted for abstinence for periods of time, choosing to develop relationships without the complications of sex. Of course not all ravers choose abstinence or even practice safe sex all the time but generally speaking, these trends in rave culture show a level of sophistication and maturity rarely seen in young people of previous generations.

photo: tristan o'neill

Another area where ravers are pushing the envelope of sexual expression is with the acceptance of homosexuality and bisexuality. Because house music developed in the gay clubs of North America, ravers have shed the last vestiges of homophobia and are able to accept gay lifestyles as just another sexual choice. It is important to note that many of the pioneers of electronic dance music including Frankie Knuckles and Ron Hardy have come from the gay community and continue to do so. Joe LeSesne a.k.a. 1.8.7 is a popular DJ and jungle music producer based in Philadelphia who recently surprised his fans by having a sex-change operation. Joe is now known as Jordana. For most artists in the popular eye this would probably create some fairly serious PR problems and some loss of support from the audience but within the tolerant and accepting climate of rave culture, it is unlikely to cause much of a ripple.

The rave movement has done more for gender relations than any other popular movement in history, and continues to this day to provide a bridge between the worlds of gays and straights. Many heterosexual ravers regularly attend house music nights at gay clubs and gay people regularly attend raves. This cross-over has resulted in an increasing number of ravers experimenting with bisexuality and it is not uncommon to see normally heterosexual ravers kissing and cuddling with members of the same sex, though it is far more common with girls than guys.

Kim Stanford of The Toronto Raver Information Project (TRIP) has attended many raves, distributing information on safe sex and drug awareness. *"Within rave culture there is a lot more openness around sexual experimentation and especially bisexuality. I've sat with gay friends at the booth and normally their "gay radar" will tell them who is gay. But at raves they have a hard time spotting gays because there is a blurring of those sexual labels and identities. It is pretty common for ravers, especially women, to have had sex with members of their same gender, even if they are normally heterosexual."*

Kim also notes that one of the most popular pamphlets on the TRIP table is one on safer S and M. She believes that the interest goes beyond mere curiosity and reflects rave culture's openness to new forms of sexual expression.

As well as the blurring of sexual orientations and erotic experimentation, rave also embraces a broader definition of sexuality that includes and embraces the sensual. Ecstasy is well known for producing profound sensual experiences that for some can be as satisfying as sexual experiences. In fact, at the height of an ecstasy experience the sexual drive is suppressed, and in men, can result in a shrinking penis effect that makes sex out of the question. Women also report a decreased sex drive while under the influence of ecstasy. But despite the lack of libidinous motivation, raving is an incredibly sensual experience and it is this kind of intense sensuality that is most prevalent at raves. People are discovering that you can have a wonderfully satisfying sensual experience just *dancing* with each other.

Ecstasy produces a profound sensual awareness coupled with feelings of universal love causing people to openly express love and affection. Ravers love to massage each other and complete strangers can easily find themselves hugging or sharing feelings. These open demonstrations of affection are intensely sensual but are rarely complicated with the pressures of sexual politics commonly found in the bar scene. For women especially, raves are a much safer and trouble free environment than most social gatherings where women are apt to be spending a lot of time fending off unwanted advances. Even though the atmosphere at rave parties is sensually power charged, it is not a pick-up scene. At raves, women experience increased freedom to be themselves and an intimate encounter with a

In a society that seems obsessed with objectifying the sexual act as some sort of universal yardstick for success and power, rave offers a refreshing antidote by emphasizing the importance of the sensual, humanistic and universal qualities of our sexuality rather than the simplistic and egotistical pay off of a one night stand.

member of the opposite sex is likely to go no further than a warm hug and a big smile.

Personally speaking, as a highly sexed man, I find it a unique and wonderful experience to dance with complete abandon in a sea of ravishingly beautiful, scantily clad, nubile young women and think only of universal love and beauty. In a society that seems obsessed with objectifying the sexual act as some sort of universal yardstick for success and power, rave offers a refreshing antidote by emphasizing the importance of the sensual, humanistic and universal qualities of our sexuality rather than the simplistic and egotistical pay off of a one night stand.

photo: trent warlow

For both men and women the holistic perspective offered by the rave generation can transform the way we think about our sexuality and ourselves. Increased sensual awareness and intimacy coupled with the sensibilities of universal love has the potential to bring a new understanding between men and women, one that will inevitably lead to deeper, more meaningful relationships on all levels. To rise above our sexual conditioning in this way may prove to be the most sexually liberating experience of all.

"I love the fact that everyone runs around and openly shows their sexuality, it's refreshing, you don't see that in every day society."

- Nicole A. Tobias, music major, festival director, raver, New Jersey, USA.

"I think that ravers have a very mature attitude towards sex. There's an appreciation of that special moment of two people spending time together."

- DJ Davie, The Vibe Tribe, Canada.

"Men don't try to pick up women at raves even though they dress much more daringly than usual. If a man starts to talk to a woman, it's usually not because he is trying to pick up the woman, but because she is a fellow raver and just happens to be there. The response is also never impolite. This is one of the main characteristics of the famous "rave-vibe". This is something so totally different from disco/restaurant/bar culture that outsiders find it hard to believe."

- Janne Leino, raver, Helsinki, Finland.

"I think that everyone is a closet case of some sort. They may be curious and the rave scene gives them a chance to experiment to whatever level they want. It could be a guy giving a guy a back massage or a blowjob. I don't believe that everyone lives their lives never wondering what it's like to do this or that. At a rave you can enjoy being massaged by a guy and not have to worry about being labeled."

- Surfer Bob, The Vibe Tribe, Canada.

"Even though few sexual unions take place at raves in Yugoslavia, raves do happen to be a place where sexual barriers become diminished. The rhythm enhances your sexuality, while at the same time reduces the perception of people as mere sex objects."

- Ferid Abbasher. a.k.a. DJ Lord Ferdi the Despiser, Nexus, Indjija, Yugoslavia.

"Going for it at a rave is like having sex with everyone around you. Because ravers don't go out with the intention of picking someone up - they don't have to. I feel safe in the knowledge that I won't be tapped on to by some drunken lout when I go out raving."

- Vix, music major, rave promoter, London, England.

"I still haven't come to terms with how people act in the clubs and bars, at a rave you are "safe". You know you can go there without risking being raped or having tons of guys trying to chat you up, etc."

- Chrissie, student, raver, Malmö, Sweden.

"In the rave scene you can have sex with your best friend and not feel bad or guilty about it, but at a party if someone gives you a nice massage on the dance floor, you're not necessarily going to have sex with them. You can just love them for what they are or who they are. It's not about wanting to bang someone like in the club scene. It's just about having an honest interaction with people."

- Logan a.k.a. Beats Off, The Vibe Tribe, Canada.

"Being a gay male, I can tell you that the rave scene is very open to sexual issues and very accepting and tolerant of a persons sexuality. The rave scene has been able to let people explore their sexuality without fear of retribution."

- Albert Mancuso a.k.a. DJ Science, Florida, USA.

"The beauty of sexuality in the rave scene is that everyone is equal. No one is ashamed of who or what he or she is. They just go for it!"

- NoRuleZ, web designer, raver, Nijverdal, Netherlands.

"When you are at a rave, you aren't there to find the most beautiful girl or guy to follow you home so that you can have nice sex and then forget about them for the rest of your life. The concept of rave is much more then just sexual lust and stone-age intelligence."

- Fredrik Larsson, electronic musician, raver, Stockholm, Sweden.

"Love plays a big part in rave culture, sexuality too... but you don't see much sexual stuff at raves. It happens, but people pay much more attention to love. This is the lesson of rave culture. You will definitely learn about love!"

- Scotto Ba Gotto a.k.a. The Glow Stik King, New Hampshire, USA.

"I used to be homophobic and through raving I found that I've now become comfortable around gay people. It took a while to get over being afraid of what people might think. Now it doesn't bother me what any one else might think."

- DJ Davie, The Vibe Tribe, Canada.

"There's a lot of androgyny going on in the rave scene. It seems to be less about girls and guys and more about people loving each other. There's a lot of bisexuality especially amongst women. Ravers are already pushing the boundaries of what's acceptable to society so people feel more free to experiment."

- Raevn Lunah Teak, designer, raver, Brisbane, Australia.

"I think that rave offers us a new and powerful understanding of the equality between men and women which can have a big impact on the current sexual revolution. In every day life there are not too many opportunities to show love and I think that we tend to suppress it. Rave gives me a venue for my love. A chance to really get inside of my love and experience it and express it and experiment with it. There's a lot of contact at raves, a lot of massage and hugging. It's much more sensual than sexual."

- Leandre, raver, Victoria, Canada.

"Sexuality is more open and undefined in the rave scene. People are not so concerned about the social precepts that have been impressed upon them for their whole lives."

- DJ Drenalin, Salinas, California, USA.

"Men wear pretty baggy clothes and females tend to take most of their clothes off. This is because women like to do that, but they only have the courage to do that at raves, because in bars men would drool over them and try to hit on them. Of course, men are trying to meet women and vice-versa everywhere, but it is much more hidden at raves and somehow more intelligent."

- DJ Jules Nerve, Helsinki, Finland.

"Ravers are not afraid to touch or hug somebody and when they do, it doesn't necessarily have a sexual connotation. It doesn't mean that you are going home with that person later. Ravers are less inhibited and embarrassed. At parties you might see girls dancing topless, but they take their shirt off because they're hot, not because it's a sexual signal."

- J, The Trip Factory, Saltspring Island, Canada.

CHAPTER 10: THE TRIBAL EXPERIENCE

- neo-tribalism
- quotes
- the moontribe collective

"Rave is simply a natural step in an evolutionary process of trance through dance. In ancient times the human animal would beat on a hollow log for hours, even days, in order to free the mind from the survival orientated thoughts of the day, thus allowing for abstract visions for the individual, while creating emotional bonds within the group. The tools have changed, yet the function remains the same. We dance the tribal rhythms of our ancestors while celebrating technology and all it does to enhance our scope of living."

- George Storm, raver, citizen of the world.

10. The Tribal Experience

Since human beings have walked on this planet they have demonstrated a need to connect with one another in some sort of group activity. For a community to be psychologically healthy there must be a forum where the members can come together, exchange information, review common goals, solve problems, hold council and generally keep in touch with each other. At the simplest and most basic level, the communal fire pit provided the focus.

Our primitive ancestors spent an enormous amount of time sitting in groups around a fire staring at dancing flames and smoky forms. Anyone who has done this will know how relaxing and meditative it can be, how it can slow down our overactive minds and cause our thoughts to wander and become more fluid and abstract. In this trance-like state of mind we have different priorities and see the world and our selves from a different perspective. This type of fluid mind-state has long been associated with stimulating creative thought processes that lead to new ideas. It is precisely this ability to alter the way we think that has enabled us to adapt to a changing world, expand our consciousness, and develop the intelligence necessary to solve our civilization's most complex and abstract problems.

In a group setting, a relaxed and creative mind state also brings about a heightened sense of intimacy. We share a feeling of belonging that makes our superficial differences seem less important and the things we have in common more meaningful. Group intimacy also makes us feel safe and protected. This can be thought of as an extension of the parent-child bond, which is the basis for the family. Just as we need to maintain the bonds within a family, we have the same needs with our extended family or community.

Most, if not all of our social ills today can be traced back to the break-down of the parent-child relationship, which in turn leads to the break-down of the family, the community and ultimately the collapse of society. If we are to solve the problems that are undermining our society we must first heal the relationships within our families and communities. Because we are motivated by our need to love and be loved, we have invented many rituals throughout history that provide us a venue where we are able to express our most fundamental drives. In prehistoric times we painted our faces and danced around the fire, but as our level of sophistication grew, so did our rituals. Every culture on earth has developed a wealth of rituals designed to fulfill the basic need we have to bond with each other.

Most, if not all of our social ills today can be traced back to the break-down of the parent-child relationship, which in turn leads to the break-down of the family, the community and ultimately the collapse of society.

These three elements: altered states of consciousness, group identification and ritual can be thought of as the tribal experience. And our need for this experience is as strong today as it was forty thousand years ago.

photo: tristan o'neill

NEO-TRIBALISM

Though the trappings may be quite different, in today's modern world we are still striving for the same tribal experience engaged in by our ancestors. Although many of our efforts at tribalism these days seem somewhat distorted and egocentric, people are still flocking to group events where they can directly or indirectly make a group connection. Sporting events, social clubs, movie theatres, nightclubs, etc., all demonstrate we have not lost our desire for the tribal experience. But in today's society, with the collapse of the family, rising crime rates, unemployment, addictions, environmental destruction, and a myriad of other social ills, it is becoming increasingly difficult to find the real thing. More and more, our tribal gatherings are dominated by commercialism and egotism and lack the heart felt connections that we instinctually crave. With rave culture, our tribal needs are once again being met and people are responding with growing enthusiasm as the ancient tradition of the tribal gathering is being resurrected on a global scale.

Rave culture is the embodiment of today's neo-tribalism with the rave party as its ritualistic centre. And although rave is considered a modern or even futuristic movement, not much has really changed in the last few thousand years. Some of the superficial trappings may be different, but the intent and the outcome are much the same. As human beings, we have a basic need to transcend our own personal perspective and goals to the point where we can experience and identify with the collective group consciousness. In this state we become one organism with a common perspective and the rewards of this type of tribal activity can be enormous. When we identify with other people on this level, conflict within the group is greatly reduced because the individual's needs become subordinate to the needs of the group. By developing a group consciousness we become less selfish and therefore more compassionate and understanding.

To achieve the group mind states of tribal ritual, we must first transcend the ego which anchors us in our sense of self. Normally, we tend to perceive ourselves as separate entities from the world around us. We see the world in terms of opposites, good and evil, me and you, black and white, up and down, God and Devil and so on. This egocentric point of view creates a dualistic model where opposites cannot be reconciled. When we superimpose this model on our view of the world, it creates polarization and therefore conflict.

To move beyond this limiting perspective we can employ methods that enable us to let go of our previous conditioning and tap in to a higher state of being. One of the most useful tools to achieve this end is a trance state. Throughout history people have used trance states to access their subconscious and superconscious minds. The word trance comes from the Latin, *transire* meaning, "to go across" which has come to mean crossing the boundaries from one level of reality to another. There are many meditation techniques and yogic practices designed to promote trance states, but the neo-tribalism of rave culture, following in the well-worn footsteps of many tribal cultures, uses music, dance and mood-altering drugs. At a rave, the combination of these three elements provides the necessary context for attaining powerful transformative states.

Although many younger ravers may be unaware of the tribal roots of the rave movement, or even fully understand the mechanics of trance states, they are instinctively attracted to the scene because it gives them something they can not find anywhere else. For a few hours they are able to leave behind a world full of contradiction, conflict and confusion, and enter a universal realm where everyone is truly equal, a place where peace, love, unity and respect are the laws of the land. For most people, this may be the only time they truly experience peace of mind. For many others it can provide an illuminating perspective on their own lives and their place in the world.

"The role of the DJ is to understand the power that exists. It's ultimately a role of responsibility to understand that you are wielding incredible amount of potential power and you have to be aware of where you are taking people. In a tribal sense it's a fundamental role, like a magician or healer or diviner or shaman. Like the shaman, the DJ is a facilitator of a transformative experience. It's all about controlling the pulse and rhythm of the party and guides the level of consciousness and awareness from one reality to another. A DJ rides the energy between themselves and the participants and guides the journey like an expedition. With techno or house music, the four-on-the-floor rhythm acts as the shamans drum."

**- Andrew Rawnsley,
musician, DJ, Editor
of XLR8R magazine,
San Francisco, USA.**

With rave culture, our tribal needs are once again being met and people are responding with growing enthusiasm as the ancient tradition of the tribal gathering is being resurrected on a global scale.

"I think that the music sets the dancer up to fully let go, to allow the body to do the magic and let the mind create an epiphany of group dynamics. Everyone becomes a sea of rhythm and that creates a phenomenal feeling of being one, which is the essence of our own being. It's about realizing and remembering that we are not separate."

- Gena Womack, founding member of Moontribe, Los Angeles, USA.

"Raves are just an evolution of the tribal 'raves' you can find in every primitive society. It's well known from the beginning of history that certain kinds of sounds, low and cadenced, stimulates unused parts of our brain, inducing an ecstatic state. In that mood, some people have visions or mystical experiences or just feel very relaxed and in total peace."

- Federico Sommariva, rave promoter, DJ, Milan, Italy.

"At a rave, the DJ is a shaman, a priest, a channeller of energy - they control the psychic voyages of the dancers through his choice of music and their skill in manipulating that music. A large part of the concept of raves is built upon sensory overload - a barrage of audio and very often visual stimuli are brought together to elevate people into an altered state of physical or psychological existence."

- Norman NG a.k.a. Nomskii, rave promoter, writer, Singapore.

"We are the part of human culture that still practices dancing into a trance state, reminiscent of the Indians and aborigines."

- Frank Zelaya a.k.a. DJ SoR, Los Angeles, USA.

"Shamans have traditionally used certain substances to break through the doors of perception. In the case of rave, the shaman's sacrament is ecstasy or mushrooms or LSD. It's exactly the same kind of transcendental tribal experience. People have same tribal needs today as they have ever had and the rave scene is providing people with those same basic human needs with technology in the mix."

- Leandre, raver, Victoria, Canada.

"I am blessed to be part of a generation that is starting to truly learn from the wisdom of the tribal cultures of the past and combine that with the marvels of modern technology - a potent synthesis."

- Vix, music major, rave promoter, London, England.

THE MOONTRIBE COLLECTIVE

One of the many manifestations of neo-tribalism in rave culture can be found in the numerous collectives formed around the world which are supported by huge dedicated groups of followers. In England this began with "posses", groups of ravers that traveled around the country following a specific DJ. Spiral Tribe were one of the early tribal collectives from Britain that are still traveling the world today, staging impromptu raves in out of the way places. In recent years, Moontribe from Los Angeles have gained a worldwide reputation for producing monthly full moon parties with a spiritual or tribal focus.

Gena Womack, one of the founding members of Moontribe, moved to San Francisco in 1990 and started attending a weekly rave event called Come Unity whose mission statement was to change the world through dance. Soon afterwards, San Francisco promoter, Alan Mcqueen of Wicked Productions, along with his wife Trisha, started to put on small full moon parties at Bonnie Dunes beach featuring local DJs, Garth and Jeno. Gena remembers the effects those early parties had on the people who came. *"It was amazing to see the transformation in people who came to those parties. People who were normally quite reserved would come in their designer clothes and gradually they would start opening up and start wearing bright colours."*

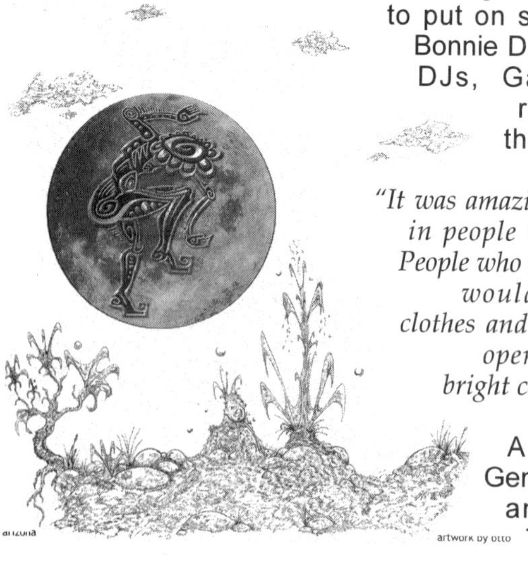

A couple of years later Gena moved to Los Angeles and met DJs Daniel and Treavor at a Kundalini

Yoga workshop. Daniel had already started promoting full moon parties with James Lumb of Electric Skychurch. At first, the events were attended by a group of about twenty regulars and the DJs would play for up to eight or nine hours at a time. Daniel remembers the first event. *"We heard about the full moon parties in San Francisco and I always wanted to go to one. I was frustrated at the time because I wanted a place to play and experiment. We wanted to do a party but keep it tight and vibey and spiritual and also have a place where we could really let go. So in June of '93, I got together with Treavor, Heather and Electric Skychurch, rented a generator and sound system and headed off into the desert. The first party was really trippy and attracted some weird urban city vibes, but it was a good learning experience and made me realize that what we were doing was very powerful and spiritual."*

The focus of the group was to create a sacred space **where people could come together and have an** *epiphany* **of** group consciousness.

Gena remembers attending one of the first full moon parties in Los Angeles, *"When I got to LA in '93, I hooked up with Daniel, Treavor and Heather and they had been doing tiny desert parties. I went out and there was about twenty of us who had a really good time. And then John Kelly got called into the circle and then John Kavoolick came along and took responsibility for finding the locations and Dallas became the group facilitator. Daniel and I were out there all the time, bringing new people in. Then we decided that we would call ourselves Moontribe. It all happened very naturally. The full moon parties in LA were much more profound for me because I was going in knowing what I was doing. We would facilitate energy circles where the entire party would be holding hands and dancing together, giving each other energy and love. It was wonderful to see all these different people coming together through music, dance and psychedelics. We had some very profound group experiences."*

The focus of the group was to create a sacred space where people could come together and have an epiphany of group consciousness. The kids showing up at the full moon parties were fairly young and Moontribe felt a responsibility be a positive role model taking it upon themselves to educate newcomers about the spiritual aspects of rave and the responsible use of psychedelic drugs.

The Moontribe council was now made up of eight members, Daniel, Gena, Treavor, Dallas, John Kavoolick, John Kelly, Heather and Brian. As well as the full moon parties every month, Moontribe were also organizing sporadic Sunday daytime events featuring out-of-town guest DJs like Mark Farina and Derek Carter. These five-dollar parties would also include acoustic drumming sessions, body art and catering by the local Hare Krishna temple.

But the main focus of the group was always the full moon parties. The parties started off with less than a hundred people and grew steadily in size. By the collective's third anniversary party the crowds had swelled to over three thousand strong, and the logistics of dealing with such large numbers of people were beginning to create some problems. The park rangers frequently investigated the gatherings and came to know the Moontribe members by name. They were generally supportive and were impressed by the fact that the sites were always cleaned up thoroughly and returned to their pristine condition. But when the numbers increased the police started to close parties because of safety concerns. At one event attended by over four thousand people, the police and the National Guard were called in. They arrived overland en masse and sent several helicopters to close the party down at a remote location deep in the Mojave Desert. After that the Moontribe council had their own concerns about protecting the environment and providing sufficient resources for so many people.

photo: tristan o'neill

Around this time there were other people that saw the money making potential of such large turnouts and began to promote desert parties with a less spiritual focus. Gena remembers the bad press. *"We had a lot of bad press at one point. The press would report on national television and relate our parties with other parties that were run badly and encouraged the use of nitrous oxide. They would be overdosing on drugs and getting taken out by helicopters. They didn't clean up either, so in the morning there would be a sea of rubber balloons (used to inhale nitrous oxide or laughing gas.) Those promoters had no consciousness at all and all the bad press hurt what we were trying to achieve. That's when we decided to have meeting points and caravan in. No directions would be given out. But they were posting the locations on the net and thousands of people and cars would still be streaming down the road."*

Moontribe's efforts to curb the number of people coming to the full moon parties were largely thwarted by the collective's incredible popularity, which eventually proved to be its downfall. Also, producing thirteen parties a year for five years is an enormous amount of work and as the demands on their time and energy became stressful, the group began to move on to other ventures.

Although the monthly full moon desert parties are now over, the members of Moontribe still come together occasionally for full moon raves or appear at events to raise awareness on political issues. Recently several Moontribe members joined forces to protest a proposed nuclear waste dump in California. This year they also performed outside the federal building in Los Angeles in support of a free Tibet, and have given their time and energy to protest an unpopular curfew bylaw in LA that confines youth to their homes after eleven p.m. The Moontribe DJs are still in demand and in recent years have performed all over North America and in Ireland, Holland, Germany and Japan.

The phenomenal success of Moontribe and the many other rave collectives around the world speaks volumes about a new generation's search for tribal rituals. In a world that has lost sight of its ancestral origins, the global culture of rave is providing a powerful and meaningful group connection for millions of disenfranchised young people who are striving to create a better world.

"Looking back, I'm amazed at the amount of people that were affected by Moontribe and who hold those experiences we had together near to their hearts. In that sense, Moontribe will never be over, it will just take on different forms."

-Gena Womack, founding member of Moontribe, Los Angeles, USA.

CHAPTER 11: RAVE AS RELIGION

photo: tristan o'neill

"And David was dancing before the lord with all his might..."

- 2 Samuel 6:14, The Bible.

11. Rave as Religion

The dictionary gives the definition of religion as "The expression of man's belief and reverence for a superhuman power recognized as the creator and governor of the universe" or "Any objective attended to or pursued with zeal or conscientious devotion." I have talked to many ravers about this issue and have become convinced that raving does indeed meet all the requirements of a grass roots, people's religion.

Although ravers don't feel the need to give their superhuman power a name or personality, when a rave "goes off," everyone has a shared experience of connectedness and hundreds or even thousands of people can feel like one being with a shared purpose and direction. This direct experience of oneness is a fundamental aspect of the religious experience and is well documented in all religious doctrines. Whether we call it samadhi, enlightenment, grace, nirvana, Godhead or satori, this state of being is considered to be the point of contact with the divine, the place in which Man and God become one. Every religion has its devotional practices to achieve this condition and spiritual representatives to act as advisors and guides.

Although there are no formal priests in rave culture, DJs can be thought of as the equivalent. They officiate at the head of the proceedings, at the altar of the turntable, and administer the sacrament of music. They are a respected and revered element at any rave, providing a focal point and serving as a conductor by guiding the dancing devotees on their inner journey. An experienced DJ will tune in to the audience and instinctively know when to increase the intensity of the music, or when to alter the direction of the musical journey for maximum impact. Some DJs do this intuitively while others are quite aware of their shamanic role as a facilitator leading people from one level of consciousness to another.

In the last few years some DJs have taken advantage of this privileged position, asking excessive amounts of money to perform and making outlandish requests. One DJ in England demands to be led into the arena in a sedan chair carried by a group of humble followers. When we think of modern religious leaders like Jim Baker or Gerry Fallwell, this kind of egotism and self-righteousness could also be considered consistent with a religious model. However this type of perversion is more likely to represent a corrupt few rather than the will of the majority whether in rave culture or in some modern religious movements. For the most part, rave DJs are extremely aware of their position of power and take the role very seriously indeed.

The religion of rave embraces the spontaneous and intuitive, seeking to commune with the infinite through ecstatic revelation.

As unorthodox and esoteric as a rave party may be, it is not uncommon to see the trappings of traditional religions at some events. Images from Buddhist and Hindu religions are the most prevalent and are often used in the collage of projected images cast on to giant screens. Sanskrit symbols or meditating Buddhas are often used to illustrate flyers. At a recent solstice event produced by Full Circle there was an altar set up at one end of the dance floor festooned with rose petals and other offerings such as those found in a Hindu temple.

The most "religious" - some would say the most pure - group of ravers are the followers of Goa trance music also known as psychedelic or psy-trance. These electronic devotees are famous for creating psychedelic, black light environments for their mostly underground parties, and are solely dedicated to the spiritual benefits of raving. Gil Oliveira Santos, a.k.a. Ravehunter, is an electronic musician from Sao Paulo in Brazil. He has had two albums released in Germany and Brazil and now specializes in Goa trance with a group called Mahadeva. *"In Brazil we follow the philosophy of peace, love, unity and respect. We are developing our spiritualism and evolution. A lot of people have discovered spiritualism while they are just having fun. That's the way it has worked for me. Psy/Goa trance is the music I like the most. It is intelligent music and in the right atmosphere it can transport you to another dimension where all is bliss. There is spiritualism in the music. It is energy... It is dharma... It is a state of mind..."*

Ravers generally prefer to sample their religious imagery and motifs from eastern or mystic traditions whose exotic and mysterious aspects have more allure than the more familiar Christian beliefs. For most ravers, eastern religions have a much stronger tendency towards tolerance and acceptance than ridged, restrictive Christian traditions. But for the most part, ravers do not cling to the religious models of the past, preferring instead to create something new. Structure, conformity and subservience have given way to a more personal and free-form model. The religion of rave embraces the spontaneous and intuitive, seeking to commune with the infinite through ecstatic revelation. In this sense, rave has more in common with the mystic traditions.

Mysticism has been described as the science of union with the absolute. Mystics believe that to know God we must transcend the self and connect with a larger whole and the dissolution of the ego or sense-of-self is essential in order to experience God as a direct reality rather than an abstract mindful concept. Spiritual practices such as counting rosary beads, repeating prayers or mantras, singing hymns, chanting, staring at candles etc., are all devotional practices designed to turn the mind away from daily concerns and redirect awareness towards the unity of God consciousness. Rave incorporates many of the same practices and techniques and can achieve the same results.

photo: tristan o'neill

Tim Laughlin is a forty-two year old rave promoter from Devon who toured the South of England with a collective known as The Vibe Crew throwing free parties and playing in clubs. At one such event on the South Coast he had the kind of religious experience that is common among ravers. *"I was going off at a club in Torquay, Devon called Face to Face. It was in a seventeenth-century church with the DJs in the pulpit and a bar at the altar. They were playing intelligent techno and I experienced what I thought it must be like when someone has a deeply religious experience. The atmosphere was indescribable. The whole place became one. By the end of the night people were crying with joy and utter elation. It was one of the most amazing experiences I've ever had in my life and*

I value that experience like people value their religion. It's way beyond just getting off at a party. It's something that's in you and stays with you forever.

Since that time I've had several experiences like that on E and now I find that I can have similar experiences without E by using the music as a trigger. I think it's very much like tribal experiences where everyone from the tribe gets together to celebrate a good harvest or some other ritual. Everyone comes together and gets into a trance state with music and dancing."

artwork: virginia smallfry

For the past five thousand years music has been used as a common religious tool for achieving spiritual focus. From simple Hindu mantras to the complexity of orchestral hymns, we have been singing and playing our way to God for centuries. The continuous, repeating eight bar cycle and persistent beats of electronic dance music are reminiscent of the cyclic nature of the reverent music of many cultures. In fact, the pious drumming and singing of aboriginal cultures are regularly sampled in the music played at raves. An electronic duo called Deep Forest has built an entire career out of sampling the UNESO library of indigenous recordings from around the world. These talented musicians take recordings of a Peruvian Indian folk song or a Gypsy lament and weave them seamlessly with electronic ambient music, creating deeply moving and original compositions. Deep Forest's next CD promises to be based in part on the spiritual singing of North American Indians. From pygmies in Borneo to chanting Tibetan monks, ravers are resurrecting and embracing holy music from the four corners of the planet.

From simple Hindu mantras to the complexity of orchestral hymns, we have been singing and playing our way to God for centuries.

Another function of religion is to bring the community together regularly with the intention of submitting to a higher power. This common purpose and practice serves to strengthen community bonds and create meaningful links between the individual members of the congregation. People are given an opportunity to meet their neighbours and a chance to create an extended family. DJ Billy from Canada has this to say: *"I remember playing at a rave with Stacy Pullen and the police came by, so Stacy turned the music way down low and everybody in the room was so in synch and in tune with what was happening. That was the night I became aware of the larger picture. People really coming together, going on a massive journey and forming deep connections with each other. That night was a huge moment for me."*

As our communities become larger and more fractured it is becoming more difficult to form the kind of relationships that are essential to a healthy society. Raves provide venues where a large number of different kinds of people can meet and bond together. The ritual of the communal dance and the effect of the music create a powerful context for group connection, but it is the use of ecstasy that catapults the experience into new realms of possibilities.

The Dionysians were well known for openly using mind-altering substances in traditional, structured rituals aimed at self-growth.

The effects of ecstasy can enable us to see beyond our superficial differences to a place of commonality. Deep down we have an understanding that we are all the same, that there is a place within us common to us all. It is at this point of collective contact that the whole can become more than the sum of its parts. A new dynamic is reached where individuality is transcended and group awareness takes over. The Christian ethic of "Love others as yourself" takes on a renewed meaning as it moves from the conceptual to the practical. We can choose to agree or disagree with theories but we cannot deny our own personal and direct experience.

But can ecstasy make claims to be a bona fide spiritual aide? Here is a quote from a Benedictine monk who has experimented with ecstasy. *"Ecstasy opens up a direct link between myself and God and has the capacity to put one on the right path to divine union. It should not be used unless one is really searching for God. Prayer is communication with God but tends to be blocked by the internal dialogue. Using ecstasy while trying to pray removes these obstacles."*

And here is another comment from a Zen monk of the Soto tradition who has also incorporated ecstasy into his meditation practice and has recommended it for some of his students. *"Being still when taking MDMA helps you to know how to sit, as it provides you with experiential knowledge. It is like a medicine, a wonderful tool for teaching. For example, I had a very keen student who never succeeded in meditation until ecstasy removed the block caused by his own effort when trying to meditate. That one experience helped him to make fast progress and he has since been ordained a monk."*

And here is a letter written by a Buddhist monk to Rick Doblin of The Multi-disiplinarian Association for Psychedelic Studies in California. The letter is from Volume 5, Number 3, MAPS Newsletter, page 44.

Dear Rick,

Thanks for sending the latest issue of MAPS and congratulations on the breakthroughs in your research.

Well, I not only had a ball in England at the rave but also got an education and personal liberation. I had not been to a dance since I became a monk yet I used to love to dance and was part of the scene in the 60's.

What blew my mind was the fact that I'll be 70 this year. I was so taken by the MDMA and the music that I danced from 11 p.m. to 7 a.m. It had a very strong impact on me, since I could totally give myself to the rhythm and was in a sort of trance, which reminded me very much of the Native American dances which I witnessed in New Mexico. It also occurred to me that the DJ was a kind of shaman. Having gotten over the initial 'shock' of the rave, I have had time to muse over the whole experience. I've come to the conclusion that rave dancing could be a very important aspect of the spiritual path. It is not only fun and relaxing but is also creative, that is, liberating. The other night I went to a nightclub to dance with three visiting monks from Mt. Baldy!

The effect MDMA has on me is like a magnifying glass. I use it only once or twice a year (my supply is very limited) for meditation. I can focus more sharply and the content becomes more magnified and I see more with my mind's eye.

Hope you are happy and well,

H.

It has been said that this is the first generation to be raised without religion, but it may be more accurate to say that the old religious models have lost touch with the youth of today. Young people today are rejecting the traditional religions followed by their parents and are busy creating new contexts for their devotional needs. A Rabbi from the USA agrees. *"Traditional religions have lost the ability to provide their followers with mystical experiences. Instead, young people are far more likely to have such experiences while on LSD or ecstasy. If priests really want to understand young people, they should try these drugs themselves. Then they would learn that certain drugs can produce the same quality and potential value as other mystical experiences."*

It is also an interesting and common phenomenon that many young people who have had no previous interest or awareness in spirituality start to develop an interest in religious matters after going to a few raves. Their experience with the trance states at parties can often lead to an interest in spiritual pursuits. Having had a powerful or moving experience at a rave, they now have to find the terminology and context with which to describe and communicate the experience, and religious or spiritual systems often provide the framework necessary to explain and define these profound experiences.

And who is to say that an ecstatic raver is not just as close to God as someone who dutifully visits the local church every Sunday? There are many so-called religious people who, on the surface, faithfully follow the practices of their chosen church but in reality are only going through the motions of what they believe is expected of them. They may never have had a religious experience themselves and so are forced to rely on the testimony of others. A direct experience is worth far more than any didactic story, no matter who the teacher may be. It seems evident that many people subscribe to a religion for other reasons than spiritual growth. Many people simply inherit their parent's religion or subscribe to one doctrine or another to fulfill social needs. The true religious practitioner, however, is looking for a direct experience of God. We only have to look to religious leaders - who teach by example - to know this.

Jesus spent prolonged periods of time fasting and praying in the wilderness and was no stranger to altered states of consciousness or intense hallucinations. The Buddha reportedly sat and meditated under a Bo Tree for seven years until he had a direct experience of Godhead. Previous to this, he had tried scores of other ascetic practices in his search for an experience that was beyond the senses and therefore beyond the ego. The spiritual leader of the Muslims, Mohammed was renowned for his faith in ascetic pursuits, passing down to his followers the practice of regular fasting, one of the most common (and cheapest) ways to alter your mental state and a pre-requisite for becoming a Muslim. Mohammed was also an advocate of all night trancing and is reported to have channeled Islam's holy book, the Koran, during nocturnal trancing sessions. Any raver will readily identify with this excerpt from the Koran:

> *"You that are wrapped up in your mantle, keep vigil all night... It is in the watches of the night that impressions are strongest and words most eloquent; in the day-time you are hard pressed with the affairs of this world."*

- Sura 73.1-8 from the Koran.

For centuries, saints and sages have been using a multitude of techniques to transcend their ordinary states of consciousness. Whether it's fasting, sensory deprivation, fire walking, endless repetition, psychedelic drugs or self-mutilation, the goal is the same: to tap into something bigger than ourselves, rise above our own selfish concerns in the search for inner meaning, and transcend our own consciousness so that we might attain personal contact with God.

Pagan religions also have a long history of ecstatic rituals designed to put practitioners in touch with the divine. In the Dionysian tradition, emotions, fantasies, and even sexual urges are summoned forth and embraced as inherent parts of the self. In the practice of the Dionysian mysteries, the essential unit is not the isolated individual but the group-in-action which manifests its collective energy through throbbing patterns of music and dance. In these shared patterns of rhythmic energy ones ego overlaps with that of others, dissolving the barrier between the individual and the outside world. The Dionysians were also well known for openly using mind-altering substances in traditional, structured rituals aimed at self-growth.

In the end, religion or reverence for a higher power comes down to a state of mind. If we can truly love and identify with our fellow human beings as we do with ourselves, we will automatically take their needs into consideration. Once we come to the realization that at some deeper level we all have the same basic needs and desires, we will be more likely to overlook our superficial cultural differences and learn to live in peace.

In India, a common greeting is "Namaste". It means, "I respect and honour the light within you." It implies that we are looking beyond the superficial details that make up our perception of a person and acknowledging a place of light or clarity that is common to us all - a spiritual place where we are one with ourselves, with others, and ultimately, with God. Most people are familiar with this concept through religion or higher philosophy, but for the majority it remains an abstract idea or theory. For most people, deep and meaningful connections with members of our families and communities remain elusive. The rave experience can actually give us a direct experience of unity with others, achieving the same effect as hundreds of hours of meditation or other spiritual practices. The combination of group trance and ritual dance has been used successfully for hundreds of years as a gateway to God and rave is merely a continuation of this tradition.

"Religion is the sum of the expansive impulses of a being."

- Henry Havelock Ellis, British psychologist, author, 1859-1939.

"Raves are comparable to American Indian religious ceremonies and also the concept of the shaman in Eskimo and Siberian society - where music is the key towards pulling oneself into a unique emotional and psychological state, a state in which one experiences a wash of sensations and visions. The hypnotizing effect of techno music coupled with the seamless transitions and thematic progressions of rave DJs as the night progresses can be quite intoxicating, resulting in what could be closely compared to a religious experience."

-Brian Behlendorf, founder of SFRaves and Hyperreal.com, San Francisco, USA.

"For some people attending a rave is like going to an evangelical church. It's a chance to participate in a deeply emotional experience with people who share your beliefs."

- Nicole Makin, raver, writer, Canada.

"At raves I have had feelings of oneness with everything and a deep sense of calm and warmth."

- Maya Berelowitz, student, raver, Cape Town, South Africa.

"I had an experience at a rave on ecstasy where I was contemplating the idea that a benevolent God exists in a world where babies die and families are destroyed and dogs don't live to be ninety. I couldn't get my head around the injustice of it all. But I came to a realization that maybe my perception of it was too extreme and the truth was somewhere in the middle. I came to peace with the fact that I didn't have to know all the answers and that maybe this was the way it was meant to be. I never had a clear idea of God, but that night I came closer to a better understanding of what God might be."

- Leandre, raver, Victoria, Canada.

"My first complete rave experience changed my life forever. The MDMA experience makes you perceive by a kind of intuition, the real essence of your being. It's not something elaborated by your conscious or unconscious mind, it's something you suddenly realize you know without any doubt. You know the truth because you have experienced it. Now you know that you, me, everything is one, or God as you wish to call it."

- Federico Sommariva, rave promoter, DJ, Milan, Italy.

"Rave culture is like a religion without a God. God is the music."

- Stevan "STeW" Fryd, manager, raver, Budweis, Czech Republic.

"Though I must admit that acid and ecstasy are probably what brought me to understanding God and the intricate nature of our universe, over the years, I've realized that my vulnerability at the time is what brought God closer. What makes you feel like God is there with you is probably what helps you let go of yourself enough to notice he's been there all along."

- Frank Zelaya a.k.a. DJ SoR, Los Angeles, USA.

"I was out partying with my best friends, talking and chilling on the day before Christmas when I suddenly got all quiet and stopped breathing! I had this wonderful experience where I understood it all: why the grass is green and why the sky is blue, the whole package!"

- Veny Veronika Vere, secretary, raver, Oslo, Norway.

"Rave is the worship of music and art, which is the creation of the mind, which is the creation of the creator. Ravers go to church just like anyone else. They just go twelve hours earlier."

- J, The Trip Factory, Saltspring Island, Canada.

"Goa-trance music is closely connected with religion. At a Goa-party you can see a lot of images of Shiva, Buddha, Om, etc. Music is our religion!"

- Stardiver a.k.a. Alex, student, raver, Moscow, Russia.

"The big raves are becoming like a mass communion with thousands of people facing the DJs with their hands in the air."

- Topher, underground rave promoter, BC, Canada.

"Going to the desert parties with Moontribe has definitely been a religious experience for me."

- DJ 608 a.k.a. Michael Angelo, Los Angeles, USA

"My mind is my own church."

- Thomas Paine, American political philosopher, 1737-1809.

CHAPTER 12: THE RAVERS

photo: tristan o'neill

" ...fairies never say 'We feel happy.' What they say is, 'We feel dancey.'"
- J. M. Barrie, from Peter Pan.

12 THE RAVERS

Ravers are an incredibly diverse group.

They are musicians and artists, laymen and lawyers, psychologists and psychonauts, leaders and loafers, dreamers and scammers, students, bus drivers, nurses and nerds. They can be rich or poor, from any social class, ethnic origins or religious background. A raver might be an aging New Age guru or a thirteen-year old school girl.

Even if you have never been directly exposed to rave culture, you will almost certainly have come into contact with a raver or two on a daily basis. They may be serving you behind the counter at the bank or lurking in the halls of justice. They may try and sell you a newspaper, or the Brooklyn Bridge. Or they may turn out to be your cousin or brother or even your grandmother.

This kind of diversity is maintained in part by the fact that for many people raving is a part-time occupation. People are generally attracted to rave culture because of the experience they have at parties. In between events, like Superman's alter ego, Clark Kent, they revert back to their mundane, everyday lives, until the next flyer comes around, miraculously transforming them back into "super raver." This kind of split personality is fairly common among ravers and may account for the fact that the scene has been able to remain underground for as long as it has. Up until quite recently, ravers have been relatively invisible to the public eye. In the last couple of years however, there has been a huge proliferation of full-time ravers and

artwork: virginia smallfry

recognizable rave fashions, making it easier to identify people associated with the scene and giving rave culture a higher public profile. These full-time rave enthusiasts - usually the younger crowd - can now be found hanging out in electronic music stores or dedicated rave cafes and restaurants all over the world. These people represent the heart and soul of the movement. They are the keepers of the buzz about what's hot and what's not. They are a clearinghouse for current information, a word of mouth communication center that can make or break a party or CD release. Dedicated ravers are completely devoted to the music and philosophy of rave culture, which they will fiercely defend in the face of ignorant opposition. As well as maintaining a constant state of readiness for the next party they will also strive to keep the party energy going in between events. Often they will live in shared accommodation with other ravers forming a communal family model. The ubiquitous two turntables and a mixer will invariably be set up at one end of the living room and at any given moment, day or night, someone will be spinning records. Mini house raves can spontaneously erupt at any time and can sometimes continue for days. Or at least until the noise complaints begin to roll in.

photo: jason dyck

The ubiquitous two turntables and a mixer will invariably be set up at one end of the living room and at any given moment, day or night, someone will be spinning records.

Most serious ravers will attend parties on a weekly basis - every Saturday night - and maybe one or two club nights during the week. This can get quite expensive, so unlike the alleged lazy loafers of the so-called generation X, ravers tend to have jobs. The average rave can cost around twenty-five dollars. A dose of ecstasy will cost the same or more. Allow another twenty for

photo: jason dyck

DJ arizOna

transportation and miscellaneous expenses like water, snacks, glow sticks etc., and a night out will cost you seventy-five dollars minimum. If you like to do two hits of ecstasy and go to the club before the party it is very easy to spend over a hundred dollars. This is comparable to a conventional night out with dinner and drinks but at a rave you are far more likely to have an unforgettable experience that will stay with you for forever. Conversely, you are less likely to have revelations that may improve the quality of your life while stuffing your face or drinking booze at the local watering hole. For this reason, raving can be thought of as excellent value for your entertainment dollar.

photo: jason dyck

Raving can be thought of as excellent value for your entertainment dollar.

In the early days, ravers tended to be between 16 and 22 years of age but in recent years the demographics are expanding as more and more older people are discovering the scene. Nigel Tasko from the Alien Mental Association has been promoting raves for the last seven years and has noticed the change. *"A few years ago ravers were more of a fringe group with very little other connections with society at large. Now we have university students, lawyers, rockers, athletes... it's more of a mixed crowd from all areas of society. We are seeing more older people coming to parties but also an increase in the younger crowd. I think that this is a positive trend because it's great to have an environment where all kinds of different people can not only have fun together but can also learn from each other."*

Tim Laughlin of England's Vibe Tribe agrees that the age groups are expanding in both directions. *When I first started going to parties in England it was mostly*

photo: tristan o'neill

younger people from the middle and upper-middle classes, because they had money to go out and party. The age group has gone from 18 to 20 years old, to 16 to 60 years old. So there's more younger people and more older people as the appeal of dance music spreads."

This kind of inclusively is the cornerstone of the rave ethos and what attracts many people to the scene in the first place including West Coast underground promoter, Topher. *"I was attracted to the scene because everyone was welcome. It didn't matter how old you were, or whether you were a punk or a geek. There was no status quo, you could mingle and meet people no matter what you looked like or what scene you came from. Although there is more fashion consciousness now, I think that it's still a very inclusive scene."*

photo: jason dyck

DJ Mis-Chief, a.k.a. Jen Jen from England, records for one of the top hardcore and trancecore music producers in the United Kingdom and has been attending raves since 1990. *"I always thought that it was amazing that this huge cross-section of people who normally wouldn't have anything to do with each other would be dancing side by side and having a great time. You'd see bad boys from Bristol dancing next to hippies and women with their teenage children. There's such a wide cross section of people and ages. I'm a mother of two teenagers myself."*

Even in Brazil everyone is welcome, illustrating that the broad demographics found at raves is truly an international trait. *"Many kinds of people go to raves. There are no rules. We see hippies, cyber-punks, goths, trancers, druggies and clubbers. It doesn't matter who you are. Everyone who loves the music and people who are curious come to raves in Brazil."* says Gil Oliveira Santos, a.k.a. Ravehunter, a Goa trance musician from Sao Paulo, Brazil.

DJ K-Rad a.k.a. Damien (right) with Davin/arizOna (left)

And DJ K-Rad, a.k.a. Damien from Canada has this to add: *"There's more and more people getting involved in the scene now. More mainstream people and outsiders are discovering rave. I think we have to welcome new people just as I was welcomed when I first got involved. I remember the people that were a little bit more patient with me at the beginning and I want to be like that rather than some crusty old raver who doesn't want to make eye contact."*

One thing that ravers do have in common is a spirit of fun and adventure and a willingness to meet and mingle with new people. Ravers are generally a spontaneous, fun-loving bunch open to new experiences. Politically, they are likely to be left leaning, although many ravers shun conventional politics all together and see it as an outdated system that is no longer useful. They prefer instead to deal with political issues on strictly humanistic terms. But although they may shy away from the structure of traditional party politics, ravers do have a strong sense of fair play which dictates that it is far more important how issues directly affect people than whether or not the bottom line is taken care of or even considered at all.

Shortly before his death, Timothy Leary described ravers as high-tech hippies because while they subscribe to the sixties ideals of love and peace, unlike their Luddite sixties counterparts, they are completely at home with new technologies. It is significant that this is the first generation that has grown up with modern computer technology. Unlike previous generations who were either struggling to keep up with the never-ending learning curve or suspicious that machines would eventually take over and ruin the world, this new generation, born into a world of technology, have no such fears. They not only embrace new technologies, but openly celebrate them.

Rather than being pessimistic or cynical about the inherent dangers that come with emerging technologies, ravers only see the endless possibilities for making the world a more interesting and fun place to live. Rave culture and in particular, rave music has helped enormously to build bridges between the once antiseptic, sterile world of science and the humanistic world of tribalism. It's all the same thing to ravers who have a deeper understanding of technology and a realization that it is people who create conflict and not machines, thus relegating technology to the status of a useful tool and nothing more.

It is hardly surprising then, that ravers are generally computer literate and many spend time surfing the net. If you do a search on the word "rave" you will find thousands of web sites, businesses and services that relate directly to rave culture. Apart from flyers and word of mouth, the net is one of the few places to find information on upcoming events. The net is also a great place to find electronic dance music and get information about DJs and producers. There are bulletin boards to post and read messages. There are several sites that offer virtual raving, where people can mingle and meet at a rave that exists only in cyber-space. (See: Recommended reading and web sites.)

People are drawn to raves for different reasons. For some it is a chance to have a great time, let off steam and relieve stress. For others it is the opportunity to have a spiritual or religious experience. Some people are just there for the music and others may just like to mingle and socialize with friends. But whatever brings someone into the rave scene initially, before long they will invariably begin to explore all that rave has to offer. Many will be changed forever by the experience. Though the people who attend raves may have disparate lives, it is the rave experience that draws them together again and again. A rave is an environment where individualism becomes subservient to the expression of the whole community or tribe. For many people this can be a powerful lesson and one that gives ravers their strong sense of bonding as a community and extended family.

Though the people who attend raves may have disparate lives, it is the rave experience that draws them together again and again.

Here are a few comments on what draws people to raves:

"I go to raves because it is a place where I am free to express myself without all the constraints society sets for me. I can smile at the stranger next to me and have them smile back without any strings attached to those good feelings. It is rare that in a world like ours that so many people from all walks of life can come together and experience such unity and acceptance towards each other."

- Maya Berelowitz, student, raver, Cape Town, South Africa.

"I think people go to raves at first because they are curious. We see all kinds of people from different groups and cliques. A lot of the press is bad so people come to see for themselves. We see punk rockers, rappers, white people, black people and children."

- DJ Davie, The Vibe Tribe, Canada.

"I go to raves to reach a feeling of freedom and enlightenment, to dance myself into trance and for at least a short while, forget the feeling of personal impotence at solving any of the major problems that surround me."

- Ferid Abbasher a.k.a. DJ Lord Ferdi the Despiser, Nexus, Indjija, Yugoslavia.

"I go to raves because after the first time my life was changed for the better and now I just have to go because when I'm at a rave I'm having the most fun I've ever had in my life!"

- Dave Waterhouse a.k.a. SkyCriesX, raver, Seattle, USA

"Initially I went to raves for the love of freedom and the lack of convention, but it turned into the love of the music and the feeling of adventure."

- Rich, computer analyst/programmer, raver, London, England.

"Here in Mexico all kinds of people go to raves. From poor men or girls to the more elite people, and everyone comes together and are joined by the music."

- Marco Antonio Pimentel a.k.a. DJ Marcore, Mexico City, Mexico.

"I go to raves strictly for the music. To relax and to become one with the music, WITHOUT any foreign substances."

- Nicole A. Tobias, music major, festival director, raver, New Jersey, USA.

"I go to raves because I really love the music. It gives me butterflies in my stomach and my spirit rises. I have become very fond of moving my body on the dance floor while raving! There does not seem to be any limitations."

- Veny Veronika Vere, secretary, raver, Oslo, Norway.

"I go to raves because of the music, the people, the camaraderie, the connection, the syncronicity, the release and a great time. I love the sense of community and the feeling that you are a part of something worthwhile."

- Leandre, raver, Victoria, Canada.

"At raves in Finland I see 60's hippies, old men, Japanese business tourists, a lot of people in wheelchairs, but of course it's mostly young people from different areas of life. Most of them are well educated."

- DJ Jules Nerve, Helsinki, Finland.

"I go to raves to feel the unity, to be with the people and to communicate with them through dancing."

- Daniel a.k.a. Earthguy, raver, Johannesburg, South Africa.

"People go to raves because they're fun. There's no violence. You can dress up any way you want, do what you want. No one is pointing fingers. If you're gay you're gay, if you're straight you're straight. If you want to do drugs you can, but no one is pushing anything. It's a very open and tolerant environment."

- Surfer Bob, The Vibe Tribe, Canada.

"I go to raves because I feel happy and relaxed with positive and happy people. I love the music too and prefer Goa trance and drum & bass parties. I go to raves in Skopje every weekend."

- Veteroski Goran, raver, Tetovo, Macedonia.

"Going to raves is how I express my humanity and delight in my spirituality."

- Vix, music major, rave promoter, London, England.

"I go to raves because my mind and body needs it. The dance is healing. All negative thoughts and pains disappear. I feel completely in contact with myself. My mind is clear and positive, it feels like I can go anywhere, do anything, I feel like I am at one with myself. And I have never taken the drug ecstasy."

- Fredrik Larsson, electronic musician, Stockholm, Sweden.

"I think everyone can go to raves, everyone who knows what this music is about. Anyone can try it..."

- Marek, student, DJ, Leszno, Poland.

"I go to raves because I love the music, I love the people. I love to go with many friends and meet new friendly people. Rave is my life style. I think rave, I love rave, I compose rave, I make rave sex. "

- Stevan "STeW" Fryd, manager, raver, Budweis, Czech Republic.

Another group of people that can be found at raves are those who come to simply observe. They are often adults who have heard about the rave phenomenon and are curious to see what all the fuss is about. Sometimes they are parents of raving teenagers curious for a first-hand look. They may be indirectly related to the rave scene by some professional connection, or they may even be there in some official capacity such as an undercover police officer or a concerned city counselor on a fact-finding mission. Whatever the reason, at any given party there will be a small percentage of non-participating spectators. Although these visitors are welcomed, unfortunately raving is not a very satisfying spectator sport and casual observers are apt to miss the point altogether. Raving is not something that can be experienced vicariously.

Raving is not something that can be experienced vicariously.

Health conscious ravers are generally in good physical shape. One of the things that has always struck me at raves is how healthy, strong and vibrant everyone looks. The practice of providing smart bars at raves began in California in the early nineties and has since spread throughout the world. Along with providing copious amounts of bottled water - the preferred tipple of ravers - smart bars also serve fresh fruit and vegetable juices with additives such as spirulina, ginseng, gota cola or other herbs with nourishing or energy boosting properties. This trend also carries over to life outside the rave with a significant percentage of ravers choosing to eat a health food or vegetarian diet.

Rave culture and in particular, rave music has helped enormously to build bridges between the once antiseptic, sterile world of science and the humanistic world of tribalism.

An athletic look is the norm and it is rare to see an overweight person at a rave. Even if they start off with a few extra pounds there's nothing like regular, all night, aerobic sessions to fight the flab. But although some regulars may find raving to be all the exercise they need, it is also common for ravers to be involved in some sort of formal exercise program or sport. Many also value the outdoor life and are avid hikers or campers. These types of health orientated activities seem to go hand in hand with rave philosophy. Even if people have less than a healthy life style when they first discover the scene, the chances are that before long, they will find themselves slipping into some spandex or sampling the latest spirulina cocktail.

Like the hippies before them, ravers are prone to question and challenge authority. The source of this friction is often caused by the opposition to loud music and experimentation with drugs. Even though statistically raves cause the least amount of problems for the police than any other type of public gathering, ravers continued to be persecuted and harassed by authorities. Ravers find this constant game of cat and mouse with the police and city hall frustrating, but for the most part are able to maintain a positive attitude towards the problem and rarely become bitter or cynical. Ravers tend to accept opposition as part of the territory and take it in their stride. Even when subjected to extreme harassment, a raver is more likely to shrug it off and walk away than become loud and belligerent. Although it is hard to imagine the rave movement spawning militant or pro-violence groups like The Weathermen or the Black Panthers of the sixties, in recent years we are beginning to see political organizations emerging that specifically address the rights and freedoms of ravers. If opposition to rave culture continues, it is probable we will inevitably see a proliferation of these kinds of groups. (See: The Politics of Rave.)

Openness to new ideas and experiences is another common raver attribute. The rave experience is about taking us beyond our ego-centered reality and expanding the horizons of our consciousness. It is about changing the way we see ourselves and the world around us. In a complex and often confusing world it is all too easy to cling to familiar but out-dated, rigid models and mind-sets. Many of our problems, both personal and social are due to our resistance to new ideas, and it is precisely this inflexibility that prevents us from creating new and more effective paradigms.

Ravers have a willingness to view the world through fresh eyes and are therefore freed from the traps and restraints that come from obsolete patterns of thought. As we develop as human beings, the solutions to many of our most serious and persistent problems, from the environment to economic issues, will come from looking beyond the well-worn paths of the past in an effort to discover new and fresh approaches. Rave culture, with its positive and optimistic attitudes, represents a new generation of free thinkers who have the potential to contribute a great deal to solving the problems of a world in crisis.

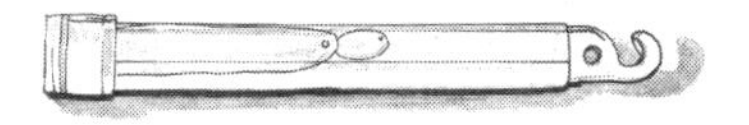

CHAPTER 13: THE PHILOSOPHY OF RAVE

artwork: virginia smallFry

"The philosophy of one century is the common sense of the next."

- Henry Ward Beecher, American clergyman, abolitionist, 1813-1887.

13. The Philosophy of Rave

The basic philosophy of rave culture can be summed up in the acronym PLUR which regularly appears on rave flyers and tickets all over the world and has recently turned up on various clothing products from some of the leading sportswear designers. The letters stand for peace, love, unity and respect. This simple mantra has been widely accepted as the guiding principals of rave culture. To trace the origins we must go back to New York, circa 1991.

Frankie Bones was a DJ from Brooklyn, New York and was the first American DJ to play at one of the London orbital parties held in and around London, England in 1991. When he returned to the US, he was inspired by his experiences in England to produce a series of raves in Brooklyn known as the Storm raves. Although house music had originated in Chicago and Detroit four or five years earlier, up to that point the scene had been developing exclusively in the clubs. The Storm raves are said to be the first full-scale all night rave parties to be held in New York and were responsible for launching the rave scene on the East Coast of America.

The story goes that at one of the Storm raves there were two groups of rival street gangs who were about to start a rumble. Frankie Bones saw trouble brewing, so he brought the music down and got on the microphone to deliver a heart-felt speech pleading for peace, love and unity. The speech ended with the music being turned back up to full volume and a sea of ecstatic ravers waving their hands in the air. The fight was thus averted and the party went on without incident. Another report suggests that the speech was not quite so eloquent and that Frankie had simply shouted out, "I want to see some peace, love and unity here or I'll break your fucking necks!" This account also ends with everyone laughing and the party continuing in high spirits. Whichever account is closer to the facts, the end results were the same and the incident gave birth to an important piece of rave history. Frankie used the phrase, peace, love and unity repeatedly after that and became known as its originator. But it was some time after that the "R" for respect was added.

Laura La Gassa and her husband, Brian Behlendorf of the SFRaves mailing list and the Hyperreal web site had a conversation at a small renegade party in Washington DC in the summer of 1993. Brian suggested that respect should be included and inspired Laura to write a piece for the web site entitled, The Four Pillars of the House Community, a term that she had borrowed from a message posted by Geoff White on the SFRaves site. Geoff was one of the original members of SFRaves and was also active with the San Francisco DJ collective Wicked, famous for their monthly outdoor full moon parties. Laura also gives credit to Rishad Quazi and Dan Philpot, members of the North East Raves mailing list for first using the acronym PLUR. Laura's original essay can still be found at: www.hyperreal.org/raves/spirit/plur/PLUR.html

The doctrine of PLUR has since been embraced by rave culture throughout the world and now forms the philosophical foundation of the global movement. From the freezing fjords of Finland to the baking beaches of Brazil, peace, love, unity and respect have become a potent and positive catch phrase of a new generation.

From the freezing fjords of Finland to the baking beaches of Brazil, peace, love, unity and respect have become a potent and positive catch phrase of a new generation.

Kind Gatherings are a company that produces raves in Toronto, Canada. Last year they staged a party called Sky High at the world trade center. One of the organizers, who goes by the name of Papa Smurf, likes to add an "F" to PLUR making it PLURF. This is in keeping with the Smurf's annoying habit of adding an F to everything, but in terms of rave philosophy it is appropriate, because for ravers having fun is just as important as any high-minded philosophy. In a world where we are valued and rewarded for what we can achieve or acquire, fun has been relegated to the status of a pastime or hobby, something to be pursued in our spare time that does not interfere with more important concerns such as education or employment. But to ravers, fun is an important part of the equation and the pursuit of fun is considered as noble a cause as any. Even in well-established rave organizations or record labels where there may be considerable amounts of money at stake there is a playful element that, rather than slowing down productivity, seems to grease the wheels of industry and actually increase efficiency. This is a lesson that the rest of the business world would do well to learn. Since the industrial revolution we have been taught to separate our lives into business and pleasure. This has resulted in our business activities becoming less pleasurable and our pleasurable activities becoming less productive and therefore less meaningful. Rave culture offers us a refreshing alternative that advocates blurring the lines between work and play and consequently getting more satisfaction from both.

Spontaneity is another trait that can be included in the philosophy of rave culture. Ravers are prone to doing things in an instinctual and casual manner and like water, they will often take the path of least resistance to achieve their goals. This is in stark contrast to the way that business is usually conducted in today's high stress work environment. Rave culture is far more concerned with reducing stress in all areas of daily life, even if it means sacrificing a measure of efficiency. This is not to say that rave promoters will not get stressed out if they have put thousands of dollars into an event that gets rained out or shut down, but it does mean that they are far less likely to develop an ulcer than their Wall Street counterparts.

Rave culture, like so many social revolutions, seeks to expand our personal and collective rights and freedoms and a rave party is the ultimate expression of that ideal.

Many smaller parties are often conceived on the spur of the moment or thrown together at the last minute. Even the larger parties which obviously require a higher level of organization are often approached one stage at a time. Each step of the planning is done with the belief that the following stages will fall into place when the time comes. This kind of faith and trust are rare in the world of conventional business, where every last detail is tested and examined before the first step is taken. This approach is not new and can be directly related back to the here and now philosophies of the mystic traditions later adopted by hippy culture. Indeed, within rave culture you will find many followers of eastern mystic traditions like Zen Buddhism or Taoism. Many ravers also pursue spiritual practices such as yoga or meditation, though nothing is preached or pushed and everyone is free to find their own way.

Freedom is probably the most important philosophical issue for ravers. Freedom to believe what you will. Freedom to dress however you want. Freedom of expression. Freedom of speech and action. Freedom to dance all night long. And the freedom to decide what to put into your own body. Time and again, people will describe their experiences at raves in terms of feeling free. The unrestrained and unfettered climate created by the rave environment is an essential element for a successful party and an important prerequisite of the rave experience. Every revolution in history has demanded the right to freedoms previously denied and each has eventually resulted in attaining a few more freedoms. Rave culture, like so many social revolutions, seeks to expand our personal and collective rights and freedoms and a rave party is the ultimate expression of that ideal.

For ravers, philosophy is not merely an intellectual pursuit to be expounded or debated but something to be experienced directly. Rooted in the heart rather than the head, the philosophy of rave is more about the way we feel rather than what we may think. Ravers talk a lot about the vibe. Parties are judged by their vibe. Music creates the vibe. In many different countries you will find collectives named Vibe Crew or Vibe Tribe and flyers will often urge people to "keep the vibe alive." To ravers, the vibe is a central pivot around which everything revolves. It describes how you feel about yourself and others and comments on a state of emotional well being that is inextricably linked to the surrounding social climate. Not limited solely to the mind-set of the individual, the vibe is about a positive and optimistic group dynamic. The rave party is the vehicle that provides a direct experience of that ideal. The ultimate goal of rave culture is not to isolate this group vibe to secret nocturnal gatherings, but to use the rave as an epicenter from which to spread the positive and powerful vibrations generated at the party out into society at large.

"San Francisco has always had that philosophy of peace and love and I think that the people that were attracted to that part of the scene came to San Francisco. From day one, that was the mission and purpose, to be role models and facilitate that kind of philosophy."

- Gena Womack, founding member of Moontribe, Los Angeles, USA.

"Each individual is responsible for finding and maintaining and giving peace, love, unity, and respect. It isn't just handed to you. It doesn't just magically appear because you've arrived at a rave. You have to find it and generate it for yourself and then give it away to anyone and everyone to jump-start them into generating it. The giving away of it is what makes up the vibe."

- Laura La Gassa, SFRaves, San Francisco, USA.

CHAPTER 14: FASHION

photo: tabatha lee

"Beware so long as you live, of judging people by appearances."

- Jean de la Fontaine, French writer, 1621-1695.

14. FASHION

Like the music, rave fashions are a synthesis of old and new, embracing equally the past, present and future. Rave culture's inclusive tendencies attract people from a wide variety of musical and social backgrounds, so rather than one defining fashion to which everyone subscribes, rave fashions tend to be a lot more diverse. As with music and art, fashions are "sampled" from a wide assortment of influences that have originated in other social circles.

Many people come into the rave scene from the club scene and so bring with them all the glitter and gloss that has been characteristic of night clubs since the golden days of disco. Traditionally places where people gather to engage in public mating rituals, nightclubs reflect a preoccupation with fashions that emphasize celebration and sexual attraction.

Club fashions that have migrated into the rave scene include tight-fitting short dresses with spaghetti straps, "baby doll" dresses, pseudo-metallic material for dresses and shirts, skimpy halter-tops, cut off chemises that display bare midriffs and brightly coloured feather boas. Exaggerated and flamboyant make-up jobs augmented with silver and gold glitter abounds, as do Technicolor and fluorescent hair colours. One of my personal favorites and a common accouterment at larger raves are over-size silver or gold foil eyelashes.

The clubbers, and especially the gay clubbers, have also brought with them a fetishistic element, so it is not unusual to see a little creative leatherwork and a metal stud or two on the dance floor. In the rave scene fetish attire is more likely to be worn in the spirit of fancy dress rather than denoting any real sexual preferences. A friend of mine once noted that at fancy dress parties people tend to dress up as their alter ego or at least something that reflects their own hidden desires. Kurt Vonnegut once said, *"We are who we pretend to be, so be careful who you pretend to be."* This is especially true of the club scene where people are making a conscious effort to impress or influence each other for one reason or another. At a rave superficial social barriers have a tendency to fall away giving people more freedom to be themselves. For this reason, fashion in general is relegated to a lesser status and is exploited more for its fun factor than any serious attempt to impress. The fact is, at a rave you really can get away with wearing anything at all, no matter how flamboyant or outrageous.

One of my personal favorites and a common accouterment at larger raves are over-size silver or gold foil eyelashes.

Many people including a good number of DJ's have migrated to the rave scene by way of hip-hop culture, bringing with them some of the fashions long associated with black American, urban society. Oversized baggy pants and shirts, ski caps, baseball hats and hooded sweatshirts or "hoodies" are now common dress for ravers. The ubiquitous plastic chains, now associated exclusively with rave, also originated from hip-hop culture. Originally made of metal, these mock manacles are now brightly coloured, large link plastic chains, strung from a belt loop to a back pocket. They dangle down to the knee or even lower and

photo: tristan o'neill

have become a common rave accessory with both sexes. Plastic baby building blocks or small plastic toys strung together are also worn as an exclusive rave variation on the plastic chain.

Retro fashions are another common crossover style found in the rave scene. These are clothes that have been recycled from the past and include bell-bottom pants with huge inserts to exaggerate the flare, jet black, tight fitting, slim line pants and tops, and raised heel, platform soled shoes and boots. Retro colours are also coming back in the form of pale, sickly oranges and greens, mustard yellows, muted ochre and washed out browns. Retro hair is chopped and dyed jet black and retro accessories include plastic barrettes for your bangs, shinny black hand bags from the fifties, and clunky, heavy framed, black rimmed or horn rimmed glasses. Piercings and tattoos are popular with a wide range of youth and are ubiquitous but far from exclusive to the rave scene.

artwork: virginia smallfry

Although rave incorporates and encourages many fashions from other cliques, over the past few years some distinct rave styles have emerged that can now be found all around the world. Slim line, tight-fitting "street style," sports wear accented or detailed with stripes are now popular with ravers worldwide. Stripes in general are prevalent and can be seen accenting almost any piece of clothing. Pants may have a thin stripe accenting the outside seam. Tee shirts and tops will frequently have a stripe of colour around the neckline or cuffs, or feature a stripe or two across the chest.

For feet that dance all night, comfortable footwear is essential. Most ravers prefer trainers or running shoes but by far the most popular brand and style, especially in North America, are blue Nike Airwalks with white trim. Nike and their omnipresent "swoop" are by far the undisputed champions of the logo wars. It is common to see the Nike check mark on shirts, pants, hats, or even underwear and socks. But serious ravers disapprove of overt support for big corporations and generally prefer their clothing adorned with anti-advertising in the form of stolen logos. For this reason, you might see less legitimate corporate logos at a rave than many other public events. This visual sampling is known as slamming or byeting. As with flyer art, high profile corporate logos are appropriated and transformed into rave slogans and printed on tee shirts, sweats and baseball caps. The familiar Coca-Cola script becomes the word Ecstasy and the familiar X files logo has the word "files" replaced with "stasy" in the same lettering. I recently saw a tee shirt with an Arm and Hammer baking powder logo. From a distance the logo looked authentic but on closer examination the words Arm and Hammer were replaced with LSD and ecstasy and the slogan below read: *Brand E cleans and deodorizes your mind.* With slamming, the colour, design and text style of the logo remain recognizable, but the message reflects rave culture's playful and irreverent lack of respect for anything that smacks of corporate control. A logo or trademark is a legal statement about ownership and authority that goes against the communal philosophy of rave.

Although rave incorporates and encourages many fashions from other cliques, over the past few years some distinct rave styles have emerged that can now be found all around the world.

One of the defining characteristics of rave culture and a conspicuous influence on its sense of style is the preoccupation with innocence and child-like fun. It is a joyful retreat to childhood and a time when play was the most important thing in our lives, a time free from the responsibilities and concerns of adult life. Children have a playful exuberance which ravers value and seek to emulate. Ravers love to play with children's toys and will even bring teddy bears or other stuffed toys to parties. Although it is usually the younger crowd that are prone to puerile playthings, there is an underlying belief in rave culture that the innocence of youth is not necessarily a trait that needs to be left behind but something that adults can also indulge in and benefit from.

This trend towards infantilism is well represented at any rave. Tee shirts emblazoned with cartoon characters, white Mickey Mouse gloves and people sucking on pacifiers or lollipops are everywhere. Girls with their hair in pigtails may be wearing clear plastic or cuddly animal, mini back packs which provide a convenient place to keep a water bottle, candy, incense, extra clothes, or whatever. Other accessories (or toys) used by both male and females include brightly

photo: jason dyck

coloured plastic or glow beads worn around the wrist or neck, glow sticks, laser pens, flashing bicycle lights and sport whistles. The whistles are used for making noise when the music rises to a dramatic climax or for punctuating musical phrases along the way. In England, whistles are augmented with party horns that serve the same purpose. At first glance, a rave can look more like a kindergarten birthday party than an all night dance event.

A favorite TV show with ravers in England is called Teletubbies which is a children's show designed for a pre-school audience. The show follows the simplistic adventures of a group of alien teddy bears who have televisions in their tummies and spend most of their time giggling and hugging each other in scenes that are endlessly repeated to the delight of four year olds and ravers alike.

Long hair is definitely out for raver guys who typically wear their hair cropped short or shaved off altogether. Girls also wear their hair short and will often use brightly coloured plastic barrettes to tame their bangs. Dye jobs usually favor the more garish end of the spectrum and are likely to include orange, red, purple or even green and blue. Jet black dyes are also very popular for a retro look. But by far the most fashionable hair colour associated with the rave scene for both guys and girls, is bleached white.

At larger more festive raves or special occasion parties such as New Year's Eve or Valentine's Day, many serious, core-group ravers also regularly indulge in full-blown fancy dress. Costumes again tend to reflect the marriage of past and future. Space themes and futuristic costumes are widespread in the form of silver suits, cyborgs, sci-fi characters and alien motifs. While at the other end of the spectrum, representing a more mythical and mystical past, fairies abound. These are one of the more common costumes for female ravers and tend to be the more traditional storybook variety, complete with lacy tutus, gossamer wings and star-tipped magic wands. Other favorite costumes include, stripped "Cat in the Hat" stovepipe hats, fast food uniforms and bright orange construction safety jackets.

Along with the regular rave crowd, there are a number of other kinds of people who might be found on or around the dance floor. Ex-hippies are no strangers to group psychedelic experiences and for many people who were changed forever by the sixties, rave culture is a breath of fresh but familiar air. Hippies are pleasantly surprised by the spirit of openness and group dynamics of the rave experience and take to it readily. These ravers of the past have since assumed a variety of disguises, and depending on their current economic status, can be seen sporting everything from Salvation Army specials to designer yuppy gear to Nordic sportswear. In recent years there has been a resurgence of hippy culture in the form of the rainbow movement, and once again young people can be seen wearing tie-dyed t-shirts, long hair and other hippy fashions of the past. This new generation of hippies find it easy to relate to what is happening in the rave scene and find the transition an easy one to make. If they happen to find the right parties early on, they may soon find themselves cutting their hair and bleaching it white. The fact is, there are many similarities between rave culture and the modern hippy or rainbow movement. In the past few years there have been many crossover events which blend the two groups.

photo: tristan o'neill

Fraser Clarke, a promoter from England, recently organized an event called The Omega Rave in Arizona's Kaibab national forest that welcomed ravers, hippies, new age practitioners, rainbow people and environmentalists. Fraser coined the word Zippies for the attendees in an attempt to unify the group. Other events like the annual Burning Man festival in Nevada's Black Rock desert also represent a move towards a fusion of sub-cultures with similar neo-tribalistic tendencies. Drum circles and pagan rituals are starting to show up at some rave events and electronic dance music may be heard wafting through the air at a rainbow gathering. In the future, we are sure to see a lot more blurring of the boundaries that separate these movements.

In the end, rave is about being yourself and having the freedom to express yourself however you please.

Many ravers will deny that fashion is an integral part of the scene but it is evident for any one who attends a party that some sort of group consensus is taking place. Like any social clique, ravers conform to certain unwritten rules in order to identify and show solidarity with the group, and ravers are certainly more community-minded than most. In most scenes that

photo: tristan o'neill

identify with a specific look, fashions are worn to be judged. They are proof that the wearer is sufficiently knowledgeable and connected to "get it right" and the right look is proof that they are tuned in or in the know. No one is more aware of this than the purveyors of fashionable merchandise who are only just beginning to see the huge potential of marketing to ravers. Dance and clubbing magazines are filling up fast with ads for fashionable clothes and sportswear specifically designed to appeal to the rave crowd. Accessories, from bags and shoes to sunglasses and laser pens are finding their way into full page glossy magazine ads in an attempt to part ravers from their cash. Time will tell whether the efforts of mass marketers will woo the corporate-phobic rave crowd. My guess is that as soon as they catch up with what's happening in the rave scene, it will already have moved on to something else.

Although you will see many of the fashions previously mentioned at any given party almost anywhere in the world, in rave culture you also score points for originality. Rave is far more relaxed about fashion than many other social groups and is far more likely to create and foster a climate of freedom where it is okay to break the rules. Besides, anyone who begins the night with a little fashion consciousness is likely to transcend such trivial concerns by the time the party is in full swing. As people are swept away by the music and ambience they will care less and less about what they or anyone else is wearing. In fact, as things heat up, interest in clothes, and sometimes even the clothes themselves, begin to fall away. It is not uncommon to see both guys and girls stripped down to their underwear on the dance floor.

In the end, rave is about being yourself and having the freedom to express yourself however you please. And this spirit of acceptance and tolerance that is key to the movement dictates that you will not be judged too harshly if you do not have cropped, bleached hair, a string of glow beads or gossamer fairy wings.

photo: trent warlow

CHAPTER 15: THE POLITICS OF RAVING

artwork: virginia smallfry

"The world of politics is always twenty years behind the world of thought."

- John Jay Chapman a.k.a. Johnny Appleseed, American pioneer, 1774-1845.

15. The Politics of Rave

It could be said that rave culture is essentially a revolutionary political movement in that it represents the will of a significant portion of society to organize and gather for the purposes of creating a new community model and that these activities are carried out despite fervent opposition from existing governing bodies. In this sense, rave parties themselves become political acts that demonstrate the united, political will of the participants.

Ravers could also be described as apolitical, in that they do not subscribe to any form of traditional party politics. But even the rejection of politics is a political statement and rather than having a well-developed, formal political manifesto or set of policies, the rave itself becomes a political statement. It is an expression of political will which seeks to show by example that people of disparate social, cultural or religious backgrounds can transcend their trivial differences and truly connect as a global community through the celebration of music and dance. In this way, raves

photo: tristan o'neill

are a public demonstration of mass cohesion and solidarity that goes far beyond the narrow focus and selfish concerns of conventional politics which tend to create more division than unity. A rave makes the political statement that we are all equal, and that no matter how different we may think we are, on a more tribal level, we all have the same basic needs as human beings. In this light, rave culture offers a firm foundation on which to build a new political order which may, in the not so distant future, lead the way to a more humanistic and personal system of government.

In the summer of 1987 in England, a series of raves in and around London called the Summer of Love were the genesis of the rave movement. These illegal parties involved thousands of people meeting at secret locations to dance through the night. Huge convoys of vehicles raced through the English countryside staying one step ahead of the police who were caught off-guard by the sheer numbers and determination of the ravers.

These parties, which represented the birth of the rave movement, became known as the Free Party Movement and began a tradition that continues to this day in various forms around the world. Free parties are a true model of grass roots democracy and one of the few political models that are truly for the people and by the people. There are no entrance fees and everyone involved, from the promoters to the DJs, donates their time, energy and resources without pay. DJ Mis-Chief, a.k.a. Jen Jen, was first introduced to electronic dance music at the free parties. *"I first heard the music at a free party in the south of England in 1990. Free parties were a natural progression from the free festival movement. That was where the people with the energy and positivity went. Two of the main promoters of free parties were Circus Warp from Bristol and D.I.Y. from Nottingham. The music was mostly house, garage and old school and there would be two or three thousand people show up for a weekend. More and more they started to get shut down but there is always a friendly farmer or someone who was into the vibe and willing to take a fine. People would come from all over the country to a clearing in the woods or a disused quarry."*

Rave parties themselves become political acts that demonstrate the united, political will of the participants.

Since the beginning of the movement, ravers have been forced to defend their unconventional actions in the face of relentless opposition from city officials and the police. Because of this, there have been a growing number of organizations and groups over the past few years who are striving to give the rave movement a united political voice while trying to deal with some of the issues that affect everyone involved.

Information groups like Ravedata from Boston, Massachusetts are forming in countries all over the world to increase awareness of rave culture and to provide useful information to ravers and non-ravers alike. These groups provide a focus for ravers to examine the scene in which they are involved and open lines of communication to other groups including the authorities. Harm reduction groups are another kind of political rave organization that is becoming a common presence at parties. These organizations are involved in educating people about safe sex and drug use in order to reduce the impact of the potential problems associated within the scene.

Since the beginning of the movement, ravers have been forced to defend their unconventional actions in the face of relentless opposition from city officials and the police.

Kim Stanford is a registered nurse with a background in street nursing and many years experience as an AIDS outreach worker. Since April of 1995 she has been staffing information tables at raves and heading up The Toronto Raver Information Project. T.R.I.P. is an organization whose goal is to provide a safer rave scene in Toronto, Canada by giving out information on drugs and sexuality to help people make informed and considered decisions. They are also equipped to administer emergency first aid and crisis counseling when necessary and hand out free condoms and information flyers. Kim explains T.R.I.P.'s approach: *"Our approach to safer drug use and safer sex is known as harm reduction, which started in the 1950's with methadone maintenance treatments for addicts. As a public health approach it has been growing since the advent of HIV and now it's branching off into other areas. We talk to people about the drugs they are doing in the rave scene, the reasons they are doing them and the possible negative effects. We encourage people to take breaks regularly if they are doing amphetamine-based drugs and to drink water to prevent dehydration. We teach people to party with friends so they can look after each other and give people advice on how to know what drugs they are buying."*

T.R.I.P. was founded in 1995 by Ken Quale who later founded a similar organization on the West Coast of Canada called MindBodyLove that does the same kind of work for the Vancouver rave scene. The organization is mostly funded by The City of Toronto with additional support from The Queen West Community Health Center and now has a core group of around twenty-five volunteers who first attend a series of workshops to prepare themselves with the necessary knowledge and skills. Kim requires that volunteers are ravers because they are already part of the rave community and are committed to the scene. Another important trait that ravers possess more commonly than members of the general public is their ability and willingness to stay up all night.

One of the biggest problems and potential dangers in the rave scene is the quality of drugs available. Many of the drugs that people are buying at raves are adulterated with cheaper substances to extend them and therefore increase profit margins. Unofficial testing has proven that most of the substances used to cut MDMA have similar effects, such as MDA or ephedrine and although there have been rumors of harmful or even deadly additives, this has never been substantiated. I asked Kim Stanford about a recent rumor that claimed broken glass was being mixed with ecstasy. *"I think the rumors about ecstasy being sold with ground up glass in it probably come from the fact that there are kinds of meth-amphetamine called glass or ice because they have a sparkle like glass, but I think that someone just heard about that and got it mixed up. It would be an awful lot of work to grind up broken glass that small and fine."*

Although so far there have been no deadly additives proven, with no way of telling what you are buying, it seem likely that it is only a question of time before we see some serious casualties. One of the hopes of T.R.I.P. is to provide drug-testing facilities at parties. This is already being done in Amsterdam where some drug testing stations are now available to ravers and other recreational drug users. There are also portable drug testing kits that can be bought in Amsterdam and similar kits are now being made and sold by the Green Party of Great Britain (See: Ecstasy Buying Tips). Kim believes that these kinds of kits are an important tool for harm reduction. But to get an accurate reading of which drugs are present and in what dosages requires an expensive piece of equipment called a spectral analysis machine. There is only one such machine in Toronto and it is owned and operated by the police. Kim has been trying for some time to get access to it but the politics of drug policies are proving to be a major hindrance. "*The majority of politicians and policy makers are really reticent to advocate funding for harm reduction drug testing. The prevailing attitude among the*

photo: jason dyck

general public is that if you choose to take a drug then you live (or sometimes die) with the consequences. The problem is, the only spectral analysis machine in Toronto is owned by the police. We have met with them and they have told us that they are willing to test samples but they couldn't guarantee that who ever brought in the samples wouldn't be arrested for possession. We were also advised that if we take ecstasy from ravers, shave a bit off to test, and hand it back, we are technically trafficking."

RaveSafe is another example of the many harm reduction groups that are organizing worldwide. Their mandate includes the research, production and distribution of drug harm reduction information as well as promoting safe raving practices in Cape Town, Johannesburg, Port Elizabeth and Durban in South Africa. Founded in 1993, RaveSafe is a volunteer organization modeled on similar harm reduction groups in Europe. They believe that each individual has the right to accurate and honest information about drugs and their effects in order to make informed decisions about their own lives and health.

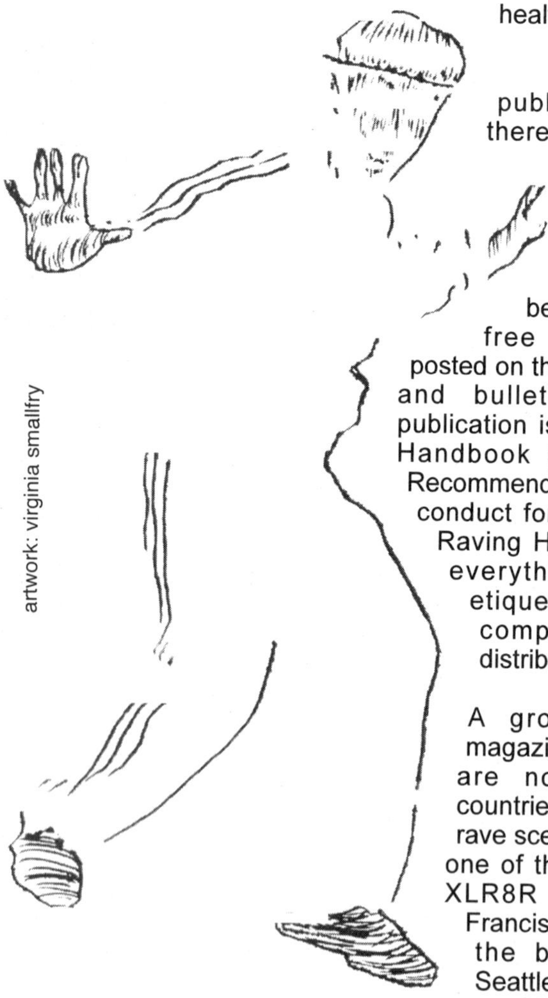

artwork: virginia smallfry

As well as literature being published by various groups, there are a growing number of pamphlets and flyers being produced by the ravers themselves about all aspects of the rave scene. This information is being created and distributed free of charge at parties or posted on the net on personal web sites and bulletin boards. One such publication is The Responsible Raving Handbook by Kirk Cameron (See: Recommended Web Sites.) A code of conduct for ravers, The Responsible Raving Handbook offers advice on everything from dance floor etiquette to dealing with noise complaints and has been distributed widely in the US.

A growing number of rave magazines and other publications are now available in many countries which have a developed rave scene. One of the first and still one of the most comprehensive is XLR8R magazine out of San Francisco. Andrew Smith founded the bi-monthly magazine in Seattle in 1991. Smith had been working at the University of

Washington Daily newspaper when he got involved in the rave scene and saw the need to document what was happening. In 1993, he used his credit card to put out the first twelve-page issue. With the first few issues successfully off the press he partnered up with Andrew Rawnsley and today the magazine has a well-earned reputation as one of the best electronic culture publications in North America. Andrew Rawnsley graduated in 1986 from Middlesex University, England, where he majored in electronic music. I asked him about the approach of the magazine. *"One of the things we try and do with the magazine is present an honest, real assessment of what's going on in the face of sensationalist TV reporting and so on."*

Magazines like XLR8R are now being published around the world, providing a voice for rave culture and a forum where people can share information about the scene. There are scores of rave publications in North America today and a growing number of international publications including, Hype (Australia), The Vibe (South Africa), ReMix (New Zealand), No Limits (Israel), Machina (Poland), Tutti-frutti (Italy), Dream (UK), Raveline Magazine (Germany) and Mix Mag (US and UK).

Another form of political event that is becoming increasingly prevalent worldwide is the protest party. These are events that seek to bring public awareness to rave issues by openly defying laws that are felt to be unfair. The protests take the form of raves that are staged without warning in public places such as city centers and public parks. Last year in Oxford, England a demonstration/party was held in the busy Cowley Road area. A sound system and lights were set up and over a thousand ravers danced in the street. Police arrived to break up the party but eventually had to give up. A similar protest was staged the same year in downtown Sydney, Australia and drew a crowd of more than three thousand. The Australian police were also powerless to deal with the situation and in the end, could only wait for the party to wind down in its own good time.

A protest party in England, organized by a group called Reclaim the Streets, involved blocking the M41, a major highway. A truckload of sand was dumped in the middle of the highway making a giant sandpit for a crowd of children to play in. The sandpit was then surrounded by a throng of six hundred ravers who danced to techno music. These acts of disobedience sparked a series of similar protest parties around the world including major events in The Netherlands, Hungary and Finland. The flurry of political activity culminated in 1998 with a global protest called the International

Street Party, which consisted of protest parties staged simultaneously in over twenty major cities around the world.

B-SIDE, a non-profit society in Canada, is dedicated to free parties and political demonstrations and regularly stage protest events in front of the public library in downtown Vancouver. The events are called Make Friends Not War (A Rave for Peace) and represent a collective of rave organizations including MindBodyLove, Alchemist Productions and Bee Tribe. Make Friends Not War began on a sunny Sunday afternoon in the wake of the Gulf conflict and has been running every Sunday ever since.

The objectives of B-SIDE are representative of many like-minded organizations throughout the world. This is a mission statement taken from their website:*"To inform, organize, represent and support the Vancouver rave community, as well as inform, cooperate with and contribute to the rest of the local community. B-SIDE intends to encourage participants in rave culture to play a more active and responsible role in their communities. B-SIDE also intends to create awareness of the healthy and positive influence of the music, activities and synergy of rave culture, thereby dispelling the myths and stereotypes about the rave community which have been the cause of negative media attention and discrimination."*

No matter how fierce the opposition may be, no matter how stringent the laws become, ravers always seem to find a way to exercise their right to engage in the modern tribal ritual of rave.

Groups like the Right to Dance Movement in California, another promoter of protest parties, are springing up all over North America and around the world as ravers organize to demand the right to rave. In many places like Holland and Canada, these organizations are tolerated and take their place among the political landscape like any other civil rights group. In other places like America and Britain, there is considerable opposition to rave culture. But no matter how fierce the opposition may be, no matter how stringent the laws become, ravers always seem to find a way to exercise their right to engage in the modern tribal ritual of rave.

Israel, famous for its harsh treatment of ravers and zero tolerance of drugs, has recently gone all out on a war against ravers and in particular, the followers of Goa trance music. Some Israeli politicians have gone as far as to call Goa trance the Devil's music in an all too familiar replay of the rock-and-roll paranoia of the fifties. One Israeli minister ranted on television, warning parents against the evil influence of Goa itself. This caused some parents to travel to India to save their poor children from the clutches of the evil spirits that forced them to stay in the tropical paradise. The United Kingdom's legendary trance pioneers, Return to the Source, tried to stage a party in Israel last year that was shut down by the police within the first hour. In 1998, Israeli immigration officers interrogated and deported Juno Reactor, a trance group who were in Israel for a party that had pre-sold five thousand tickets. They were arrested without cause at the airport, thrown into jail and deported the next day. This followed a similar incident where Serge Souque of the French trance group, Total Eclipse, was also thrown in jail with no formal charges. The last time DJ Mark Allen played in Israel, the fully licensed club got raided by police looking for drugs. They found none, but did manage to confiscate some antibiotics. When politicians were questioned as to the motives of the raids and arrests it was claimed that arrests were made at the request of the Israeli Musicians Union who were concerned that visiting musicians were scooping more than their fair share of the work. The musicians union however, denied making any such statements and other kinds of musicians have been entering the country with no problems. These incidents and others like them have prompted the Israeli ravers to form their own political group called The Israeli Freedom to Party Organization.

To demonstrate their commitment to making a positive impact on society, raves are being used more and more as the tools of social change, bringing awareness to a wide variety of social issues.

In Britain, there has been a decade long war between the government and the rave community. Amendments to the Criminal Justice Act in November 1994 created a national law that effectively outlawed raves and similar gatherings. In 1997, Tory MP Barry Legge promoted a bill that would give local councils and the police the power to shut down any club where there was evidence that drugs were being sold or used. Barry cited that "evidence" could mean providing free drinking water, the promotion of drug awareness information or the presence of harm reduction groups. It is no coincidence that the bill appeared in an election year.

Matt from Sunnyside Posse, a promoter and photographer involved in the free party movement in England was also politically active in the campaign against the amendments to Britain's Criminal Justice Bill that brought a whole slew of changes specifically designed to prosecute rave

The Love Parade has become the biggest cultural event in Europe and in 1999 attracted well over a million people.

club owners and rave promoters. Matt organized marches and protest parties to bring awareness to the issue and was also a leader in the Reclaim the Streets movement that regularly stage public raves in the streets of London. Although primarily a political rave organization, Reclaim the Streets also brings awareness to environmental issues.

One such protest against The Criminal Justice Bill was held in Hyde Park in the heart of London. An estimated five thousand people filled the park and neighbouring streets, dancing to electronic music pumping out of a huge sound system. Eventually the police rushed into the park on horseback to break up the event but things did not go as planned. As the police charged they were met with a hail of bottles and sticks and were forced back outside the park. Hundreds of police officers in riot gear surrounded the area and waited as the party continued. Inside the park, a carnival atmosphere prevailed as fire-eaters and jugglers performed, poets ranted through megaphones and a crowd of thousands danced to electronic tribal rhythms.

Unfortunately the protest did little to change the outcome of the amended bill which went ahead regardless. One of the first casualties of the crack down was Megatripolis, a well-established rave night at a London gay club called Heaven. Here is the public notice that was posted on their web site shortly after Megatripolis was shut down:

"We communicate this live from our beloved club in London as a transmission of truth, intent, and clarification. On behalf of those who have worked so hard and achieved so much here. There is a quest of change blowing across the United Kingdom. This is from those who demand change, the key word in any understanding of the people who generate Megatripolis is the simple word 'liberty'. Throughout our brief life, through many changes and vicissitudes, Megatripolis and its people stand for liberty. We intensely dislike and react non-violently against all attempts to dictate opinion. We believe profoundly in the freedom of the spirit and the liberty of mankind to work out his own salvation and to be himself in his own way. We demand for ourselves the freedom to follow our own stars and we stand out for a like liberty for all mankind. We are being asked here in Britain, the most independent of lands, to give up being free. We are here working for our freedom. We are here because we must find freedom for our native peoples first. We are those who are real. Love. Magic. Freedom."

- Megatripolis, London, September 29th 1994.

It seems amazing that in spite of every effort to inhibit the rave scene in England and in other countries around the world, it continues to grow and thrive. This is a testament to the spirit, fortitude and determination of the ravers themselves and a hand full of officials that have lent a hand along the way. One such sympathizer, Lorna Cohen, is a councilor in Leeds, England and is known to her constituents as the "Raving Granny". Cohen is in her sixties and not only embraces the rave scene but actively promotes it. When the City of Leeds decided to celebrate their centenary with twenty four hours of entertainment in the city center, Cohen sent a note to all the dance clubs in town encouraging them to apply for a 6 a.m. license. Cohen also believes that the rave scene provides a lot of good business for the city with many spin off benefits like record companies and fashion sales. Consequently, Leeds has the most vibrant rave scene in the United Kingdom. It also has one of the best safety records.

photo: jason dyck

Unfortunately, most cities do not share Lorna Cohen's enthusiasm for rave culture. In the City of Milwaukee, a vigorously enforced anti-rave ordinance has been on the books ever since the grave fiasco of 1992 when nine hundred and fifty ravers were arrested without cause. Drug Enforcement Agency investigations are said to have played a role in scores of busted parties in the Eastern US between 1994 and 1995. Chicago police in particular have been responsible for a number of brutal shutdowns in the last few years and in the Baltimore and Washington DC area there is now an official anti-rave task force. Even the City of Stockholm in Sweden has appointed a special police force to deal with rave parties called the "ravekommissionen."

But as mainstream society's resistance to rave culture increases, the rave movement itself responds with increased political will and awareness. And to demonstrate their commitment to making a positive impact on society, raves are being used more and more as the tools of social change, bringing awareness to a wide variety of social issues.

In recent years, rave culture has developed a keen social conscience and we are seeing a marked increase in events designed to bring awareness and raise money for community groups of all types. A party called Rave for Choice recently donated its proceeds to local abortion clinics and a national pro-choice women's group. In Boulder, Colorado, Rave for the Rain Forest raised money for a number of ecological organizations. A group called Raves To Benefit Aids has raised over $75,000 to date by staging parties in Detroit and New York and a San Francisco rave called Unleash The Queen was specifically designed to raise awareness of homophobia. Events like these are now taking place worldwide and are a good example of rave culture's commitment to creating a healthy community.

One of the most impressive public displays of the solidarity that exists in the world scene is The Love Parade, an annual event held in the city center of Berlin, Germany. Started by Dr. DJ Motte in 1989, the first parade attracted 150 people who marched through downtown Berlin behind a VW bus pumping out techno music. From its conception the march was to stand for peace, love and pancakes, a German expression which DJ Dr. Motte explains like this. *"Peace stands for disarmament, Love stands for better understanding between people through music and Pancakes for the fair distribution of food throughout the world."*

The Love Parade has since become the biggest cultural event in Europe and in 1998 attracted well over a million people. That's a lot of people (and a lot of pancakes.) If we consider the number of cities worldwide that are staging raves almost every Saturday night, and the fact that those parties are attended by anywhere from two hundred to twenty thousand people, it doesn't take a mathematician to figure out that there is an enormous universal, popular support for rave culture.

Earthdance is another global event that grows bigger each year. This is an international event organized by a global collective of party promoters whose aim is to promote world peace and the freedom of the Tibetan people. The concept is to create a global dance floor by simultaneously staging parties in twenty-five countries around the world. At the climax of the event at 12 a.m. GMT, every DJ in every country will play a specially created track for world peace at the same time. Conceived by Return to the Source producer and Medicine Drum member Chris Deckker, this groundbreaking event is a powerful testament to the commitment and dedication of ravers worldwide to help create a better world to live in.

Considering the long history of opposition and hostility towards the rave movement, it is a wonder that the culture exists at all. But are ravers really that much of a threat to the moral standards of a society rife with consumerism, poverty and violence? Is it really so unacceptable to elevate one's mood and dance to electronic music in large groups? Is the moral majority just not ready for peace, love, unity and respect?

Apart from a little recreational and mostly responsible drug use, ravers are not inclined towards any other kind of criminal behavior. In fact raves have a universal reputation for being peaceful events. Reports of violence, accidents and other problems usually associated with large gatherings are almost unheard of. But in spite of this, police and lawmakers are engaged in a disturbing trend to persecute ravers while condoning sporting events, rock concerts and other events attended by large crowds that create many more problems with violence and drugs (mainly alcohol) than any rave event.

With the tremendous number of people now involved in the global rave scene and as ravers become more involved and active in the political arena, it is only a question of time before we begin to see ravers elected to public office. When that happens, we will hopefully see a move towards a more tolerant and understanding attitude towards what we must now accept as one of the most significant cultural movements of the twentieth century.

"The unity of freedom has never relied on uniformity of opinion."

- John Fitzgerald Kennedy, 35th president of the US, 1917-1963.

"There are some sustainable values emerged as a reaction to intrusions by the law of a State into personal freedoms in areas such as homosexuality and drugs. This adversity, created through intolerance, is what defines rave; it is about overcoming the adversity, about being free, and about allowing others to be free too."

- Norman NG a.k.a. Nomskii, rave promoter, writer, Singapore.

"I had a conversation with a police officer outside a rave club and he said that I seemed normal so what would I be doing hanging around these people. I assured him that these people were my friends and that they were normal too and it's not necessarily abnormal to want to dance all night."

- Anne Marie, raver, nurse, Victoria, Canada.

"Since the war ended, raves are restricted to discotheques. There are no problems, sometimes parties go on for 2 or 3 days with no police trouble. Every party is allowed, none are forbidden."

- Petar Mimica, student, raver, Mimice, Croatia.

"The law tends to stay out of it in New Zealand. The only problems we've really encountered are noise control."

- Olivia, DJ, trader, Auckland, New Zealand.

"America is not very open to information on harm reduction or responsible drug taking. Any organization that has that kind of a mandate will immediately come under attack. Just the idea of anything pro-drugs is really hard to get across."

- Dennis Barton, Skylab200, Los Angeles, USA.

"Raves are well accepted in Austria because there is almost no violence. I, for my part, have never seen any fights at raves. Moreover, the system of security provided by the organizers of raves is very efficient."

- Sebastian Zillinger, soldier, raver,
Amstetten, Austria.

"At first the Law prohibited raves, but not for long and not every party. Since there have been no bad incidents at raves, nowadays we don't have to have any special permission from the law."

- Mladen Alajbeg, electrical engineer,
DJ, Trogir, Croatia.

"One gram of hash is a "big amount of narcotic stuff." We have terrible laws up here. The police are a fully corrupted organization and the clubs are controlled by the Mafia. The only good places are gay clubs."

- Oleg Ilyushin a.k.a. DJ Vint, Moscow, Russia.

"Eventually they shut the party down for not having a business license. So now you have a couple of thousand kids on the street, no buses running and you cause a much bigger problem than the party itself. People should be grateful that we can provide a safe location for their kids to party. The City wants kids off the street and they want them to have somewhere to go and stay out of trouble. They don't want them to drink alcohol but they are not giving them any alternatives."

- JC, rave promoter, Sideline Productions, Canada.

"In the beginning there was a lot of trouble with the police because of drugs and all that stuff. But now we don't have much trouble. Now the authorities understand more about raves."

- Marco Antonio Pimentel a.k.a. DJ Marcore,
Mexico City, Mexico.

"I don't like the fact that the police walk in and claim that promoters didn't get certain permits, then a week later, when a different group is in there for another type of event with just as many people, they don't get bothered."

- Nicole A. Tobias, music major, festival director,
raver, New Jersey, USA.

"The cops have been quiet until recently, about one year back, they got a new chief and started raiding raves. Nowadays the newspapers work with the police in order to destroy the culture. But they will never succeed. One day we will be the cops and the law makers."

- Janne Leino, raver, Helsinki, Finland.

"We aren't just a bunch of screwed-up kids out to do drugs all night. There are a lot of us who go sober to parties. We are just there to enjoy the music and dance and groove to the beats."

- Alison Maria Clemens, raver, Michigan, USA.

"A lot of Israeli ravers came to Goa and stayed because they didn't want to do their mandatory army service and the Israeli government was putting pressure on the Indian government to eject all Israeli citizens from Goa. The Indian government responded by shutting down the parties and in '94 there were almost no parties at all in Goa and the parties that did happen had to close by three a.m. The police were also searching everyone's houses for drugs. By '95 they eased up and the scene started up again."

- Chika, Solstice DJ, Tokyo, Japan.

"The problems with the authorities stem from the fact that there is no dialogue. They really don't know what's going on because we don't tell them and they don't ask. Ignorance breeds contempt and this creates conflict."

- Leandre, raver, Victoria, Canada.

"I've been involved in the fight against the radioactive waste dump in Ward Valley near the Arizona border. I've been on demonstrations, signed petitions and played a benefit to try and prevent nuclear waste being dumped in the desert."

- Daniel, Moontribe DJ, Los Angeles, USA.

"People are starting to realize that we're not just about taking "E" and "spacing out." We're about being loving, living life, and understanding."

- Katherine Wheatley, raver, Melbourne, Australia.

"The by-laws in Toronto were recently changed so that the police could shut down parties without contacting the fire marshal if they thought that the venue was not up to fire code. Previous to this, the police needed to check with the fire marshal before they could act. Since then, the police have been shutting parties down and they have mostly moved back into legal venues."

- Kim Stanford, The Toronto Information Project, Canada.

"The feeling is like, if you are a raver you are a suspect."

- Fredrik Larsson, electronic musician, Stockholm, Sweden.

"In San Francisco there is not much tolerance for unpermitted, underground parties. We have had equipment confiscated and parties shut down. With city permit fees being so exorbitant in the larger cities, it's nearly impossible for someone to consider throwing a cheap, small party."

- DJ Drenalin, Salinas, California, USA.

"The situation could be worse, though on the other hand, you don't see many illegal warehouse parties in Finland these days. The local tabloids are trying to create rave and drug hysteria from time to time, of course, but in general we don't have anything like the Criminal Justice Bill in Britain. Fortunately it's still pretty liberal here."

- Erkki Rautio a.k.a. pHinn, DJ, web master of pHinnWeb, Tampere, Finland.

"For the first couple of years in Los Angeles we never had a problem with parties getting shut down until '92 when the fire marshal's sixteen year old daughter was discovered at a rave, high on ecstasy. Then they started to crack down and there started to be some problems."

- Gena Womack, founding member of The Moontribe Collective, USA.

"Russia is a police country! Now there is a law: if police find drugs at a club, the club will be closed. But it's not a problem if the club is supervised by criminals. Open-air parties after 23:00 are also forbidden! But it's possible to make a big open-air rave in afternoon. In July we had a rave with 55, 000 people!"

- Stardiver a.k.a. Alex, student, raver, Moscow, Russia.

"I think that the average raver is pretty educated in the political scene. Because it's a persecuted, underground movement we tend to bemoan the injustice of it all and become more informed as to why city hall does this or why the police do that. Also, a lot of ravers have traveled and experienced other political systems and can see what's working and what's not."

- Leandre, raver, Victoria, Canada.

"In all the parties I've done, I've hardly ever had any real problems with drugs or violence or anything else. In twenty-five parties, there have only been a couple of minor incidents. I ran an after-hours club for a year and only had to call the police twice. A police officer told me one night that raves were by far the least amount of problems for the police."

- Nigel Tasko, rave promoter, Noble House, The Alien Mental Association, Canada.

"In eight years of going to raves at least once a week, I have never seen any violence. Raves are much safer than a bar."

- Wayne Grimwood, raver, underground promoter, England.

photo: tristan o'neill

"Toronto has screwed most warehouse parties in the last year by rigidly enforcing fire codes, necessitating either clubs for smaller gatherings or large expensive legal venues, putting the existing money-oriented groups in the driver's seat. Ottawa actually organized an anti-rave task force about two years ago. I had my SMURF booth at a party and was giving out lots of toys and treats. Twenty-six cops showed up with video cameras and poked and prodded everything. The house lights had been put on when they came in which noticeably dimmed the vibe, but I was so proud of the kids 'cause they kept on dancing."

- Pappa Smurf, rave promoter, Kind Gatherings, Toronto, Canada.

"There are no big problems with the police in the Czech Republic. We can have free festivals and street parties. Of course, there are always cops, but there is no paranoia and no one arrests you for playing your music and you can do what you want at a party! There are cops, but they just stand there and watch people selling drugs to each other and are glad that they are not attacked."

- Tomá1 Rádl, writer, web designer, raver, Praha, Czech Republic.

"In Tokyo we had a three thousand people party in a field and in the morning everyone picked up their garbage and left the site relatively clean. Two months later there was a rock music festival and the next morning there was garbage as far as you could see. That is the difference in consciousness between the rave scene and the rock scene."

- Chika, Solstice DJ, Tokyo, Japan.

"The beauty of an underground party is that you only tell the people you want to come. Basically with an underground or illegal party you are free to do what you want. But it's a trust issue. You trust the people who are organizing the party, you trust the DJ to do his job, you trust that the right kind of people will be there. But in a free country, how can it be illegal to have a party? I think all parties are legal and it's the authorities who are confused about the law."

- Surfer Bob, The Vibe Tribe, Canada.

"There are no problems with the law and club culture in Yugoslavia. Actually, some of the biggest parties like Enlightenment, The Prodigy or Teknosys were supported by the police and there have never been any incidents."

- Marko Vajagic a.k.a. DJ Mark Wee, architect,
Belgrade, Yugoslavia.

"It's time that the police and the city councils started working with promoters to ensure that the venues are safe."

- Nigel Tasko, rave promoter, Noble House, The Alien Mental Association, Canada.

"I'm not a big fan of political activism because ostensibly the rave movement operates outside of the existing political system so to go back into that system to change it is a non-sequitor. It's like when people try and play by the rules and get all the right permits and try to do everything legally and then still get shut down. It happens a lot. I think that the politics of rave operate outside of the mainstream and acts as an antithesis to political demonstration."

- Andrew Rawnsley, musician, DJ, Editor of XLR8R magazine, San Francisco, USA.

"The law is very strict in Austria. No drugs are permitted. Under cover police are at all the parties but they try to catch the dealers and not the users."

- Stargate Group, rave promoters, Vienna, Austria.

"Here we are, listening to music and doing what we do. Give us an environment where we can do it in a responsible manner and let us enjoy ourselves."

- Troy Roberts, DJ, Platinum Records, Seattle, USA.

"We have problems with the police in Macedonia and the reason is drugs. In the beginning we had more problems with the law, but now it is getting better. I'm sad because the police shut down the two best parties last year."

- Veteroski Goran, raver, Tetovo, Macedonia.

"You can't have a revolution without oppression."

- Ian Hunter, political activist, Canada.

"The prestige of the government has undoubtedly been lowered considerably by the prohibition laws. Nothing is more destructive of respect for the government and the law of the land than passing laws which cannot be enforced."

- Albert Einstein, physicist, philosopher, Nobel laureate. 1879-1955.

CHAPTER 16:

RAVING AROUND THE WORLD

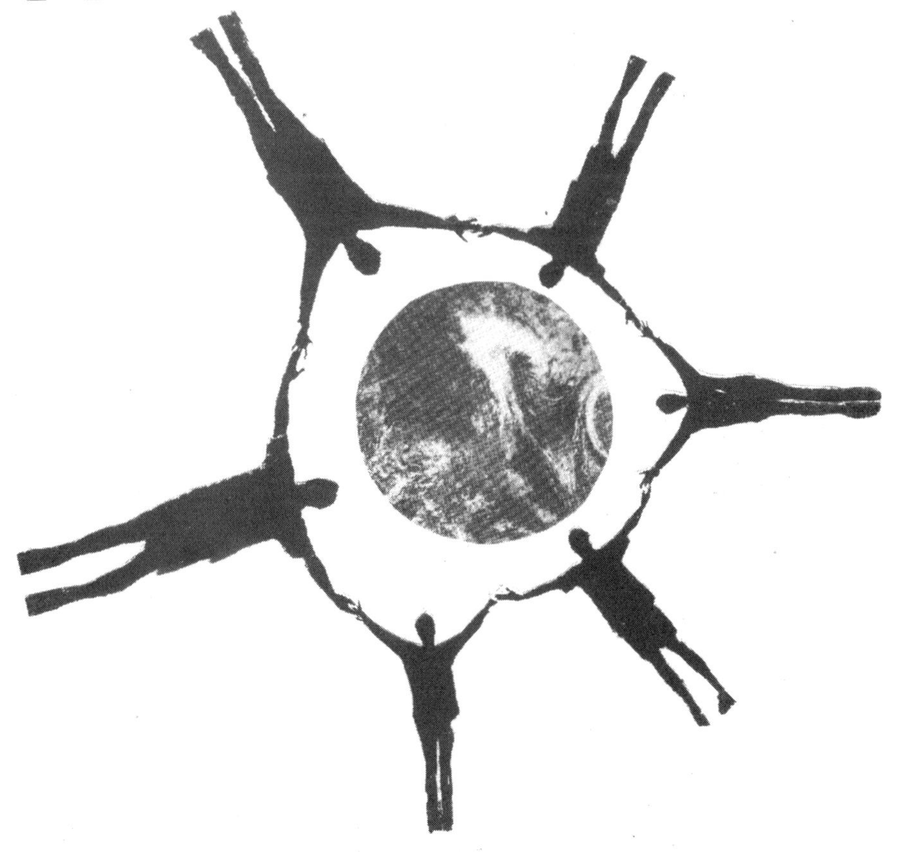

artwork: virginia smallfry

"Borders don't mean anything. DJ's are on the road every weekend. Not just in Europe but the whole world. The Internet is helping us to be connected with ravers all over the world."

- Mladen Alajbeg, DJ, electrical engineer, Trogir, Croatia.

The phenomenal growth of rave culture throughout the world over the past decade has been astounding, proving that regardless of cultural conditions or bias, the appeal of rave is truly universal. Here is a summary of what's happening in various countries around the planet...

Argentina

Next to Brazil, Argentina is the rave capitol of South America. In recent years, Buenos Aires has become famous for large, well-organized parties that retain a strong tribal focus. There are big production parties every weekend and lots of club events to choose from. This year in Buenos Aires, 12,000 people attended The Ultimate Rave '98 featuring five dance floors, dozens of DJs and several live acts.

Australia

With a reputation for having a good time, it is no wonder that Australia has embraced raving with open arms. Well-developed rave scenes are now established in Melbourne, Brisbane, Perth, Canberra, Adelaide, The Northern Territories, Tasmania, Newcastle and New South Wales on the north coast. Large parties attracting many thousands of people are the norm and most large cities have a vibrant club scene. This year marks the sixth year anniversary of Earthcore, a huge, three-day event billed as Australia's ultimate outdoor adventure dance event.

"More and more party crews are starting up. Today we have about four or five big production crews doing big parties for between 2,000 and 8,000 people. That's a long way from the 100 to 300 people parties of 1989-91."

- Brewster B., Weird World Recordings, Melbourne, Australia.

Austria

Austrians have been raving for about ten years already and the scene is still growing today. The Stargate Group, along with Danube Raves and Gazometer are the three main rave organizers in the country producing regular events that cater to the estimated 20,000 ravers in and around Vienna.

"Austria's scene is rapidly growing. Concerning different styles of music, in Linz and Vienna new genres of raves are invented. Many organizers of raves discover overwhelming locations like old gas-towers, industrial areas, ships, airports or subway-stations."

- Sebastian Zillinger, soldier, raver, Amstetten, Austria.

Belgium

The rave scene in Belgium has been well established since the late eighties and has become one of the strongholds of gabba techno. Antwerp has a thriving party scene that regularly attracts crowds of up to 20,000 and is also home to many well-established clubs such as La Rocca, Fuse, Boccaccio, Cafe D'Anvers & 55. Today in Belgium there is also a small hardcore scene filtering across the border from Holland and a variety of smaller scenes into speed garage and drum and bass.

"I discovered the dance scene in 1989, when "new beat" was born in Belgium. Clubs like Boccaccio and 55 seemed like heaven to me! The atmosphere was great! I organized my first night in January 1993 which was still one of the best parties ever!"

- Nico Claes, rave promoter, Antwerp, Belgium.

Brazil

As a country famous for wild parties, it is no surprise that Brazilians have taken to rave culture. Like Goa in India, Brazil is famous for its huge beach raves that started on the coastline south of Sao Paulo in 1994. Electronic dance music of all kinds is thriving in the clubs but trance is the music of choice for the mostly outdoor beach parties that have been known to attract crowds of up to 20,000.

"In Brazil, raves already have a long history. It began with a very few people who loved the music and the vibe and now we have super raves for 6,000 people with swimming pools and expensive tickets. The beach raves at Trancoso and Caraiva in Bahia are known for being mythical parties. The people who are going to the raves are everyone - from rich teenagers to the poor guys from suburbia. Everybody parties together."

- Lubna, raver, web designer, Sao Paulo, Brazil.

"I think if the party is happening far from the city, buildings, cars or police, then there is no difference if the party is in Brazil or any other country. If there is a difference then maybe raves in Brazil have a more spiritual atmosphere."

- Gil Oliveira Santos a.k.a. Ravehunter, Goa trance musician, Brazil.

Bulgaria

In the last five years Bulgaria has come a long way to establishing a buoyant rave scene. The capitol city of Sofia now has several electronic music clubs including Club Lipstick, Garbage, Graffiti and Club Alibi. Even smaller towns now have rave clubs such as the Club Underground in Blagoevgrad and smaller clubs in Stara Zagora. The Metropolis Group that includes Ivo Rachev and DJ Steven are the main rave promoters in Bulgaria who have successfully staged numerous large parties over the past few years. Most recently, Metropolis rented the Winter Sports Palace in Sofia and attracted 6,000 people for a party featuring Berlin's top female DJ, Marusha, Mark Wee and Sugar Daddy O.

California

The scene in California began in San Francisco in 1989, quickly spread to Los Angeles and is now one of the most vibrant scenes in the US. In general, California raves tend to have a more spiritual focus, but the scene has since diversified and there are numerous promoters producing many different kinds of events from high-powered club nights to full on arena parties to small underground events. Parties in San Francisco and Los Angeles regularly attract around two thousand people and big parties can attract up to fifteen thousand. Musically, California has been a melting pot of styles. Californians tend to like their house deep and mellow but in the last few years have become known for pioneering new directions in trance and breakbeat.

"In '92 the rave scene seemed to die in LA. There was a city crack down on raves so the scene moved to the after hours clubs for a couple of years. Then in early '94 there were a few people that had started to do small parties again and that grew until now, when we are seeing the scene get really big again."

- Michael Angelo a.k.a. DJ 608, Los Angeles, USA.

"I've always had the time of my life in San Francisco. The kids there like to have fun and listen to good music. Even older people are staying out and having a good time 'til five in the morning."

- Troy Roberts, DJ, Platinum Records, Seattle, USA.

Canada

Windsor and Toronto are just across the border from Detroit and Chicago, so these cities felt the influence of electronic music early on. Canada now has one of the most exciting rave scenes in the world. Toronto has several capable promoters who stage huge multi-room parties on a weekly basis. Vancouver, on the West Coast, has a well-earned reputation as one of the vibiest scenes around. In Quebec, Montreal is fast becoming the rave capitol of North America. There are also well developed rave scenes in Ottawa, Calgary, Edmonton and other city centers across the country.

"There are about 10,000 regular ravers in Toronto and most of the bigger parties get 5 to 6 thousand people. There are also smaller parties almost every weekend."

- Kim Stanford, The Toronto Raver Information Project.

Chicago/Detroit

The birthplaces of house and techno, Chicago and Detroit are the world Meccas of electronic dance music. Many of the world's leading producers and DJs come from these cities and even today, Chicago and Detroit labels remain world leaders in the production of electronic dance music. Rave culture however, was late to arrive in this part of America where electronic music has been showcased mostly in the clubs and in private "cabarets." This was probably due to the heavy-handed attitudes of the police and some serious urban social problems with youth violence, poverty and race relations. Despite this, peace, love, unity and respect are playing their part in healing the wounds of urban America and today, the rave scene is alive and well in both these cities that have given so much to the world of music.

Colombia

The rave scene in Colombia has recently been severely hampered by a 1 a.m. curfew. Previous to this there was a burgeoning underground scene developing with a preference towards trance music. For now, the scene has retreated to the clubs (which also close by 1 a.m.) In Medellin, the hottest club is Plataforma with an outrageous light show and resident DJs, Juanito and Diego Mezclaz playing everything from underground to deep house, hard house and trance. In Bogota, the place to visit is The Music Factory and a gay bar called The Cinema. Ecstasy and LSD are difficult to find in this part of the world where coke is cheap and a pound of pot can cost as little as $10 a pound.

Croatia

Rave culture spread to Croatia in early 1993 a short while after the civil war ended. Small free parties began to spring up with local DJs spinning hardcore and techno. Some of these early parties were held in disused bomb shelters. The first large rave was held in February 1994 in the city of Split. After that, the big discotheques began to play techno and before long, almost every club on the Dalmatian coast was playing electronic dance music and attracting international DJs such as Derrick May, Wesbam, Marusha, Darren Price, Sonic and many others. Large international style parties with thousands of people are common in and around the capitol of Zagreb and on the Adriatic coast. This year a company called Astralis will stage a three-day ethno-rock-trance, open-air party on Krk Island also on the Adriatic coast.

"Today in the Split area, techno parties are every weekend. Sometimes two or three, and the quality of the parties are very good."

- Mladen Alajbeg, electrical engineer, DJ, Trogir, Croatia.

Cyprus

There have been some reports of small underground Goa trance parties on Cypress but most of the action is still in the clubs. The biggest electronic dance music club on the island is The Kool Club in Ayia Napa that features 3 floors, 6 bars, a huge sound and lighting system and a capacity of 1,500. Another stop for international DJs on Cypress is called Pzass.

Czech Republic

The rave scene started in the Czech Republic in 1990 nudged along by two club DJs, Bidlo OO FX and Loutka. Today the scene is booming with six rave clubs in Prague alone, Radost FX being the biggest and oldest. A series of free open-air parties in 1994 saw a proliferation of underground raves that continue to be the most popular form of party. Today, the Czech Republic boasts many international DJs and world class musicians with burgeoning rave scenes in Pardubice, Brno and a number of smaller towns around the country. Ecstasy is very expensive and so many ravers use an amphetamine called pervitin.

"The first party I visited was the first house music party in our region in 1992. There were only a few people, we didn't know exactly, what sounds we are listening to but the atmosphere was great. Then I went to a party 3 years later in Pardubice. We listened to Paul van Dyk, Marusha, Westbam, Darren Price, Luke Slater and the best Czech DJs."

- Petr Nejedly, economics student, raver, Hradec Kralove, Czech Republic.

"The best parties in Prague are free parties. There are several groups of techno freaks like NSK, Cirkus Alien, Technical Support, Direct Drive, Hiipno Gong Pakt and Balistix who have a sound system and do free parties outside in meadows and so on. No one pretends anything, everything's so rough, there are no smiling girls giving us cigarettes from sponsors. It's just us and nature."

- Tomá1 Rádl, writer, web designer, raver, Praha, Czech Republic.

England

England is famous the world over for its long and illustrious history of rave. From the "summer of love" in 1987 to the present, England has proved to be one of the most fertile environments for rave culture. In recent years, there have been a number of legal measures enacted against the rave scene. But despite the official opposition, England remains one of the world leaders in the production of electronic dance music and still hosts some of the biggest and best organized rave events in the worlds as well as being a world center for the production of new electronic dance music.

"There's a huge difference between the scene in England and the scene in North America. In England there's a greater variety of music because there is more people creating music. People are more committed to the music, more prepared to travel to find it. I think that ravers party harder in England. It means more to them. English ravers are more faithful to DJs as well. It's common for DJs to have their own "posses" who follow them all over the country from party to party or club to club."

- Tim Laughlin, Vibe Crew, England.

Egypt

Egypt is well known for its Goa trance following, which means vibey, underground parties with a spiritual focus. In recent years there have been a number of successful outdoor raves near the pyramids that have inspired the plans for a gigantic world rave scheduled for New Year's Eve 2000 at the foot of the great pyramid of Cheops.

Estonia

Estonia has a very active rave scene that continues to grow every year. Visited regularly by international DJs, this Baltic country has a thriving underground scene as well as some larger events and a growing club scene.

"The population of Estonia is 1.4 million and the population of the capital, Tallinn is 500,000, but we still have a very active rave scene here."

- Sonic Intervention, Tallinn, Estonia.

Finland

The Finnish rave scene started in 1988 when the now-legendary Berlin Club in Helsinki held its first acid house nights. The Hyperdelic Housers posse from Turku organized the first illegal techno parties in 1989, the same year that MetalBassOrganisation held the first full on rave in Helsinki. DJ Elliot Ness has been instrumental in building the scene in Finland and has been organizing and promoting parties since the early 90's. Today there is a lively rave scene in Helsinki, Turku, Tampere, Lahti, Vaasa and many other smaller towns throughout the South. Finnish raves usually attract anywhere from 100 to 2,000 people. Like the Swedes, Finns have a reputation of using drugs in moderation or not at all. There are an estimated 5,000 - 10,000 ravers in the Helsinki area and another 5,000 - 15,000 in smaller cities around Finland.

"Where I live, in a small place called Ilomantsi near the Russian border, "Ultrasonic" was one of the biggest rave parties in our area. There were over 450 visitors and there's only about 7,500 people in our whole village!"

- Esa Ojansivu, student, raver, Ilomantsi, Finland.

Florida

In recent years Florida has become a prolific production center for electronic music and in particular, progressive house and trance. The rave scene was booming up until a few years ago but because of America's fervent war on drugs, the rave scene has since been forced back into the clubs. Raving is now outlawed in several counties in Florida where establishments have to close by 3:30 a.m.

"From talking to Kimball Collins and Jimmy Van Malleghem, Florida was really the place to be a few years ago. It was all very new and people went out for the music."

- Nigel Tasko, rave promoter, Noble House, The Alien Mental Association, Canada.

France

Despite the fact that the French police have a reputation for breaking up parties with fire hoses, the rave scene in France has a long history that continues to this day. Over the years, France has gained a worldwide reputation for the production of Goa or psy-trance music and is also known for its preference towards a more sophisticated form of house music. There is a vibrant club scene all over the country and in recent years there has been an increase in large, well-organized outdoor events.

Germany

Germany has been very influential in the creation of electronic music and is the home of Kraftwerk, reputed to be the founding fathers of techno. Germany was one of the first European countries to adopt rave culture back in 1987 and its popularity has been spreading ever since. Large parties which regularly attract crowds of 10,000 to 20,000 people are common. Germany is also host to the biggest rave event in the world, The Love Parade, which attracted over a million people in 1998. Germany remains one of the world's leaders in the production of techno music and is home to some of the best DJs in the world.

Goa, India

The beaches of Goa have been home to a community of international travelers since the sixties and have been staging monthly full moon parties for thirty years. When rave culture hit the beaches in the late eighties it was a marriage made in electronic heaven. Thanks to people like Frankfurt DJ/Producer Sven Vath, Goa Gil from San Francisco, and English record labels like TIP and Blue Room who started some of the first parties here in 1989, Goa has become the Mecca of psychedelic trance music. In the last few years there has been pressure from foreign governments to curb the scene but it continues to this day to be one of the spiritual homes of global rave culture. The early scene began in the Calangute and Baga beach area and has since spread to Vagator beach, Spaghetti Beach, El Aviv, Disco Valley and the trance fortress in Anjuna.

Greece

Greece is fast becoming a favorite rave destination for many Europeans. There is a very well developed club scene in Athens with venue capacities between 500 and 2000. There are also numerous clubs to be found around the country including The Paraiso in Faleraki, Plastik in Rhodos and clubs on the Islands of Mykonos and Crete. Although much of the action is in the clubs, Greece also has a faithful following of Goa trance supporters who regularly stage underground rave events around Athens or on the Island of Mykonos. There is also a growing following for jungle and drum and bass.

Holland

Holland has a long history as a tolerant and free society so it is no surprise that it has welcomed rave culture with open arms. One of the first European countries to foster rave, Holland now has a well-established scene and some of the most progressive drug policies in the world. Most of the best ecstasy in Europe is manufactured in Amsterdam and exported around the world. Holland is also home to gabba techno, which means "mate" in Dutch. With a large healthy club scene and a thriving warehouse party scene, Holland is one of the world leaders in the culture of rave.

"The scene is extremely big in The Netherlands. It started underground in 1988 with parties under viaducts but now it's as big as it can get. Raves of well over 30,000 people in huge stadiums are nothing special any more. There are several raves every weekend which is a lot for a country with only 15 million people."

- NoRuleZ, web designer, raver, Nijverdal, Netherlands.

"The scene in Amsterdam is so much more educated and organized. The ravers are a lot more involved in the scene. They know the DJs, the history of the movement etc. There's so much more information. The Dutch know that the drugs are out there and that you can't prevent people from doing them so they try and make it safer by giving people information and a support system to allow you to do them properly or not do them at all."

- Michael Elewonibi, musician, rave promoter, Canada.

Hong Kong

Despite the takeover by China, rave culture is alive and well in Hong Kong. There are now several clubs that cater to electronic tastes and this year, the world famous Ministry of Sound Club in London, England opened a sister club in Hong Kong. World class local talent such as DJ Joel Lai are now touring the world and new talent is emerging daily. Large parties are also beginning to be staged, thanks to the likes of promoter Andrew Bull with The Arena Group who recently promoted a party called Unity with Paul Oakenfield, Boy George and Pete Tong at the Hong Kong International Trade and Exhibition Centre in Kowloon Bay. The party featured 12 hours of non-stop music from two stages and attracted a capacity crowd of 3,000.

Hungary

In the past few years, the rave scene has been growing steadily in Hungary. A large following for psychedelic trance music has spawned The Eclipse Festival, a weeklong trance event in Ozara. This open-air event features an impressive line-up of international DJs as well as camping, a circus and a cinema.

Ibiza

The Balearic Island off the coast of Spain is where it all started but Ibiza has since moved away from a purely rave vibe to become the clubbing capital of the world. The party paradise was recently touted as finished but in 1997 came back with a vengeance to re-established itself as a twenty-four hour a day, international dance destination with an estimated 500,000 visitors per season. In recent years, the police have cracked down on the beach parties but the club scene is legendary. Manumission, Pacha, Space, Es Paradis, Privilege and Amnesia are just some of the many mind-blowing, extravagant, clubs that are providing an important platform for the best international DJs. The club scene in Ibiza remains one of the most lively in the world, despite the fact that if you get caught with five or more doses of ecstasy, you could be looking at five to eight years in a Spanish prison.

Israel

In the nineties, many young Israelis traveled to Goa and brought back Goa trance music and rave culture with them. The Israeli government has made it clear that they disapprove of the movement and have done everything in their power to stamp it out. Amazingly, rave culture continues to grow in Israel with a healthy club scene and a growing number of party promoters. The music in Israel is still almost exclusively trance and the young Israelis have a reputation for being some of the most colourful and energetic ravers anywhere.

"Israel is one of the most progressive trance cultures in the world! Rave culture is increasing and almost every year it doubles. I've seen it go from the smallest parties of 30 to 40 people, to the biggest Goa trance parties in the world for 30,000 people!"

- Amit K., electronic engineer, raver, Haifa, Israel.

Italy

Italy is the home of Italo, a kind of electronic disco that was instrumental in the birth of house music. It was also one of the first European countries to embrace rave culture as early as 1987. The scene is mainly centered in the northeast and on the Adriatic coast where there are many clubs with capacities of 1,000 to 5,000. The opening night of a Tuscany club called Insomnia recently attracted 8,000 people and The Cocoricò club in Riccione features a gigantic glass pyramid and Sven Vath from Germany as a resident DJ. In a country of 55 million it is estimated that there are 4 million ravers. Today, due to government crackdowns, the scene is going through a dark period. Raves have been effectively banned and clubs are must close by 4 a.m., forcing promoters to stage parties across the border in neighboring Slovenia.

Ireland

The Irish have long been known for their love of music and now have one of the friendliest rave scenes in Europe. Smaller, intimate parties are the norm here but there have also been some bigger events all over the country. Outdoor parties are common in the summer and there is also a good club scene in most of the major cities. Ireland is a favorite stop for many international DJs.

"There is a really beautiful scene in Ireland. I played in Gallway last year and there's a really tight core group of people who just want to dance and have fun. I played in clubs, but I hear they have really cool outdoor parties as well."

- Daniel, Moontribe DJ, Los Angeles, USA.

Japan

The rave scene in Japan is divided into the club scene and the party scene. The huge, well-equipped clubs in and around Tokyo are expensive and frequented by immaculately dressed Japanese clubbers. Clubs are open all night, every night and generally specialize in one type of electronic music. The rave scene almost exclusively features Goa trance or hard trance. Some of the biggest names in trance music come from Japan including Tsuyoshi, Suzuki, Prana and Matsuri. Nowadays 6,000 people parties are common in Tokyo. These big events are held in arenas and massive public event halls with no opposition from the police or city officials. Ecstasy is fairly hard to find and penalties for possession are harsh. In recent years crystal meth has become a major social problem in Japan and is also widely used in the rave scene.

"The first rave parties in Tokyo started in about 1991 but were held in the clubs. In Tokyo the clubs are licensed and open all night so it was no problem to find locations for parties. DJ Tsuyoshi started the first Goa Trance parties in Tokyo in 1992. The first party was called Wanna Dance and there were only 50-100 people. In Japan we have no problems whatsoever with the police, it's like Germany, people in Japan are more business minded, if it's good for business it's okay. There is no violence or any problems at the parties so the police are okay with it."

- Chika, Solstice DJ, rave promoter, Tokyo.

"Tokyo is really full-on and so cool. The people are great, the technology is amazing and the parties are amazing. I played five nights in a row in different clubs. Some clubs go until 5 or 6 a.m., some open at 8 a.m. in the morning and go till 3 p.m. in the afternoon. It was a great time and I had some really good connections with people."

- Daniel, Moontribe DJ, Los Angeles, USA.

Latvia

The first full-scale rave in Latvia was held in1994 and since then the scene has continued to grow. Pulkvedim Neviens Neraksti or Pulkvedis for short, is a Latvian city known as the underground pearl of the Baltic's with a strong following from the large student population. Promoters like Underbeat are consistently producing large, quality events with international DJs and dedicated electronic music clubs like Metro in the capitol city of Riga are proving that Latvia is a country that loves to rave.

Macedonia

Rave culture has been flourishing in the ex-Yugoslav Republic of Macedonia since 1992. It's capital city, Skopje is home to several world class clubs including The Metropol, that regularly showcases DJs from England, the US, Holland, Germany, France, Greece and Yugoslavia. There are also a number of rave organizations such as PMG, Trance Experience, Creative and others that are working to expand the scene. The Macedonian Tribal Gathering is a massive annual rave event that attracts visitors from all over Europe. Recently, 6,000 people showed up to see The Prodigy at the Skopje Fair. Musical preferences lean towards techno and trance with a growing interest in drum and bass. Ecstasy is very expensive and so many Macedonians prefer to party sober.

Malaysia

South East Asia is fast becoming a new world center for rave culture and in recent years there has been an explosion in the underground rave scene in West Malaysia. Large parties are now attracting thousands of ravers and international DJs. A recent party featured a six-hour set by Jon Carter of the United Kingdom. If you turn on a radio in Malaysia, one out of every five songs will be a dance track or remix. Electronic music clubs like Zouk in Singapore are making Malaysia a place to look out for in the new millennium.

Malta

The rave scene arrived in Malta three years ago and already some people are predicting that it could become the next Ibiza. Clubs like Mirage are leading the way along with a handful of promoters bringing in international DJ talent. In 1998, parties in Malta were host to Advent, Jeff Mills, Luke Slater, Johannes Hail, Carl Cox, Dave Clarke, Paul van Dyk, CJ Bolland and many others. Raves are now being staged on a monthly basis and the club scene continues to grow.

"In my opinion, Malta is slowly evolving into one of the major clubbing places for tourists to visit."

- Neil Cassar, computer programmer, raver, Zabbar, Malta.

Mexico

Rave has been happening in Mexico for some time but it's only in the last few years that it has developed into a truly international scene. Its proximity to the US gives Mexico a huge pool of world class DJs to choose from and more and more DJs are discovering that Mexico is a fun place to play. Like most countries the scene began with warehouse parties but because of the warm climate, there are now many outside events in remote locations or public parks. This year, a huge party called Union Fest will feature Juan Atkins, Oliver Lieb, Richie Hawtin, John Aquaviva and twelve other international DJs.

"I just played a party in Mexico City with about 500 people. It was really a great vibe with good people. The scene is just starting there. They're still into alcohol and that whole thing but people are definitely opening up and starting to catch on."

- Daniel, Moontribe DJ, Los Angeles, USA.

New York

Home of the Paradise Garage Club and Frankie Bones' Storm Raves, New York has long been an important center for the production of new electronic dance music. Stamina and endurance have long been characteristic of New York nightlife, and it's no surprise that New York DJ's have become known for marathon sets. Twilo is a club in Chelsea's warehouse district where resident DJ Junior Vasquez is famous for his extended sets that can run from 1 a.m. to noon the next day. Danny Tenaglia is revered by DJs and dancers alike for his Saturday night marathon mixing sessions at The Tunnel and Jonathan Peters regularly plays ten to twelve hour sets Friday and Saturday nights at The Sound Factory. Known more for its club scene and innovative music producers than for its rave scene, New York is currently experiencing a revival of the all night raves that began the rave scene on the East Coast in 1991.

Philippines

In the past few years there have been a number of large events staged in and around the capitol city of Manila, which is also the home of a lively club scene. Party promoters such as Consortium, Groove Nation, Natural Born Klubber's and Beat Surrender are promoting large indoor and outdoor parties with the likes of Derrick May and many other top international talents. Recent events by Natural Born Klubbers, an outfit known for lavish and imaginative events, include a two day party with Britain's Mark Luvdup and a now legendary Ministry of Sound event at Star City in Manila. Many of the larger events in The Philippines are sponsored by Lucky Strike cigarettes.

Poland

Rave culture in Poland began around 1991 with small parties being held in abandoned bunkers and disused factories. Later, the scene was kick started by a series of raves called the New Alcatraz Parties. Lodz, in the center of the country, is now the capital of the Polish underground rave scene and has several "techno pubs" that have regular Saturday night events. The Parade of Freedom, an annual event modeled on Berlin's Love Parade, attracted 15,000 people last year. Musical tastes favor hardcore, Detroit house and minimal techno and although there are still no electronic record labels in the country, the success of Polish groups like Tromesa and Ventylator are putting Poland on the international musical map.

"People in Warsaw like listening to house music. In Lodz we are listening to hardcore and breakbeat. In Katowice in the South they like hardcore and jungle, and in the North in Gdańsk it's gabba and hardcore."

- Peter, student, raver, Lodz, Poland.

"In Poland a lot of people go to techno parties. We do not have to organize many raves because techno parties in clubs are legal."

- Tomasz Wileński, media planner, electronic musician, Warsaw, Poland.

Portugal

Rave culture arrived in Portugal as late as 1995 but quickly grew in popularity. By 1997 the trance scene was in full swing with a series of large parties and festivals including The Boom Festival, an annual trance party attended by 4,000 Portuguese ravers. The capitol city of Lisbon is home to several rave clubs including The X-Club, an important showcase for international DJs.

"The trance scene is very big in a small country like ours. Perhaps because we are a free country with friendly people and a belief in God."

- Foka, administrator, DJ, raver, Alverca, Portugal.

Russia

DJ Vint was playing house records in St. Petersburg's Ton Studio as early as 1988. The first raves were held in Moscow and St.Petersburg shortly afterwards and the first major party called, The Gagarin Party was held in Moscow in 1991. This led to a plethora of clubs in Moscow including LSDance, Ermitage, MDM, Penthouse, Aerodance and many others that were mostly closed in 1994 due to government intervention. By 1995 the scene recovered and there are now fifty clubs in Moscow alone. The recent success of a series of parties known as the Planetarium Raves of St. Petersburg and many other huge underground parties popping up around the country have established Russia as a world center of rave culture. A large party in Moscow this year pulled in a record crowd of 55,000 and Russian DJ's like Lena Popova, Space Girl and Russian techno acts such as New Composers are now touring the world. Russia is also said to be one of the main ecstasy producing countries but it is too expensive for the locals who prefer LSD or nothing at all.

"Moscow is the second biggest city in Russia. In St. Petersburg rave culture is going on another way, it's not as " pop" as Moscow. In other cities of Russia, rave is germinating like it did in Moscow in 1993."

- Stardiver a.k.a. Alex, student, raver, Moscow, Russia.

Scotland

Scotland has a well-earned reputation for quality dance music with more clubs, producers, DJs, and labels than you can shake a kilt at. Record producers like Chris Cowie, DJ Q, Daniel Ibbotson and Domenic Capello and labels like Glasgow Underground, Hook/Bellboy, Sole Music and Soma are fast gaining an international reputation for producing world class dance music.

"Scotland is quite a small country with only six million people but it's produced a lot of good music of all genres. There are hip-hop labels here and trip hop and house and techno. Glasgow is known for a deep house sound and most of the clubs there play house music. Here in Aberdeen you can hear anything you want to hear any night of the week in the clubs. Scotland does its own thing but gets its influences from all over the world."

- Chris Cowie, producer, DJ, Hook Records, Scotland.

South Africa

South Africa got their first taste of acid house music in 1988 following the Summer of Love in England. Danny Schreiber, a new age shaman and rave promoter was instrumental in stimulating the early scene which moved into high gear with The World Peace Party in September of 1991, a 36 hour rave on Paarden Island on the Cape Town oceanfront which attracted more than 5,000 people. A recent party staged by Mother Productions in Johannesburg drew a crowd of 9,000. Since then, the scene in South Africa has been growing in leaps and bounds and as with the US, rave culture has done much to heal the racial wounds in South Africa. There is now a huge multi-racial following and a well-developed rave scene in Cape Town, Johannesburg, The Transvaal and Durban. Huge dedicated rave clubs are now well established in the cities and large-scale outdoor events are becoming common as South Africans are fast gaining a reputation as some of the most enthusiastic ravers in the world.

"In South Africa we have the larger, commercial, money making efforts that pull international DJ's and make lots of money, smothered in cigarette advertisements and overrated VIP tickets (for those that can afford it.) And smaller, more underground parties are becoming more popular as people are feeling less endearing to the big, big balagan spenditures. Intimacy and love for one another is becoming more of a visible elements at these parties."

- Daniel a.k.a. Earthguy, raver, Johannesburg, South Africa.

"The first time Sasha and myself went down to South Africa, we played at a party with sixteen thousand people and last December I played a party with eight thousand people in a railway building. It was incredible, the place just went mad and they are really into it."

- John Digweed, DJ, producer, England.

Sweden

The first raves in Sweden were in Gothenburg in 1989. 1993 to 1994 saw the heyday of Swedish raving with many large outdoor events attracting crowds of up to 5,000 people. In Stockholm in 1995, a now famous club called Docklands opened to showcase the very best in international DJs. Before long, the club was raided and closed and the resulting press led to a special police force being formed called "ravekommissionen." The force carried out a series of brutal raids and closed every party they could find despite the fact that the results of a recent survey found that Swedes use fewer drugs at raves than any other country. In spite of the crackdown and new restrictive laws, the rave scene in Sweden continues to grow. The annual Arvikafestival in Stockholm last year attracted a record crowd of 7,000 people.

Switzerland

Bordered by France, Germany, Austria and Italy, it is hardly surprising that Switzerland has been raving since the late eighties. Switzerland is now home to a thriving Goa trance scene and some of the biggest rave events in the world. An annual event in Zurich called The Street Parade, similar to Germany's Love Parade, has been growing each year and last year attracted 450,000 ravers from all over the world. Forty parties accompanied the parade including an event called Energy '98 which featured ten dance floors in four buildings, an open air concert stage, a fun park area, two chill out gardens and a small village. 23,000 people attended the Energy party this year.

Tasmania

Tasmania, an island state in southeastern Australia, has been raving for about five years but has really only established an ongoing scene in the last two years. There are now regular full moon parties once a month that attract 250 to 400 people which is not bad for a population of less than 500,000. Tasmanian raves are usually free parties and are known as some of the least commercial raves on the planet.

"As most of the raves in Tasmania are outdoors and we have plenty of space here, police have not yet been a problem. Hobart is a small community and communication is good."

- DJ Sylk, Hobart, Tasmania.

Thailand

Thailand, like Goa, is one of the regular stops for international travelers in South East Asia, so rave culture migrated here with the foreign visitors. Koh Pan Gan hosts the infamous full moon parties, with up to three separate dance areas. Black Moon Parties can be found in Koh Samui. In Bangkok, after the clubs close, crowds of people wait on Sunrise Beach for a fishing boat to take them to Hat Yuan Bay where there are regular trance parties attended by thousands of people. In the city of Bangkok, a once lively club scene is being threatened by spot urine testing by the local police. Despite this, clubs like Narcissus, Taurus and Tapas are packed most weekends with people dancing to the sounds of local talent such as DJ Tan, DJ Num, DJ Neng, DJ Mandi, Bee and Mongkol. The most popular bar with ravers in Bangkok is Deeper, featuring hard trance, breakbeat and house music.

Venezuela

Rave is only a couple of years old in Venezuela. Techno came to the gay clubs of Caracas first then, in 1997 some underground Goa trance parties started in and around Caracas. This year there have been several outside events culminating in The Solar Eclipse Party, a week long rave in a remote mountain location in Northern Venezuela with such international stars as Sid Shanti, Pan, Mark Allen and Etnica Max. A German crew with some experience working at The Love Parade organized the party which as its name suggests, featured a total eclipse of the sun!

"There are laws which rule open air parties and raves in Venezuela and they basically ask for a permit and a 5% money of all entrance tickets. Of course, police can always be bought with money at any time if they are a threat to the event."

- Hernando, DJ, music producer, rave promoter, Merida, Venezuela.

Yugoslavia

The first rave in Yugoslavia was held in Belgrade in 1991 and was called Insomnia. There is now a thriving rave scene and in 1994 the Club Industria opened in the basement of the Philosophical University of Belgrade to become the hub of the scene in Yugoslavia. Other Belgrade clubs include Sara on the banks of the Sava River and the underground club Omen. In recent years there have been a growing number of large raves and a whole slew of rave organizers including Technokratia, Kozmik, Integra, Xperiment, TTP and Goax. Other recent parties have featured Laurent Garnier, Astral Projection and Missjah as well as popular local talent Noise Destruction and DJ Nick. There is even a national TV show called Rave-O-lution produced by Nexus, a rave organization run by DJ Lord Ferdi the Despiser and Noisemaker. The most popular music with Yugoslav ravers is techno, Detroit minimal, Goa and hard trance.

"The rave scene in Yugoslavia is maybe not as big as it should be right now, but I swear Yugoslav DJs are among the best around, trust me!"

- Marko Vajagic a.k.a. DJ Mark Wee, architect, Belgrade, Yugoslavia.

Rave culture is also alive and well in Bahrain, China, Chile, Costa Rica, Denmark, Dominican Republic, Ecuador, Iceland, Kazakhstan, Lithuania, Luxembourg, New Zealand, Norway, Panama, Paraguay, Peru, Puerto Rico, Romania, Slovakia, Slovenia, Spain, Taiwan, Turkey, Morocco, Korea, Jamaica, The Ukraine, Cayman Islands, Kenya, Ghana, Zaire and Zimbabwe.

"When people from all over the world come to the big parties and festivals every year they will meet and find out that their thoughts and "vibes" are connected in many ways and they will establish contact. No matter where you are or where you are from, we are heading for the same goal."

- Fredrik Larsson, electronic musician, Stockholm, Sweden.

"Last year, I traveled through the Middle East where the scene is definitely driven by the more psychedelic elements of techno. In Israel, they listen to a lot of Goa/psy trance and their drug of choice is LSD. The US West Coast is still listening to house and older styles of trance. Italy is into progressive house."

- Jo Fruitybits, magazine editor, Melbourne, Australia.

"The Far East and Japan now have a huge scene for electronic dance music. It's very, very big over there. It's growing all aver the world. A friend of mine recently went to a rave event in Israel and said it was unbelievable. There are now rave events in unthinkable places. Dance music is so universal. It transcends language and so many cultural barriers, which is why it is such global music. The hot spots right now are England, mainland Europe followed

by Japan and the United States. I should also mention Australia. DJs are now touring throughout the world to countries like Poland and Greece and all over. We can really see that there is a huge demand for this music."

- Dave Jurman, senior director of dance music, Columbia Records/SONY.

"I think that the international scene is unified by big parties like The Love Parade, Mayday, The Parade in Zurich and I hope it will be unified by The Parade of Freedom in Lodz in the near future."

- Peter, student, raver, Lodz, Poland.

"Many countries have rather different preferences about music. In Finland there is a lot of monotrack and Detroit techno. In the UK they have happy hardcore that isn't really big anywhere else. The Dutch have gabba, the Germans have rave and the French have their cool house scene."

- Juuso Koponen a.k.a. DJ Mekaanikko, Helsinki, Finland.

"In Germany they have so big a scene that even 100 Croatian scenes can't replace it. Every country uses what they have for raves, clubs and places for raving, for example in China they rave on The Great Wall."

- Ivan Arar, raver, Zagreb, Croatia.

"There are raves all across America. You can find them in Wisconsin and South Carolina and places that we've never heard of. We show up and there's a scene and a thousand people in a warehouse ready to party."

- Dennis Barton, Skylab200, Los Angeles, USA.

"I don't think that rave culture is divided by borders. But each culture has its own way of expressing itself. Hard beats with some, melodic themes for the Latinos, more trance grooves for the Brits, or speedy techno for Germanic people."

- Federico Sommariva, rave promoter, DJ, Milan, Italy.

"You know, when you have names like Laurent Garnier, Carl Cox, Sven Vath or John Acquaviva who play every weekend all around the world, from Germany to Russia, from Yugoslavia to Japan, from USA to Africa, you see that music is the key. That's what's understandable all around the Globe."

- Marko Vajagic a.k.a. DJ Mark Wee, architect, Belgrade, Yugoslavia.

"I think that the only thing that differs from country to country is the music and the style of dancing. The vibe is basically the same the world over."

- Brewster B., Weird World Recordings, Melbourne, Australia.

"People can dance together, no matter where you are. Many people often go to raves and techno festivals in other countries. It's the same music. The dance unites us."

- Mikael Jergefelt, raver, Stockholm, Sweden.

CHAPTER 17:

A FEW THOUGHTS ON THE FUTURE

"The future belongs to those who believe in the beauty of their dreams."

- Eleanor Roosevelt, social activist, wife of US President Franklin D. Roosevelt,1884-1962.

17. a few thoughts on the future...

"I think we can look to Europe and see that as it grows, the rave scene will become bigger and more diverse. Even now in Los Angeles there are so many different scenes. We have a hardcore scene, a jungle scene, a Moontribe scene... There's a thirty-year-old crowd who wants to hear Goa. There are big parties and tiny parties in people's houses. It's inevitable that the scene will grow. There is nothing that can stop it."

- Dennis Barton, Skylab200, Los Angeles, USA.

"Trance parties are already a bit of the future. There are people here who already call them parties from the future. So our culture will always be on the edge of the present and at the beginning of the future."

- Foka, administrator, DJ, raver, Alverca, Portugal.

"In the UK and Europe, youth culture is dance culture. You've got twenty-four hour dance radio and the biggest rock bands in the world who all want dance remixes. The majority of the pop charts are dance music. One of the biggest music publications recently reported that turntables are now out selling guitars three to one. So there's a big shift. Young people want to buy turntables and be DJs today."

- Paul Okenfold, DJ, London, England.

"The big parties will get bigger and the underground parties will get more underground. Nobody knows what will happen tomorrow but it's pretty exciting to watch the scene grow. It's a healthy vibe that's spreading."

- DJ Billy, Victoria, BC, Canada.

"I really see no end to this wonderful thing. Perhaps people will grow tired and develop into something different but it will never die, just change shape. I believe that the rave scene will leave its mark. The scene grows every year and is becoming bigger and bigger."

- Fredrik Larsson, electronic musician, Stockholm, Sweden.

"I think the scene will just get bigger. In the last five or six years I've seen it become a huge worldwide scene. I play in countries all over the world and get pretty much the same reaction everywhere I go. I think that in the future we will see more and more people making electronic music in pockets all over the world taking elements from different cultures and just keep growing. The music is truly international."

- John Digweed, DJ, producer, England.

"I think that we will continue to see more and more kinds of music merge into each other making more hybrids which will be very exciting. Also we will see all kinds of different artists embraced under the banner of electronica. I think that's very good for electronica and very exciting in general. I see this trend continuing to develop into the next decade and I definitely see the music getting bigger too as more and more kids get into it."

- Dave Jurman, senior director of dance music, Columbia Records/SONY.

"I think that I'm still going to go to raves when I am 60! What they are then will be just gatherings of this tribe and these people that share the same feelings and ideas. By that time, only the people and love will still be there because in this culture and among these fine people, I have found my place in this world. These parties are my home. From there I have grown up and there I will die."

- Jari Nousiainen a.k.a. Super attaK, Helsinki, Finland.

"I personally believe that it will evolve in to a mish-mash of styles, which in another ten years will be the mainstream pop of today. The underground side will still be pushing new sound that will filter up to the mainstream. The cycle has, and always will be there with music. Ideas spark up other people's minds to do something different. And the cycle goes on..."

- Brewster B., Weird World Recordings, Melbourne, Australia.

"I see a move to more live music and live mixing. Acts like The Chemical Brothers, Prodigy, SkyLab 2000 and The Sci-Fi Witchdoctor have started a trend which I think will continue. As the scene becomes more commercial, the true ravers will go further underground. In the future I see America learning more from Europe. The big DJs from Europe will be doing more American tours, the sub-culture will become more established and the mainstream rave movement will have to realize that it's dependent on the sub-culture, dependent on it's roots. I also see rave spreading around the globe. Promoters are moving into South America. I see Asia making a huge input into rave culture in the next few years, they move very quickly on new trends."

- Michael Elewonibi, musician, rave promoter, Canada.

"I think that there will always be those few underground parties that some of us will await for weeks or even months. But it will only get better and better with more people learning that our culture is fun and safe as well."

- Alison Maria Clemens, raver, Michigan, USA.

"I think that the rave scene will just keep evolving the way it is. More and more new scenes are starting all over the world, in Australia, New Zealand, Brazil. As the ex-eastern block countries become more affluent it will grow there too. As it spreads around the globe, we will see more musical influences from those cultures being absorbed into the music."

- Tim Laughlin, The Vibe Crew, England.

"I think that electronic dance music will survive and become the rock 'n roll of the 21st century. I do hope that the people keep enjoying the music and the dancing as much as I did and I hope that the people get the chance to feel that "good vibe" again, for a long time."

- Nico Claes, rave promoter, Antwerp, Belgium.

"I think this culture will be the main dance direction for the first half of the next century. While computers and technology grows, the sound of electronic musical instruments will dominate. There is no way to go anywhere else; if only we'll have enough electricity!"

- Oleg Ilyushin a.k.a. DJ Vint, Moscow, Russia.

"There is a whole new generation coming to hear the music now. They have been waiting in the wings because they haven't been old enough to get into the clubs and they've heard about the DJs through their brothers and sisters and magazines and they're keen as mustard to get stuck in. People that come to clubs now are a lot more aware of the scene than they were years ago. I think it's good. It's a healthy thing."

- John Digweed, DJ, producer, England.

"Rave culture will continue to develop and will be taken more seriously by the media. Different sub-levels of rave culture (jungle, hardcore, Detroit, etc.) will be getting much more attention. Others will be born to replace them as "underground". But true ravers will not abandon their house music, no matter how much it is torn apart by MTV."

- Jussi Mononen a.k.a. DJ Athens, Espoo, Finland.

"I see the music developing a more organic quality. I see more live instruments coming back into it giving it a more tribal sound. There are a lot more musicians becoming involved with electronic music which will take it to new places."

- Michael Angelo a.k.a. DJ 608, Los Angeles, USA.

"I think that we will see a lot more integration from all the music genres. I just heard Goldie's new CD and there are guitars wailing and punk elements and David Bowie! I also see a lot of different people still coming in to the scene. People with hippy backgrounds and college backgrounds. There is still a growing fascination with the movement. We used to work harder at educating people but now people just seem to get it quicker. Even the younger people seem to get it right away."

- Gena Womack, founding member of Moontribe, Los Angeles, USA.

"Before dance music came along, people would dance to bands like Duran Duran and get up and dance to one or two songs and sit down again. When dance music came along, people got up and danced all night. I think that on some kind of tribal level, people just like to dance. I don't know where dance music will be in ten years but I'm ninety-nine per cent certain that people will still want to dance."

- Chris Cowie, producer, DJ, Hook Records, Scotland.

"I believe some of the rave purists will, in the near future, break off and go underground again to look for the spirit and to get away from the material pleasures and middle-class fun. It has to happen soon because the underground people are still there and remember the old times. So I'm waiting for the reincarnation of underground rave culture, free of excessive drug use and profit-focused commercialism."

- Jari Nousiainen a.k.a. Super attaK, Helsinki, Finland.

"For every cheap-ass, radio-friendly, teeny-bopper, money-orientated producer, there's ten underground producers who don't give a monkey about sales and image, who believe completely in the soul of dance music and what it can do for people."

- Alan, raver, Buckingham, England.

"I don't think that any government or policeman or detective or rain or fire or snow or wind will stop this amazing phenomena. But I think that in Israel, they are starting to change their attitude and have started learning about us. Maybe they will get something from it in the end."

- Amit K., electronic engineer, raver, Haifa, Israel.

"I've read that already 50% of all music is somehow dance or techno influenced and the percentage is probably going to rise a lot more in the future. Even if it is unlikely that rock and roll and live bands will ever completely vanish, it is still hard to think that someday in Mars people would still listen to some guitar sounds instead of something electronic. So I guess that on some level we have the great possibility of living the future through techno music today."

- DJ Jules Nerve, Helsinki, Finland.

"Dance music is getting bigger and bigger all the time. Now we are even seeing it embraced by commercial radio stations. We now have a song like Praise You by Fat Boy Slim making top forty radio. That says that this music is now going to the next level."

- Dave Jurman, senior director of dance music, Columbia Records/SONY.

"Rave will never die!"

- Sandro Markovic, raver, Yugoslavia.

CHAPTER 18: RAVING ON

photo: tristan o'neill

"Rave culture is where I see most of the evolutionary conscious forms of spirituality today. It is a place where science, technology, global culture and youth culture meet as a spiritual pagan ritual."

-Douglas Rushkoff, author of Cyberia, Media Virus and Playing the Future.

18. RAVING ON...

So, where will rave go from here and what significance will it have on our cultural history? Will rave culture influence a generation and ultimately change the world or be remembered as just another fashionable fad on the road to a dystopic future?

A DJ from San Francisco described to me the burned out, alcoholic hippies that now panhandle at Haight and Ashbury. He told me that in recent years the has-been hippies have been joined by pooped-out punk rockers and predicts that in the next few years, ruined and ravaged ravers will take their place among the drunken derelicts and addicts strewn about the boulevard of broken dreams. While this cynical view may be understandable, I predict that raves contribution to the future will be a little more positive and far reaching. With any cultural movement there are bound to be some casualties, people who get lost along the way, people programmed for disaster. But these few do not represent the many, and with rave culture we are talking many. If we consider that raves are taking place on a weekly basis in most major centers, in more than fifty countries around the world, the figures become staggering. Even a conservative estimate would show that there are now many millions of ravers that collectively represent the biggest popular cultural movement of this century.

In retrospect it is easy to see that the social and cultural revolutions of the twenties and sixties had a huge historical impact on the evolutionary

Even a conservative estimate would show that there are now many millions of ravers that collectively represent the largest popular cultural movement of this century.

growth of our global society. And even though the fashionable and temporal trappings of those influential times are long gone, we continue to this day to feel the effects of the changes that were initiated thirty, or even sixty years ago. If we look around the world today, it is not hard to find the legacy of the sixties or even the twenties, deeply entrenched in our music, art, politics, philosophy and sexuality. Rave represents the next generation of those ideas so there is good reason to believe that the rave movement will have at least an equal impact. And given the sheer numbers of ravers, it is far more likely that rave culture will have a much larger impact.

Rave is by far the most international cultural movement of this century. The hippy movement of the sixties, though widespread, was mostly concentrated in North America and Northern Europe, whereas the rave movement has spread itself around the globe on a much wider scale, effecting many cultures outside of the so-called western world. Rave is now well established in Africa, Asia and South America and is taking hold in a growing number of other third world locales around the globe. It is also worth noting that the peace and love generation lasted for less than a decade and rave, which is only just starting to emerge and be recognized by mainstream society, is already approaching its thirteenth birthday. Given these facts, it seems that rave has the potential to have a greater social impact than all the flower-powered bohemians, turned-on hippies and radical, freethinking yippies of the sixties combined.

The influence of rave culture is now being felt throughout the societies where it is flourishing. Like most burgeoning cultural movements it is making its biggest impact in the arts. Electronic dance music, once exclusively underground, is now finding its way into more and more commercial

New ideas created by the rave generation continue to infiltrate and influence every area of society.

venues and can now be heard everywhere from TV shows and commercials to movie soundtracks and video games. Rave music is also making sweeping changes in the way the music industry does business by completely transforming the way that recorded music is produced, distributed and disseminated. Already it has been responsible for giving birth to a new era of pressed vinyl, a medium once obsolete and now the exclusive medium of club and rave DJs. More and more, we are seeing rave-related imagery being used in advertising and graphic design. Rave fashions are emerging in mainstream clothing stores and top designers are incorporating rave styles in their latest collections. This trend will no doubt continue as new ideas created by the rave generation continue to infiltrate and influence every area of society.

If put into practice by enough people, ideals become realities and can change the world.

One of the reasons that rave has spread so quickly and so far is because current technologies have given us the tools to communicate to more people and disseminate information more easily than at any time in human history. Ravers embrace this technology and are using it to maximum effect. The Internet provides instant access to anyone in any part of the world and new developments in recording technologies are making the production of electronic music accessible to anyone with a computer and the right software. More than any cultural movement in history, rave has the tools necessary to influence more people on a larger scale than ever before.

More than just a musical revolution, rave puts an emphasis on an optimistic outlook, meaningful relationships and a tribalistic approach to developing a strong sense of community. This can not help but impact positively on many of our social dilemmas, most of which are caused by the breakdown of community, be it on a personal or global level. Human relations in general have taken a serious beating in the last decade leaving us with some serious social problems. Broken families, divorce, youth violence, addiction and warring fractions around the world are all directly attributable to the breakdown of community. We have forgotten how to empathize with our fellow human beings and are consequently paying a heavy price. Rave offers us an alternative way to deal with our relationships and politics; one built on peace, love, unity and respect. We could do a lot worse (and have) than adopt such a philosophy. Idealistic? Yes. But if put into practice by enough people, ideals become realities and can change the world.

From my own personal experience, I can say that my experience with the rave movement has enriched my life immeasurably. It has given me a renewed zest for living, a lowered stress level and a more positive and optimistic outlook on life in general. As a direct result of my involvement with rave culture, I am more compassionate, understanding and tolerant towards other people and feel closer to my friends and family than ever before. In the past three years, my general health and energy level has improved significantly and at forty-four, I am stronger and more physically fit than I have been in the last ten years.

More than anything, rave culture has shown me that as human beings we can transcend our ideas and opinions about each other and make contact on a more basic human level; a place where all of us can find true equality as members of the same human family. A place where we can be free to celebrate our tribal heritage and express ourselves openly and freely without judgement. Rave has reconnected me to my tribe and I know that it has done the same for millions of other people all over the world.

Peace. Love. Unity. Respect. It's a simple formula and one that has been expounded by spiritual leaders, philosophers, free thinkers, revolutionaries and ravers throughout the ages. The real challenge is how to put these principals into action. Up until recently, rave has developed in a somewhat haphazard and spontaneous fashion but more and more we are now seeing a new generation of well-organized and focused rave groups emerging with strong political or social agendas. As the movement matures and comes of age, it will bring with it a new level of focus and commitment that will ultimately provide direction for the millions of people around the world who already subscribe to the philosophy of rave. When that happens, the influence of this important cultural revolution will be as far-reaching as any social movement of the twentieth century.

Raving may not be the answer for everyone but it is working for an enormous amount of people. People who are striving to create new tribal rituals to satisfy fundamental needs that are being left behind by a society that tends to measure success by the acquisition of wealth or power. Rave is part of an evolutionary process that began with our cave dwelling ancestors and continues to be equally relevant in today's rapidly evolving world. The sooner we learn to accept and embrace our tribal heritage, the sooner we will come to realize that we are indeed one global tribe with interdependent needs and a common destiny.

However rave culture develops from here, it has already become an indelible part of our human culture and history. Anyone who has had the rave experience, takes away with them a knowledge that they are more than just an island universe. Whether they are involved for a few months or many years, they will come away with the understanding and realization that all human beings are connected by an intangible, unified bond that points the way toward a more humanistic and hopeful vision of the future.

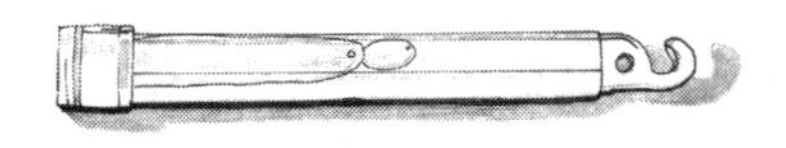

SOME FINAL WORDS...

"The value of rave culture is in the amount of energy that it's possible to create and the vibe that can be reached and made available to a significant number of people and that higher levels of consciousness do exist. That's a pretty large contribution and hopefully, if enough people take away the heart space of love they find at raves it could make a big difference in society as a whole. It's a good thing that the rave environment is available to a lot of people, especially teenagers. It gives them a safe place where they can have an experience of elevated consciousness. People discover that they are a part of a family and a caring nurturing community where they can be free. I'm excited to think what effect that can have on global societal change."

- Kim Stanford, The Toronto Raver Information Project.

"I think that rave is creating a common ground for people to come together. At parties you see punks and hip-hop guys and hippies and ravers and all kinds of people coming together to experience the music. That's got to be a good thing."

- Terrence Parker, producer, DJ, Detroit, USA.

"There are many countries, and people are different from country to country. The parties are different but the music and the kind of people are the same no matter what their skin colour or language."

- Foka, administrator, DJ, raver, Alverca, Portugal.

"The lessons to be learned from rave culture are to be tolerant, to have fun, to feel united and to spread peace."

- Sebastian Zillinger, soldier, raver, Amstetten, Austria.

"Rave culture is about global revolution through personal evolution. We have to connect with ourselves before we can reach out to other people. When we dance, we are connecting with our bodies, learning how to breathe deeper and as soon as we feel connected with ourselves we open our eyes and there is another person doing the same thing and then it spreads out to our daily life."

- Gena Womack, Founding member of Moontribe, Los Angeles, USA.

"I think there is something to learn about the fact that so many people can have a good time in a peaceful way. In Finland, there is a total absence of violence in the rave scene and I understand the situation internationally is the same."

- Juuso Koponen a.k.a. DJ Mekaanikko, Helsinki, Finland.

"I think that rave culture has brought people together. I've been DJing for twenty-one years and looking back to when I first started, people were dancing in clubs but there was never that feeling of oneness. After the rave scene happened people got into the whole vibe of it and broke down a lot of barriers. People were able to smile at each other or shake hands or give each other a hug. The people who go to events today are far more relaxed and chilled-out than the people who used to go to nightclubs fifteen years ago. If you walk into a rave club now it's a happy vibe and that's really nice to see."

- Dave Ralph, DJ, Liverpool, England.

"Raves are about the future, about globalization and emerging world culture, a culture-spanning continents and nations alike, diverse, tolerant, respectful, communicative, honest, sensitive, adaptive, peaceful, enthusiastic, open-minded, constructive and co-operative. A culture striving for ideals of freedom and choice."

- Norman NG a.k.a. Nomskii, promoter, writer, Singapore.

"Rave is a community, a place of equality and empathy. At a rave there is no homophobia, no racism, no class war and no stereotyping."

- Nicole Makin, raver, writer, Canada.

"When all of this started back in 1987 with acid house, people were saying that it was just hype. They were saying it would die after 2 or 3 years. Now, after a decade of modern electronic music scene we have the techno aesthetics in almost every aspect of modern urban life, from design to fashion to movies. So it is one of the most important cultural movements in recent history."

- Marko Vajagic a.k.a. DJ Mark Wee, architect, Belgrade, Yugoslavia.

"Every generation has to feel like they can be free to express themselves and to rebel against the establishment. The rave scene is history repeating itself. Only the music is better..."

- Albert Mancuso a.k.a. DJ Science, Florida, USA.

"The value of rave culture is an acceptance of everyone and everything. If you're black you can come to my party, if you're gay you can come to my party, if you're a beautiful woman, you can come to my party. Everyone can come and be themselves and be welcome and be free."

- Logan a.k.a. Beats Off, Vibe Tribe, Canada.

"Raving is one of the most fantastic experiences I've ever had. I'm grateful that I've been able to create a life within it!"

- Jo Fruitybits, magazine editor, Melbourne, Australia.

"The message of rave culture is one world, one love. Let's all get up and hold hands and celebrate life with dance."

- Jen Jen a.k.a. DJ Mis-Chief, Big Love, England.

"We have evolved into a community and it has a deep effect on me. The group/collective energy that we have created has eclipsed anything and everything that I thought might happen when we formed a group to throw parties. We have managed to capture a totally amazing community vibe that I have never seen recreated elsewhere."

- DJ Drenalin, Salinas, California, USA.

"Gathering together with huge numbers of us dancing, meditating and generally channeling, creates a field of love, which will spread and have a positive impact on the consciousness of the vast majority. Parties can become planetary healing ceremonies."

- From Connected Consciousness in Motion by Leyolah Antara and Nathan Kaye, USA.

"The rave scene has given me the knowledge of a greater power and I am able to assimilate the positive experiences into my every day life. It really has changed my life and the way I perceive people. I am far more accepting and tolerant of other people."

- Anne Marie, raver, nurse, Victoria, Canada.

"Rave culture teaches us to be less selfish. It's more about the group or community than the individual. Society today is so competitive. It's about being better than everyone else or having more money or whatever. At a rave everyone is much more selfless and communal."

- Raevn Lunah Teak, raver, designer, Brisbane, Australia.

"Our social system is so fragmented today and the rave scene provides a surrogate community and a sense of family. A place where people can be themselves and be accepted for who they are and not because they fit into a certain clique. I also think that the spiritual movements that are developing now and the general evolution of people's consciousness, especially young people, is directly attributable to everything that has gone on in the rave scene and I think that it will continue to have an influence."

- Andrew Rawnsley, musician, DJ, Editor of XLR8R magazine, San Francisco, USA.

"I don't know of any other group of people or social scene that puts such a high priority on friendship. A lot of social barriers are broken down in the rave scene and it brings people together. It doesn't seem to matter what background someone comes from. Everyone is treated as an individual. In that way, rave is a real force that can have a big impact on society in general."

- Nigel Tasko, rave promoter, Noble House, The Alien Mental Association, Canada.

"The rave scene opens people's minds and makes them better at dealing with other people. It's a training ground for social interaction that can put you in touch with your inner world."

- DJ Robynod, Nottingham, England.

"The historical significance of rave will be great because rave is life changing for millions and millions of people. It is not just a fashion. It is a lifestyle."

- Stevan "STeW" Fryd, manager, raver, Budweis, Czech Republic.

"For thousands of years, primitive tribes have been taking hallucinogens and dancing all night and this is the same thing. We have lost this part of our culture and we are trying to get it back. We have forgotten that our connection with nature and other people is so important and when we dance and trance, we understand this connection. Rave is like yoga or Tai Chi, it's a process of healing ourselves."

- Chika, Solstice DJ, Tokyo, Japan.

"Raving is the most fun you can have with your clothes on."

- Alan Buckingham, raver, England.

"I don't know, but I've been told. If you keep on dancing, you won't grow old."

- J, The Trip Factory, Saltspring Island, Canada.

photo: tristan o'neill

CHAPTER 19:

RECOMMENDED WEBSITES

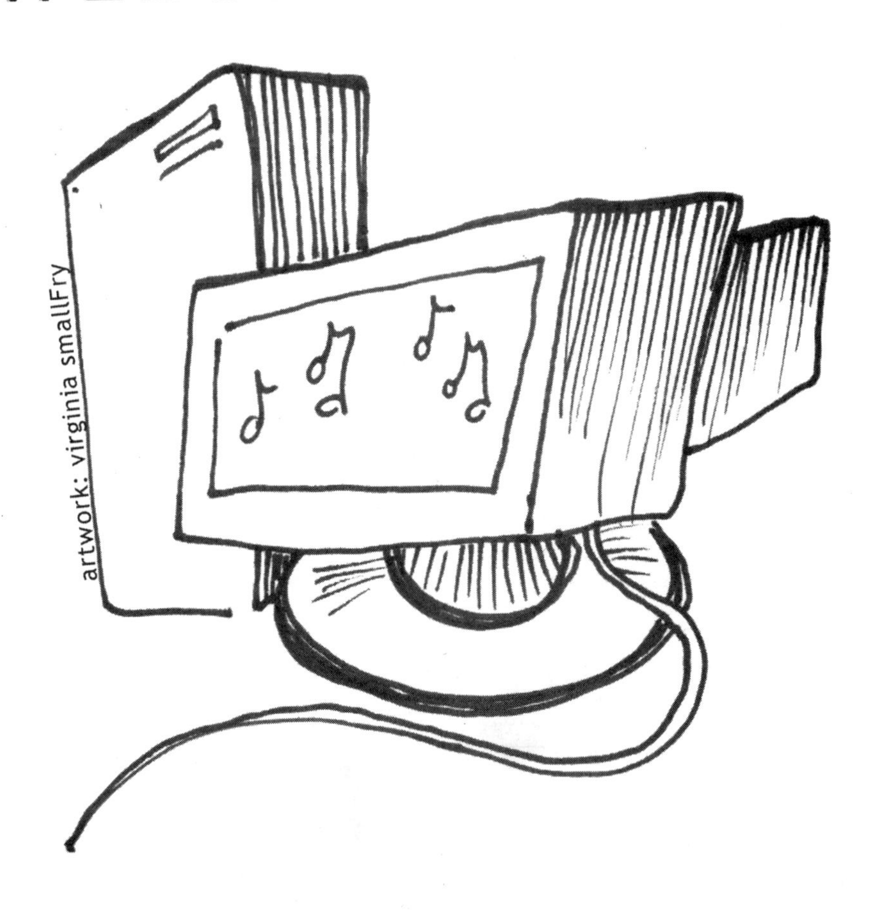

"Whereas a calculator on the ENIAC is equipped with 18,000 vacuum tubes and weighs 30 tons, computers in the future may have only 1,000 vacuum tubes and perhaps weigh 1 1/2 tons."

- From Popular Mechanics, March 1949.

Ravers typically love computer technology and so have a higher profile on the net than most other conventional media such as TV, radio or print. There are literally hundreds of thousands of rave-related sites on the net and it would take a phone book to list them all. To get you started, I have chosen sites that are well connected to other sites. If you follow the links from these pages they will lead to more and more links and so on. Theoretically, this could keep you busy for years, so don't forget to take a break and go to a party now and then. Happy surfing...

http://www.hyperreal.org

The grand pappy of all rave sites. Hyperreal is a very comprehensive site on all aspects of rave culture with many links to other sites. A great place to start.

http://www.raveworld.net

This well designed and ambitious site features lots of pictures, audio, video streaming and animations so you need a fast computer and modem.

http://www.ecstasy.org

The late Nicholas Sander's website and the best source of information on ecstasy anywhere.

http://www.housenation.com

House Nation is a non-profit organization dedicated to bringing house, garage and most genres of modern dance music to life on the Internet. A great source of information for all lovers of house music.

http://www.dancesite.com

This cyber magazine is packed with information on all aspects of dance culture. There are lots of articles to read, the latest news, music, club guide, a chat room and lots of interesting links.

http://www.cloudfactory.org

The Cloud Factory is a collective of rave promoters from the West Coast of North America. The group is known for their small 'vibey" underground parties and spreading the philosophy of PLUR.

http://www.moontribe.org

This is the home page of The Moontribe Collective with news, tour dates, info and links.

http://www.directgate.net

The home of Rave Central featuring a searchable rave database, audio and video links, a DJ info area, party reviews and loads of links.

http://www.loungex.com

A Canadian rave web-community website. Message forums, photos of raves from the West Coast of Canada, party reviewsplus a lot more.

http://www.teamhardcore.com

Another rave website from the West Coast of Canada, with DJ Profiles from all over Canada, raver chat, archive of flyers, and loads of photos.

http://vicraves.cjb.net

A complete guide to the rave scene in Victoria, Canada. Includes listings of upcoming Victoria electronic music events, photos, links, message board, a rave F.A.Q, plus a few party reviews.

http://www.erowid.org

The Vaults of Erowid is fascinating and extensive site dedicated to "Rediscovering the roots of human spirituality..." A must visit for anyone who is interested in expanding their consciousness.

http://www.pcb.co.za/users/ravesafe/

A South African harm reduction group. Lots of info on keeping the rave scene safe and a good place to start if you want to know what's happening with rave culture in South Africa.

http://www.loop.com/~rise/handbook.html

The Responsible Raver's Handbook is a complete guide to raving etiquette from Los Angeles, California. Essential reading for raving 101.

http://come.to/tsdn

Tony Santiago's Dance Nation (TSDN) is a very extensive site dedicated to all aspects rave culture. Too many features to mention but be sure to check out the great collection of over 2,100 rave site links. Schedule a week for your visit to TSDN.

http://spraci.cia.com.au/

The Sydney Party Rave and Club Info page. Loads of information on the rave scene in Sydney as well as the rest of Australia.

http://www.third-eye.org.uk/trip/

TRiP is an interactive resource web site for the global Goa & psychedelic trance scene with an amazing list of links. Also has a good message board.

http://www.wild-site.de/

A very comprehensive site dedicated to the club and party scene in Germany.

http://www.ravedata.com/

This is the Ravedata project that claims to be the world's most comprehensive collection of factual rave-related information - past, present and future. Highly recommended.

http://ubmail.ubalt.edu/~rmills/house.html

An English site dedicated to house music with some good information on the history of house and other genres of electronic dance music. Lots of interesting links.

http://indamix.com/

A site dedicated to 50 of the world's top dance DJs, producers and remixers. Features lots of music related links.

http://www.sci.fi/~phinnweb/enter.html

A very comprehensive site on the rave scene in Finland from Erkki Rautio a.k.a. pHinn. This site has loads of links to Finnish record companies, rave promoters and clubs.

http://www.techno.org

This is an independent server dedicated to all aspects of modern electronic music and club/rave culture. Also features a section on the Swedish rave scene.

http://www.third-eye.org.uk

With a mandate for enlightenment through partying, this is the ultimate resource for techno, trance and especially Goa fans. The links alone will keep you busy for a month.

http://www.innerverse.com/cosmosis/

A resource and an education on all aspects of the psychedelic trance scene with loads of info and links.

http://dj.network.at/

The International DJ Network. Features an international database of DJs that are available for your next party.

http://www.raveordie.com

A great place to find out about the rave scene in Switzerland with many links and a message board. In both German and English.

http://www.techno.cz

A great site to get you in touch with the rave scene in the Czech Republic and some other eastern bloc countries. Also has a great database of DJs and hundreds of links.

http://www.techno.de

Based in Berlin, this site will give you lots of information on the rave scene in Germany. Has many interesting features including a database of global rave sites listed by country.

http://www.deoxy.org

The Deoxyribonucleic Hyperdimension site! A fascinating collection of writings and images that attempt to describe the human condition. Although not strictly a rave site, this is a must see for anyone who is interested in expanded consciousness.

http://www.juno.co.uk/sub1.htm

Another gigantic alphabetical list of rave related sites including artists, labels, organizations, clubs, magazines and much more. Guaranteed to keep you busy for weeks.

http://users.iafrica.com/s/so/solar/

This is a site in South Africa that is organizing a "party at the end of time, a global rave event for the year 2012. Lots of interesting information about the spiritual and tribal aspects of rave culture.

http://www.flying-rhino.co.uk

A Goa trance label from the UK. Check out the link page.

http://txd.trancescape.org/

An underground rave organization in Russia.

http://x-terburg.piter.net/loveparade.htm

The official site of Berlin's Love Parade, the biggest rave event in the world and the biggest cultural event in Europe.

http://ele-mental.coil.com/ele_ment/think/

The web site of Elemental, a group from Columbus, Ohio, dedicated to the history of electronic and experimental music.

http://www.oldskool.dircon.co.uk/

An expansive site dedicated to "old skool" a vintage rave music form popular in the UK in the late eighties.

http://www.themoon0.demon.co.uk/rogers.htm

Roger's rave tent. A trip back in time to the summer of 1988 to the acid house party scene that originally started the rave scene in the UK.

http://www.yutechno.com

A site dedicated to the local underground dance scene in Yugoslavia.

http://www.ush.net/home/

A big site for the UK hardcore scene with the latest news, updates, reviews, galleries and more.

http://www.callieu.demon.co.uk/webring/dbwebringinfo.htm

If you love drum and bass, this is the starting point for you. A webring featuring a continually-growing list of drum and bass sites.

AGMV
MARQUIS
Québec, Canada
1999